The Limits of Choice

Tables with the detailed outcome of the regressions and a number of additional graphics are provided on the website http://bit.ly/campus39916.

Sahra Wagenknecht is a German economist and politician. She is Vice President of the Left Party (Die Linke) and author of several books. From 2004 to 2009 she was a member of the European Parliament. Since 2011 she has been First Vice President of the Left parliamentary group in the Bundestag. Sahra Wagenknecht studied philosophy and modern German literature in Jena, Berlin, and Groningen. With the present study, she obtained a PhD in economics in 2012.

Sahra Wagenknecht

The Limits of Choice

Saving Decisions and Basic Needs
in Developed Countries

Campus Verlag
Frankfurt/New York

Bibliographic Information published by the Deutsche Nationalbibliothek.
The Deutsche Nationalbibliothek lists this publication in the Deutsche Nationalbibliografie; detailed bibliographic data are available in the Internet at http://dnb.d-nb.de
ISBN 978-3-593-39916-4

Copyright © 2013 Campus Verlag GmbH, Frankfurt-on-Main
Cover design: Guido Klütsch, Cologne
Typesetting: Campus Verlag GmbH, Frankfurt-on-Main
Printing office and bookbinder: Beltz Bad Langensalza
Printed on acid free paper.
Printed in Germany

This book is also available as an E-Book.
www.campus.de
www.press.uchicago.edu

Contents

List of Figures

List of Variables and Abbreviations

BEA	National Bureau of Economic Analysis
CEX	Consumer Expenditure Survey (U.S.)
COICOP	Classification of Individual Consumption by Purpose (European Standard)
DIW	German Institute of Economic Research
EVS	Einkommens- und Verbrauchsstichprobe (Germany)
FoF	Flow of Funds
NIPA	National Income and Product Accounts (U.S.)
PSID	The Panel Study of Income Dynamics
SCF	Survey of Consumer Finances (U.S.)
SOEP	German Socio-Economic Panel
VGR	Volkswirtschaftliche Gesamtrechnung des Statistischen Bundesamtes (Germany)
destatis	Statistisches Bundesamt

Own Model:

Y	disposable income	
Y_j	individual disposable income	
y_j	individual relative income:	$y_j = \dfrac{Y_j}{Y}$
S	saving	
s	saving rate:	$s = \dfrac{S}{Y}$

S_j	individual saving	
s_j	individual saving rate:	$s_j = \dfrac{S_j}{Y_j}$
C	total consumption expenditure	
C^*	necessity (or: basic) expenditure	
c^*	mean necessity share in total consumption outlay:	$c^* = \dfrac{C^*}{C}$
c_j^*	individual necessity share in consumption outlay:	$c_j^* = \dfrac{C^*}{C_j}$
cc^*	mean necessity share in income:	$cc^* = \dfrac{C^*}{Y}$
cc_j^*	individual necessity share in income:	$cc_j^* = \dfrac{C^*}{Y_j} = \dfrac{c^*}{y_j}$
$\alpha 1$	propensity to save	
$\alpha 2$	propensity to dissave	
k	share of non-saving households	
$y\{ns\}$	average relative income of non-saving households	
P	price level	
p_i	price of good i	
$p^\circ{}_i$	relative price of good i	
c_i	quantity of good i	
c_i^*	quantity of basic good i	
ε	elasticity parameter	
X	welfare level (utility of a continuum of goods)	
θ	Dixit-Stiglitz-inflation of P	
$g(t)$	growth rate	
$g^*(t)$	growth of basic expenditure	$g^*(t) = \dfrac{\int_0^1 p_{it}\, c_{it}^{*\prime}\, di}{\int_0^1 p_{it}\, c_{it}^*\, di}$
$g^{**}(t)$	excess basic growth:	$g^{**}(t) = g^*(t) - g(t)$
$i(t)$	inflation rate	
$i^*(t)$	inflation rate of basic expenditure:	$i^*(t) = \dfrac{\int_0^1 p_{it}{}'\, c_{it}^*\, di}{\int_0^1 p_{it}\, c_{it}^*\, di}$
$i^{**}(t)$	excess basic inflation:	$i^{**}(t) = i^*(t) - i(t)$

Historic Path of the Necessity Share (Different Approaches):

$$c1^*_{VGR}(t) \; = \; \frac{\sum Basic\,Expenditure\,VGR\,(t)}{\sum Consumption\,Expenditure\,VGR\,(t)} \qquad\qquad 1970 - 2010$$

$$c1^*_{EVS}(t) \; = \; \frac{\sum Basic\,Expenditure\,EVS\,(t)}{\sum Consumption\,Expenditure\,EVS\,(t)} \qquad\qquad 1963 - 2008$$

$$c1^*_{NIPA}(t) \; = \; \frac{\sum Basic\,Expenditure\,NIPA\,(t)}{\sum Consumption\,Expenditure\,NIPA(t)} \qquad\qquad 1955 - 2009$$

$$c1^*_{CEX}(t) \; = \; \frac{\sum Basic\,Expenditure\,CEX(t)}{\sum Consumption\,Expenditure\,CEX(t)} \qquad\qquad 1984 - 2009$$

$$c2'^*_{VGR}(t) = [(i^*(t) - i(t)) + (g_{10year}(t) - g(t))]\, c2^*_{VGR}(t) \qquad 1970 - 2010$$

$$c2'^*_{NIPA}(t) = [(i^*(t) - i(t)) + (g_{10year}(t) - g(t))]\, c2^*_{NIPA}(t) \qquad 1955 - 2009$$

Standard Models:

CEQ	certainty-equivalent
CES	Constant Elasticity of Substitution
CRRA	Constant-Relative-Risk-Aversion
LCPIH	Life Cycle/Permanent Income Hypothesis
MPC	Marginal Propensity to Consume
$U(c)$	Utility Function
V	t-period felicity function
w	wage income
r	real interest rate
δ	discount factor
F	financial wealth
H	human wealth
λ	Lagrange multiplier
μ	dynamic multiplier

| ρ | parameter of a CES-function specifying the intertemporal elasticity of substitution |

Buffer-Stock-Model:

$x(t)$	cash on hand
$p(t)$	persistent income
$v(t)$	transitory income
TN	truncated normal distribution

Data Sources

CEX	data freely available at: http://www.bls.gov/cex/
EVS	data available on demand via: https://www.destatis.de/DE/Meta/AbisZ/Einkommens_Verbrauchsstichprobe.html
FoF	data freely available at: http://www.federalreserve.gov/RELEASES/z1/Current/data.htm
NIPA	data freely available at: http://www.bea.gov/iTable/iTable.cfm?ReqID=9&step=1#reqid=9&step=1&isuri=1
PSID	data freely available at: http://simba.isr.umich.edu/data/data.aspx
SCF	data freely available at: http://www.federalreserve.gov/econresdata/scf/scfindex.htm
SOEP -	papers and data analyses available at: http://www.diw.de/soep
VGR	historic data available on demand; recent data freely available at: https://www.destatis.de/DE/ZahlenFakten/GesamtwirtschaftUmwelt/VGR/VolkswirtschaftlicheGesamtrechnungen.html

Introduction

Despite a large amount of detailed economic research studying consumption and saving behaviour in several countries, utilizing high-level mathematics as well as highly powerful statistical software, the performance of theories attempting to explain the empirical facts still seems to be unsatisfactory. In fact, there is a clear gap between empirically oriented papers about saving on the one hand, and on the other one that part of the literature, which is primarily concerned with estimating the parameters for models of intertemporal utility maximisation that are assumed to guide consumer behaviour. While the issues raised by the latter interest only those believing in the respective models, publications with an empirical focus often reveal interesting relationships of undeniable meaning. Ultimately, these studies mostly note a conflict between their findings and the predictions of mainstream theories.

However, saving is certainly one of the crucial economic variables. Since private-household saving usually accounts for the major part of national saving, it is desirable indeed to clarify what drives an ordinary consumer to save or consume his wealth, and to understand how such decisions are affected by changes in the economic environment or by politically controlled parameters.

For decades, the Life Cycle/Permanent Income Hypothesis (LCPIH), originally formulated by Friedman (1957) and Modigliani & Brumberg (1954), subsequently highly formalised by making use of dynamic programming techniques and optimal control theory, has been the central paradigm in economics for studying consumption and saving behaviour. The LCPIH assumes households optimise the utility of consumption intertemporally, subject to permanent income or life-time wealth. In this approach, saving is merely a by-product of the optimal consumption path. The exclusive purpose of saving is future consumption since the only trade-off a consumer faces is the trade-off between current and future spending.

The mainstream models are based on the assumption of homothetic preferences and additive intertemporal utility. Preferences are assumed not to be interdependent. The optimal intertemporal consumption path is presumed to be governed by the relationship between the real interest rate, rewarding the accumulation of financial wealth, and a discount factor measuring the degree at which households depreciate future consumption compared to immediate pleasure.

The central prediction of these models under perfect foresight or certainty-equivalent conditions states that consumption does not respond to current changes in income if these have been expected in advance. The effect of an unexpected income shock depends on its impact on permanent income. If the income shock is considered to be transitory, consumption remains stable; a transitory income gain will be mainly saved, while a transitory loss will be balanced by dissaving. Only if the consumer expects the shock to be persistent, is consumption adjusted upwards or downwards. The marginal propensity to consume (MPC) out of an increase in current income is consistently assumed to be exactly the same as the MPC out of an increase of equal present value in expected future income.

Vital issues of research within such an approach are to distinguish transitory and permanent income shocks as well as expected and unexpected events. A major focus within empirical work is on estimating the intertemporal elasticity of substitution as the crucial parameter determining the curvature of the intertemporal utility function. In order to refer to aggregate data, the representative agent approach is adopted in most cases, analysing an economy as if it carries out an infinite horizon optimisation problem of a single, immortal, foresighted consumer. This approach requires a number of simplified assumptions about individual preferences.

Yet, the hypothesis of consumers monadically calculating their optimal consumption path far into the future by use of dynamic programming techniques and taking into account the probability distributions of future income streams, life-expectancy and real interest rates, is not just an approach to consumption behaviour. It is one of the cornerstones of modern macroeconomics. As noted by Hahn & Solow (1997), post-Lucas macroeconomic theory stems from two essential commitments: first, a valid macroeconomic model should be the exact aggregation of a microeconomic model; second, the appropriate microeconomic model is based on intertemporal utility maximisation subject to budget constraints and technology only.

In fact, only extremely simplified models at the micro level allow for exact aggregation as the heterogeneity of agents has to be strictly curbed. Except for some recent developments in Dynamic Stochastic General Equilibrium modelling, heterogeneous agents have been entirely excluded in the dominant range of macroeconomic theory. We are not concerned with the consequences for the modelling of firms and competition here. Concerning the theory of the consumer, excluding heterogeneity requires a presumption of homothetic preferences; otherwise distributional parameters influence the aggregate outcome and devaluate the representative agent approach. Interdependencies and strategic interactions also have to be neglected. In fact, the standard LCPIH perfectly fulfils these needs and has therefore been used as an essential module of modern macroeconomic theory.

These models, impressive due to their sophisticated mathematical apparatus impeccably concealing bizarre underlying assumptions, are often the basis for straightforward policy advice. Lucas' critique of the Keynesian consumption function (Lucas, Sargent 1981) was in fact not so much targeted at theory than at policy. Indeed, if people do immediately calculate the permanent income value of a transitory income gain, any political attempt to stimulate demand during an economic downturn by, say, improved social benefits, is simply nonsense. Generally, if forward-looking consumers translate each piece of public debt into an expectation of an additional future tax burden, public deficit spending will only force private households to become particularly eager savers due to adjusted life-time consumption plans. If preferences are, moreover, homothetic, individual saving rates will be completely independent from permanent income. Under such conditions, suggesting a policy that favours low-income families in order to encourage effective demand is just an attestation of economic imbecility.

Therefore, the choice of which theory of saving is acceptable as a description of real consumer behaviour and which should better be disregarded, has far reaching consequences. Ultimately, this should lead to a scrutinising of the reality of the micro foundation of modern macroeconomics.

Already in the early nineties, numerous papers expressed disappointment at the weak empirical performance of the standard LCPIH. It turned out that the results of the empirical tests depended crucially on the incorporated assumptions about the income process. Since income expectations are virtually unobservable, it remains an open question, whether the demarcation line between transitory and permanent income shocks, assumed by theory, corresponds to the perception of any consumer. Discount rates are also unobservable. The only time series which empirical estimations can really rely on are real interest rates. But real rates refuse to confirm a significant link to consumption growth. The striking incapability of empirical research to provide a serious estimate of the vital parameter of intertemporal elasticity of substitution, has contributed to a growing dissatisfaction.

Concerning testing of the model predictions at the micro level, empirical evidence suggests rejection of the framework. Consumption was shown to track income closely over the life-cycle. The MPC out of transitory income fluctuations was obviously significantly higher than the permanent income value of these fluctuations. Saving rates appeared to be boosted rather than diminished in the case of predictable income growth.

This led to a number of amendments to the standard approach such as the introduction of precautionary saving, liquidity constraints and habit formation. As a result, the LCPIH became compatible with a much richer variety of short-run and long-run consumption patterns. Constant-Relative-Risk-Aversion(CRRA)-utility in an uncertain environment under appropriate parameter specification can explain why consumption tracks income over a lifespan, why the MPC out of transitory income is relatively high, or why median wealth holdings are low. Parameter values sufficient to justify these phenomena are more realistic if the precautionary motive is combined with the assumption of imperfect capital markets and liquidity constraints. Habit formation provides a rationale for a positive correlation between income growth and saving rates.

However, despite the gain in realism due to the introduction of the considered amendments, numerous empirical facts remain unexplained. The most striking patterns that are still entirely dubious are: the strong and lasting disparity of saving rates across income groups; the extreme variance in wealth holdings; and the relatively high share of households that save virtually nothing during their life-time.

The buffer-stock model is able to justify why the median saver builds up relatively limited wealth. But it is entirely incomprehensible why the lowest two or three deciles seldom accumulate any financial assets. Precisely because households at the bottom of the income ladder face an over-proportional risk of negative income shocks caused by unemployment or poorly paid jobs, the precautionary motive should drive them toward a particular saving effort. To justify the strong link between income and consumption of poorer consumers by liquidity constraints implies that these consumers actually wish to borrow, but are not allowed to do so. This is also not plausible. Nowadays, most households in the bottom deciles have little reason to expect strong income growth in the future. Their desire to borrow cannot therefore be rationalised under optimality conditions. Instead, assuming poorer households to be liquidity-constrained strengthens the prediction of a strong incentive to build up a buffer-stock of wealth.

Habit formation can explain why a consumer who has just experienced a negative and permanent income shock will attempt to preserve a better standard of living at the cost of saving. But all models of habit formation assume habits to be fixed only in the short-run and to be flexible in the long-run. After some periods the saving rate of a deprived consumer should be the same as it was before. In reality it is not.

In fact, the rising saving rate curve over income in cross-sectional data as such does not challenge the standard approach. The usual explanation since Friedman (1957) has been the concentration of high transitory income households in the upper deciles, and of low transitory income consumers in the lower deciles. A similar argument has been put forward by the life-cycle approach stating that only households at the peak of their hump-shaped life-time income curve are concentrated in the upper deciles, which save most intensely for retirement. So, standard models justify the positive correlation between income and saving rate in cross-sectional data as the outcome of income fluctuations at the individual level, be it short-term or long-term.

The problem is, however, that the lifelong income variance of a typical consumer is not sufficient by far to explain the extreme variance in cross-sectional saving rates. Hence, that saving rates rise with permanent income—more correctly, with the consumer's enduring income position relative to his contemporaries—can soundly be considered a stylised fact. The effect of permanent income on a consumer's saving rate is obviously much stronger than the age effect or the impact of income fluctuations. Households in the bottom permanent income deciles save virtually nothing over their life-cycle, while the permanently rich appear to be exceptionally eager to save.

To cope with the fact of varying saving rates across permanent income groups is a serious challenge for the standard approach and the usual explanations are hardly convincing. Social security provisions are often referred to in order to rationalise low or completely absent saving by low income groups. The argument is that in the case of a negative income shock or after retirement, social security benefits cover a much higher proportion of the income of poorer households than of affluent people. Therefore, low-income consumers are assumed to have less incentive to save in order to prepare for the uncertainties of life or for retirement.

However, if this was correct, saving rate differentials in cross-section would have to be much smaller and average saving significantly higher in countries with poorer social security systems. Empirical evidence does not support such a hypothesis. While Feldstein (1980) tried to prove a negative influence of public pension schemes on private saving, his result has been refuted on empirical and theoretical grounds by subsequent studies. At least within the OECD-sample, countries with better social security and more generous pension plans tend instead to display higher saving rates. Furthermore, examining saving data from the pre-1914-era and comparing them to current saving behaviour provides strong evidence for the fact that low-income households, despite the absent social security net, saved virtually nothing in the early twentieth century. Cross-sectional saving patterns actually appear to be quite similar over long periods, in spite of vast differences in social security provisions and safety net arrangements.

Another strand of the literature considers different discount factors of different income groups to give reasons for divergent saving behaviour. Since discount factors are not observable, this approach is essentially immune to empirical refutation. However, in surveys asking people about their motives to save or not to save, poorer households would be expected to indicate that they are not particularly concerned about the future, thereby confirming the assumption of a high discount factor. In fact, these people mostly respond that they cannot afford to save, although they would like to do so.

It is not only the absence of saving by low income groups that remains incomprehensible within the LCPIH models. The same is true for the enormous assets accumulated by the rich. It has been acknowledged by many researchers that neither the standard LCPIH nor the buffer-stock model provides a reasonable explanation for the saving behaviour of the wealthiest. It is too obvious that the savings of the latter, adding dollar after dollar to already available millions or even billions, are not dedicated to a later life period and also not for consumption by their heirs. However, the wealthiest one or two percent of the population easily account for half of the financial wealth creation in a typical capitalist economy[1]. Several studies consistently conclude that only a minority of financial assets is indeed accumulated with the purpose of future consumption. As Carroll (1997) noted, if all households behaved according to, say, the buffer-stock model, the aggregate capital-income ratio would be far smaller than we observe it to be.

This is not so much a problem for a microeconomic theory of saving that might explicitly limit its scope to the 90 or 95 percent of households below the top. But a macroeconomic model, designed to reveal the essential laws of motion of an economy, must not ignore the obvious disparity in saving behaviour that distinguishes the top percentiles of richest families from the mass of common savers.

The purpose of the following book, however, is not to provide a macroeconomic theory, but suggest a microeconomic model of saving that is closer to the facts than conventional models. Our approach focuses on the saving behaviour of the majority of households that are not exceptionally rich. Hence, we explicitly do not intend to provide a theory of saving by the wealthiest.

Before offering our own model of saving, we demonstrate how the predictions of the standard models fundamentally change if one simply departs from the assumption of homothetic preferences, and introduces Stone-Geary preferences instead. *Intratemporally*, homothetic preferences lead to the prediction of a linear expenditure expansion path that goes through the origin. The *intertemporal* consequence of homothetic preferences is that the intertemporal elasticity of substitution is independent from the level of permanent income. The fact that a linear expenditure expansion path is far away from real consumption patterns is confirmed by all empirical studies scrutinising Engel-curves. The composition of consumption undeniably depends on the amount of total outlay a consumer can afford to spend. In fact, why should we consider the hypothesis of an

---

1 See: data about financial assets of the extremely rich provided by the World Wealth Report (Capgemini and RBC Wealth Management) or D.A.C.H.-Report (Valuga AG)

intertemporal elasticity of substitution that is not influenced by permanent income, to be more realistic than horizontal Engel-curves?

Although not reflected in the mainstream literature, there has been an on-going debate about the role of subsistence needs with respect to saving. One of the first authors to raise the issue was Rebelo (1992). His starting point was the implausible prediction of the standard intertemporal utility function that the optimal saving rate is identical for two countries which have the same real interest rate but different income levels. Rebelo provides a model that is based on a simple extension of standard preferences, assuming that within-period utility has Stone-Geary-form. Under this condition, momentary utility is supposed to be derived not from the entire level of consumption, but from the difference between total consumption and a certain subsistence level.

The intuition behind this approach is that, as long as their most elementary needs are not satisfied, people do not care about consumption smoothing and intertemporal optimality. Beyond the subsistence point, intertemporal reflections might be undertaken but when close to survival, other considerations are incomparably more urgent. A comprehensive check of a model of saving taking into account basic needs is suggested by Ogaki, Ostry & Reinhart (1996). Estimating the parameters of an intertemporal utility function with subsistence consumption, the authors find strong empirical evidence in favour of such an approach.

In the debate about saving and consumption in developed countries subsistence points are typically not supposed to be crucial, since subsistence in the sense of naked survival is not regarded as a major concern. However, subsistence needs determining the minimum level necessary for *social survival* in current societies are possibly almost as equally important. No one will even think about saving, as long as the basic requirements of a modern life are not satisfied. It is fully consistent with such an approach that those families who do not save always report in opinion polls that they simply cannot afford to do so, because all their money is used up to pay for the basics of living.

One of the exemptions in the debate about the relevance of subsistence consumption in developed countries are Ravn, Schmitt-Grohe & Uribe (2008), who analyse the impact of good-specific subsistence points on the price elasticity of demand. The authors explicitly support a broader interpretation of necessities, including those dictated by social norms. Yet, while the subsistence level of a human being's biological survival can be measured fairly, the question arises how necessities of social survival should be defined. Ravn, Schmitt-Grohe & Uribe (2008) suggest understanding subsistence points as an increasing function of long-run measures of output.

Indeed, expenditure devoted to satisfying basic needs according to a common standard of living should plausibly go up with this standard. A telephone or a car was still a luxury in the middle of the twentieth century, but they are a requirement for most households today. Mobile phones, computers, and internet connection have just recently transformed into basic equipment. Consequently, increases in the standard of living also boost the amount of expenditure for purchases, which are no longer a matter of choice.

To define Stone-Geary preferences this way not only overcomes the homotheticity property underlying the standard models. It also acknowledges the fact that individual preferences are interdependent. It is difficult to imagine the decision process of real people in terms of monadic processors running an optimisation program before purchasing a holiday trip or signing a life insurance contract. Actually, these models ignore one of the most essential characteristics of a human being; to be socially interconnected and to be acting in a social environment.

To consider Stone-Geary preferences with moving subsistence points is not only relevant from a theoretical point of view. The predictable response of consumers to policy changes is remarkably different under these assumptions compared to the standard approach. On the one hand, policy measures intended to encourage demand will definitely have an effect now, particularly if they concern low- and middle-income households. Since the latter's intertemporal elasticity of substitution is low under Stone-Geary preferences, their MPC out of an additional income unit will be high, even if this income increase is only transitory. On the other hand, whatever tax incentives are set, households at the lower end of the income scale will not respond with stronger saving effort, neither for private pension schemes nor for the general uncertainties of life, as long as their income does not significantly exceed the current value of the necessity basket. It is not a concern of this book to scrutinise policy implications, but they should at least be mentioned.

In the end, we depart from the entire approach of intertemporal utility maximisation. Models which explain saving as by-product of an intertemporal consumption plan do not only fail to match the facts. They additionally face serious theoretical malfunctions. In fact, those models are only mathematically solvable under extremely simplifying assumptions, and even in that case they are empirically worthless since nobody is equipped with the required information to determine the optimal consumption path. Neither is the exact probability distribution of anybody's real income process for the next 4 or 5 decades a known variable nor does a data base exist that equips us with the times series of real interest rates in the future.

In contrast to the mainstream, the core of our model of saving is a very simple rule of thumb supposed to govern the saving behaviour of rational households with basic needs, which have to be satisfied first.

The book is organised as follows. Chapter 1 reviews the major stylised facts of saving at the micro and the macro level as confirmed by the literature. At the macro level we find only few clear patterns, among them a positive link between income growth and saving. The relationship between income level and saving is weaker, significantly so in low- and middle-income countries. The most striking fact at the micro level is the steep rise of saving rates with relative income that is shown to be true for current as well as for permanent income. Another stylised fact at the micro level is the considerable share of households that save virtually nothing. Moreover, we find evidence that at a given point in time, saving rates in the lower-income deciles display less variance, while they are more volatile than saving rates of better-off people over time. Finally, the assumption of essentially two types of savers—the majority of households on the one hand, and the richest one or two percent on the other hand—is confirmed by the analysis of saving attitudes, wealth holdings and saving motives.

In Chapter 2 we consider the theoretical reasoning of the traditional models and their ability to account for the stylised facts of saving. The chapter concludes that major stylised facts of saving are not explicable within the frame of this approach.

Chapter 3 starts by introducing non-constant good-specific subsistence points into a standard Dixit-Stiglitz framework. Exploring the consequences of moving subsistence points for intertemporal optimisation, it is shown that the Euler equation in this case contains two additional variables, which are usually not considered to be relevant for saving behaviour: first, the growth rate of the necessity basket, possibly corresponding to long-term trends of income growth, and, second, the rate of excess basic price inflation defined as the difference between a particular price index gauging the inflation rate of basic goods and the general consumer price index.

Finally, we present our model. Its core is a simple rule of thumb that is supposed to govern rational saving behaviour of consumers with a hierarchy of needs, some of them elementary and basic. The rule is: When current income exceeds necessity spending the consumer saves, while he dissaves (or searches for credit) when current income falls below the expenditure required for basic needs. We analyse the predictions of such an approach at the micro and the macro levels.

Chapter 4 is concerned with the patterns of consumption shares and searches for criteria to identify subsistence points empirically. Due to a thorough analysis of cross-sectional Engel-curves, a number of expenditure categories are qualified as being dominated by necessities: food and drinks, shelter (including rents, interests on mortgages, energy, water and heating costs), transport (as far as reliable data are available: excluding new car purchases), communication, education and health care. (Due to data problems, health expenditure is neglected in the case of Germany.) On this foundation, two approximations to the historic path of the necessity share are defined and calculated for the U.S. and Germany.

Chapter 5 scrutinises whether our approach offers more satisfactory explanations for the stylised facts of saving than conventional models. Moreover, we check whether the necessity share contributes to an explanation of real saving behaviour in the U.S. and Germany. We show that a significant negative correlation between the necessity share and the personal saving rate exists in both countries.

We demonstrate that cross-sectional saving rates can be matched quite well by our approach for data of the U.S. and Germany from different periods. Finally, we find that more than 90 percent of the variation of the personal saving rate between 1955 and 2009 in the United States, and between 1970 and 2010 in Germany, can be reproduced by our model under plausible parameter values.

Our analysis concludes that the hypothesis of subsistence needs is crucial for explaining saving patterns in cross-sectional and time-series data.

Chapter 1. Stylised Facts of Saving

Paragraph 1.1
Data Sets and Statistical Issues

1.1.1 Various Saving Aggregates and Their Relationship

To scrutinise the stylised facts of saving, we review the results of the previous empirical literature about the topic at hand. In this respect, one problem deserves mention. While our goal is to uncover the determinants of saving decisions of private *households*, many macroeconomic studies do not explicitly refer to the personal saving rate, but to *private* saving, which includes saving by private enterprises. Some important and comprehensive papers even test only the relation between macroeconomic parameters and the *national* saving rate, which additionally contains public saving. Only few studies reflect on personal saving as such.

The background of this orientation is that national statistics, especially in developing countries, often simply do not collect separate figures about personal or household saving. For that reason, the data base would seriously diminish, if analyses were limited to countries and time periods, for which reliable separate saving figures of the household sector are publicly available. Moreover, even if data are provided, the definitions and the kind of measurement of personal saving vary a good deal more from country to country than those of the broader aggregates of public and private saving. In fact, a number of grey areas, where personal and business saving is hardly distinguishable, exist. Different national statistics draw different lines, thus hindering cross-country comparisons of the data.

However, household saving—at least in OECD countries—accounts for the major part of national saving and dominates the rate of private saving. Except for periods of rapidly rising public deficits, personal and national saving rates tend to move in the same direction and the relationship between personal saving and private saving is even stronger. Therefore, it appears reasonable to consider the findings of macroeconomic studies about private and national saving in order to inform our subject of

interest: saving by private households. Debating the development of the
other components of the national saving rate in detail is beyond the scope
of this inquiry.

1.1.2 Macroeconomic Data Sources for the U.S. and Germany

Our own calculations concern two countries exclusively: the United States
and Germany. For macroeconomic data we mainly employ the U.S. National Income and Product Account (NIPA) tables provided by the National Bureau of Economic Analysis (BEA) and the German national statistics (VGR) provided by the Statistische Bundesamt (destatis).
Furthermore, we refer to the Federal Reserve Board Flow of Funds statistics (FOF) and the financial flow accounts of the Deutsche Bundesbank
(DB). While the NIPA data start in 1929, German data suitable for time-
series analysis are not available before 1950, detailed data about consumption shares not before 1970.

The U.S. as well as the German statistics explicitly refer to *personal* saving or private household saving respectively. However, categorisations and
the system of measurement diverge considerably. While in Germany saving
has been derived from net financial wealth accumulation, in the NIPA
tables saving is simply the residual between personal disposable income
and consumption spending.

The NIPA saving rate is calculated as the percentage of personal saving
in personal disposable income. The latter includes the compensation of
employees, proprietor's income, rental income, personal interest and dividend income as well as current transfer receipts. This total amount is reduced by total personal tax payments and employer as well as employee
contributions to government social insurance. Saving, as mentioned, is
derived by subtracting personal consumption outlay from personal disposable income.

The NIPA saving rate has been repeatedly criticised, in particular the
NIPA definition of disposable income. In fact, the compensation of employees as part of personal income includes not only taxes and employer
contributions for government social insurance (that are subtracted to derive disposable income), but also employer contributions to employee
pension funds. In contrast to the German accounting system, the latter are

calculated as part of personal disposable income, although they are in fact not at the disposal of households. Payments from private pension funds, on the other hand, are not included in disposable income, although households certainly use them for consumption. Thus, if employer contributions to pension funds are significantly higher than pension payments, voluntary saving by households is exaggerated by the NIPA saving rate. If, in the opposite case, pension payments exceed employer contributions, the NIPA saving rate understates the real saving by households. This (measurement!) problem has contributed to the decrease in the NIPA saving rate in the nineties.

Therefore, it is advisable to additionally include the Federal Reserve Board Flow of Funds statistics (FOF) in the analysis. Here, saving is not measured as a residual between income and consumption, but is derived from wealth accumulation as in the German statistics. FOF saving by households exactly corresponds to their net acquisition of financial assets plus net investment in tangible assets minus net increase in liabilities of the personal sector. Financial assets include foreign deposits, checkable deposits and currency, time and savings deposits, money market fund shares, open market papers, U.S. saving bonds, other treasury securities, agency-backed and GSE-backed securities, municipal securities, corporate and foreign bonds, corporate equities, mutual fund shares as well as net contributions to life insurances and pension funds. Tangible assets mainly correspond to residential investment. Additionally, they cover consumer durables such as automobiles and investment as well as inventories of unincorporated and farm businesses that are included in the personal sector. The main parts of liabilities are mortgages and consumer credit. Excluding consumer durables, the demarcation of NIPA and FOF saving is comparable. The levels of FOF and NIPA saving differ considerably for a number of years, particularly in the recent past. Nevertheless, the historic paths of the NIPA and the FOF saving rate between 1950 and 2010 are correlated by a coefficient of 0.91, while their yearly changes are only correlated by a coefficient of 0.47 (own calculations). Hence, regressions upon possible determinants of the level of saving will provide similar coefficients, whichever saving rate is used. In contrast, the results of regressions that use changes of the saving rate as the dependent variable strongly diverge and might be spurious.

1.1.3 Measurement Problems—Saving Offshore or Saving Out of Realised Capital Gains

One has to take into account that the measured saving rate—even if it is based on net acquisitions of assets and not simply grasped as a residual—does not gauge all kinds of saving in the same way. A huge grey area, for instance, exists if money is shifted abroad. Although foreign deposits are reckoned in the FOF statistics, one can certainly presume that these figures are much less reliable than data about domestic saving. If saving flows are increasingly directed towards other countries, the saving rate most likely shrinks, as it does not reflect the full extent of these flows. This applies even more to those foreign investments which are motivated by the desire to remain hidden, be it for tax evasion or other reasons.

But also with respect to domestic saving some activities are not adequately recorded. If, for instance, a person receives dividends and uses the money to purchase new stocks, this action is saving out of income. Yet, if the same person sells existing assets with a capital gain of equal extent and uses the gain to buy new stocks, the realised gain is neither accounted for as income nor is it reinvestment saving. From the point of view of the respective individual, both actions appear to be almost the same, but for statisticians the difference is crucial. Hence, if companies focus on pushing up their market value by repurchasing own shares rather than distributing increasing dividends, measured saving falls, although nothing fundamentally has changed in the propensity of households to save.

For the same reason, saving tends to go downwards if banking accounts are increasingly replaced by stocks, since under these circumstances realised capital gains take on a more important role. This problem has also a distributional aspect. We will see later on that saving in stocks as well as realising and reinvesting capital gains is particularly typical for the very rich. Hence, the saving behaviour of the wealthiest households is most likely not adequately reflected in the aggregated saving rate. Therefore, redistributions of income and saving from the middle to the upper class might induce a fall in the measured saving rate.

1.1.4 Statistical Revisions

Finally, statistical revisions taking place from time to time deserve some attention. As far as they affect the measurement of the saving rate, they obviously distort the long-run comparability of figures. For the U.S. two recent examples should be mentioned. The first is the BEA's October 1998 adjustment of the definition of personal income (directly influencing the NIPA saving rate due to its definition of saving as the residual of income not used for consumption). The revised definition excludes all mutual fund distributions from personal income and counts them as business income instead. Adjusting personal income downwards, the BEA's 1998 decision accelerated the decline of the NIPA saving rate. The second revision took place one year later. This BEA's October 1999 revision, however, had the effect of increasing personal saving first by shifting government retirement plans from the government sector to the personal sector, and second by attributing interest and dividends earned on these plans to personal income. Due to this modification, personal income appears to be higher compared to consumption. Hence, saving is pushed up.

The most important revision influencing the comparability of long-run time series in Germany has been the change from the old German system, embedded in the accounting system ESA 79, to the new ESA 95 in the mid-nineties. The main difference between the two standards concerns the demarcation of the household sector. In contrast to the previous system, the economic activities of small businesses and self-employed people are included in the household sector according to ESA 95. Moreover, home purchases that previously had been accounted for as a separate sector, are now classified as an activity of private households. This enlargement of the household sector affects the measured personal saving rate in two ways: business credit and mortgages diminish net household saving, while withheld profits and checking accounts of small businesses push it up. The overall effect is not clear-cut.

Employing German saving data, one has to bear in mind that the definition of household saving used by the Statistische Bundesamt deviates from the one employed by the Deutsche Bundesbank, since they deal with pension reserves of firms in a different manner.

Those divergences and modifications obviously influence the long-run comparability of the data; however, they do not change the figures in a fundamental way

1.1.5 Microeconomic Data Sources for the U.S. and Germany

Considering cross-sectional data we use several datasets. For German figures, we focus on the German Consumer Income and Expenditure Survey
(EVS), conducted every five years since 1963. Occasionally, we employ a
set of detailed saving and consumption data for the period from 1955 to
1974 from the German Institute of Economic Research (DIW 1978).
Moreover, we refer to the German Socio-Economic Panel (SOEP) that has
been conducted since 1983 by the DIW. For the U.S. we employ the Survey of Consumer Finances (SCF), providing particularly detailed and useful
data about wealth holdings. Here, publicly available data go back to 1983.
Additionally, we refer to the U.S. Consumer Expenditure Survey (CEX)
that is publicly available as yearly data from 1984 onwards.

Of course, these panel data have to be used with care. CEX and EVS
are known to be biased towards the middle-class. The very rich are excluded since both surveys only take into account households that earn less
than the upper limit. While in the early EVS from 1962/63 until 1973 all
households earning more than 15 000 DM per month had been excluded,
the limit rose to 20 000 DM in 1978, 25 000 DM in 1983 and 1988, and
35 000 DM in 1993. According to an analysis by Merz (2003) considering
data from the 1993 EVS, households with a *yearly* net income of more than
50 000 EUR have been significantly underrepresented. However, since our
focus is on median household saving behaviour, the absence of the very
wealthy is not a major concern. The same holds for the CEX data.

The EVS income figures are considered to be reliable, since the income
aggregates strongly correspond to the national statistics. For instance, the
compensation of employees has coverage in the 1993 survey of 97.6 percent, while income from businesses and capital has 92.7 percent. Disposable household income as a whole has 93.5 percent coverage. The correspondence is similar for other years. The coverage of total consumption
expenditure by the EVS is slightly worse at approximately 87 percent of
the data provided by national statistics. This difference tends to push the
EVS saving rate upwards. Nevertheless, the general trends are widely compatible with the national data.

The situation, unfortunately, is different for the U.S. Consumer Expenditure Survey. While the CEX is focused on collecting consumption
data, the CEX income figures are regarded as possessing a relatively high
level of noise. Therefore, cross-sectional saving rates derived from the

CEX data set have to be questioned. At the aggregated level, the CEX saving rate even contradicts the falling trend of the saving rate displayed by the FOF as well as the NIPA tables for the nineties, by going upwards instead. In fact, while the correlation between aggregated NIPA *consumption* growth and aggregated CEX *consumption* growth is 0.71, the correlation coefficient between the rate of growth of CEX *income* and NIPA *income* growth is as low as 0.39. As a consequence, CEX saving data derived as a residual between income and consumption have to be used with extreme caution. Therefore, we mainly refer to NIPA and FOF saving; for cross-sectional analyses we use data provided by the SCF.

As mentioned above, the cross-section income and saving figures provided by the German EVS are more reliable. However, some serious disadvantages with the EVS data set also have to be noted. First, the survey is conducted every five years only, which considerably lowers the number of available observations. Second, and more crucial, the historic EVS data (except for the four most recent surveys) are publicly available and sorted only by the social status of households (and some other features), but not by income percentiles. Since the variance of income within the different social status groups is much higher than in the case of ordering by quintiles, this kind of categorisation fairly aggravates the difficulties at drawing conclusions. Particularly the category of self-employed households in the EVS covers quite poor people as well as rather wealthy families. The average income of the former group depends crucially on the respective upper income limit of the survey. For instance, the measured income position of self-employed households has been significantly lower in the 1998 and 2003 surveys compared to the years before. However, this has not been the result of a deterioration in the situation of self-employed people in Germany, but rather the opposite: many more self-employed households than before exceeded the income limit in 1998 and, therefore, were excluded from the sample. Due to this exclusion the average income of the entire group shrunk. The official note about the 1998 survey explicitly emphasised this phenomenon.

The measurement issues discussed in this section make it anything but simple to reveal the stylised facts of saving. Nevertheless, some patterns of saving behaviour are clearly confirmed by the data, while others are certainly rejected.

Paragraph 1.2
The Historic Path of Saving

1.2.1 General Trends in the OECD

Before we scrutinise possible factors that influence saving, let us have a look at the general time trends of the saving rate. If we review the historic path of the personal saving rate in most OECD countries, we clearly see a rising trend until a peak in the mid-seventies, stagnation at lower levels in the eighties, a slight upturn after the beginning of the nineties and a strong decline afterwards. If we compare the saving rates of the whole OECD, the G7, the Euro area, the United States and Germany, the similarity in the trends is striking particularly since U.S. and German households are usually considered being rather different in their saving behaviour.

1.2.2 Saving in the U.S. and its Various Components

This section considers the time path of the U.S. saving rate as derived from U.S. data sources. NIPA tables, as mentioned, are available for a time period of almost 80 years, beginning in 1929. The NIPA saving rate is calculated as the percentage of personal saving in personal disposable income. Since saving was extremely volatile between the Great Depression and the End of World War II, we focus on the post-war period only.

FOF saving data are available from 1946 onwards. Here, saving is not measured as a residual between income and consumption, but derived from the net acquisition of assets. The FOF data set, excluding purchases of consumer durables from saving, is conceptionally comparable to the NIPA saving rate.

The historic path of the NIPA and the FOF saving rate between 1946 and 2010 is plotted in Figure 1. We recognise a slight upward trend until the mid-seventies with a second high at the beginning of the eighties. Afterwards, both rates go down severely, approaching zero (even falling below zero in the case of the FOF series) at the beginning of the 21st century. Although the general paths are similar, FOF saving is clearly more volatile than NIPA saving. This is confirmed by a calculation of variances: while the variance of the NIPA saving rate in the period between 1946 and 2010 is 5.8, the variance of the FOF saving rate is 13.3.

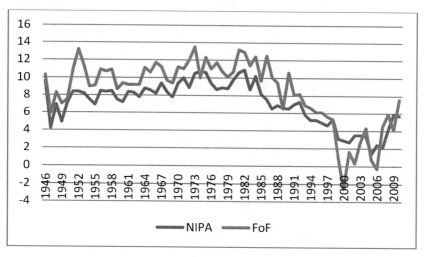

Figure 1. U.S. Saving Rate. Source: NIPA, FOF

FOF saving is in most years somewhat higher than NIPA saving. While the average NIPA saving rate between 1946 and 2010 is only 7.1, average FOF saving reaches 8.5 percent of disposable income. An exception are the years after millennium. Here, FOF saving turns negative twice, while NIPA saving, even though remaining low, always displays positive values.

Important determinants of FOF saving are the net acquisitions of financial assets and the net increase in liabilities. Figure 2 provides the historic path of these variables, calculated as percentages of disposable income. The difference between FOF saving and FOF net acquisition of financial assets is caused by two factors: the extent of liabilities on the one hand, and investment in tangible assets on the other hand. As far as these two factors correspond to each other—e.g. if liabilities are primarily mortgages that coincide with investment in owner-occupied housing—the share of FOF saving and the share of net acquisitions in financial assets in disposable income would not deviate. If, in contrast, the rate of net financial acquisitions by far exceeds the FOF saving rate, it is a sign of rising household indebtedness, which is not compensated by increased real assets.

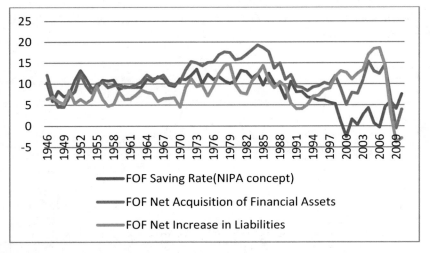

Figure 2. Components of U.S. Saving, Source: FOF

We observe an increasing difference between the two paths from the mid-seventies onwards. Net acquisitions of financial assets reached an extreme high at the beginning of the eighties; this phenomenon was not discernible in the aggregated saving rate. After this peak, net acquisitions of financial assets strongly declined until the beginning of the nineties. But while NIPA and FOF saving continued to fall until the turn of millennium, net financial acquisitions were highly volatile without a clear trend. Hence, the extreme decline in the aggregated saving rate in the second half of the nineties appears to have been caused primarily by mounting liabilities and not so much by a lack of saving efforts on the part of those households that are saving.

After the mid-nineties the value of mortgages exploded in the U.S., while residential investment showed only a moderate increase. This divergence was caused by the bubble in the U.S. real estate sector and low interest rates on mortgages that tempted consumers to refinance expensive credit card debts or consumer credit by enlarged mortgages on already existing homes. Hence, not a lower propensity to save, but soaring indebtedness was the major factor responsible for the strong decline of the U.S. saving rate during the second half of the nineties. After the outbreak of the financial crisis in 2007, the increase in household liabilities came to an abrupt end. Obviously, it was not a deliberate decision of private households in the U.S. to stop lending; instead, the downturn was caused by liquidity constraints due to the unwillingness of banks to continue to finance giant debts of increasingly bankrupt consumers.

The coefficient of correlation between the FOF saving rate and the rate of net acquisitions of financial assets is as low as 0.47. While the mean value of the FOF saving rate between 1946 and 2010 is 8.5 percent, the mean acquisition of financial assets corresponds to 11.3 percent of disposable income.

Finally, let us look at some components of saving in the U.S. The FOF statistics allows us to distinguish between three major components. The first are liquid assets in the form of checking deposits, time and saving deposits that are not tradable. The second component are the different kinds of securities, particularly corporate equities and corporate bonds, which are tradable and subject to capital gains and losses. The third component are life and pension insurance reserves. The acquisition of these different kinds of financial assets does not display a common trend. While net saving in pension funds and life insurances increases up to the mid-eighties and then slows down, the downturn of saving in liquid assets in the late eighties is much stronger, but ends at the beginning of the nineties. A substitutional relation between saving in liquid assets and saving in securities seems to exist, since the lows of one path are the highs of the other.

Saving in securities is highly volatile and does not show any distinct long-term trend. Interestingly, it decreased during the unprecedented stock market boom of the nineties. Saving in corporate equities became even strongly negative during that time. The reason for this seemingly contradictory development is the huge volume of repurchases of own assets by corporate enterprises, since the figures collected here refer exclusively to the household sector and unincorporated business.

The downward trend of saving in securities during the stock market boom confirms the existence of the measurement problem mentioned in the previous chapter. If asset values strongly increase, realising capital gains and re-reinvesting them partly or entirely becomes a natural component of saving in those households that are engaged in the financial market. Statistically speaking, however, realised capital gains are not part of income and using them to repurchase financial assets is not saving. Thus, saving in securities decreases, even as unprecedented amounts of stocks and bonds are demanded and purchased on the secondary market.

Data of real net flows must not be confused with the yearly change in the net value of those assets. The latter is further influenced by capital gains and losses. Naturally, the divergence between the flow statistics and the change in net worth is mostly relevant for saving in securities and, within this category, particularly for corporate equities and those funds that consist mainly of stocks.

1.2.3 Saving in Germany and its Various Components

In this section we consider the German savings data provided by German national statistics. The main source here is the German Statistisches Bundesamt, providing saving figures from 1950 onwards. Despite some statistical revisions (we have considered the influence of the most important one in the previous chapter), the figures are mainly comparable. Similar to the FOF saving rate, the German saving rate is calculated by the change in net assets.

In addition to the saving rate of the National Accounts, we refer to the aggregated saving rate derived from the income and consumption survey EVS. The latter is particularly interesting, since it is dominated by middle-class saving, while the very rich are excluded. Unfortunately, saving data provided by the EVS are much rarer than those of the National Accounts, since the survey did not start before 1963 and is conducted only every five years. Figure 3 compares the historic path of the German saving rate from the national accounts (VGR) and from the survey (EVS).

Obviously, the paths of VGR and EVS saving display generally the same trend. Both rates rise tremendously during the post-war period, reaching their high in the mid-seventies. The series display another peak at the beginning of the nineties, going into decline afterwards. The latter feature is similar to the paths observed in the U.S.

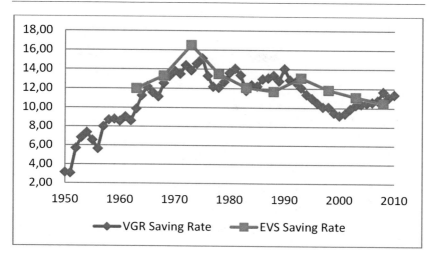

Figure 3. German Saving Rate, Source: VGR, EVS

Nevertheless, some differences are also visible. The peak of EVS saving during the middle of the seventies is even higher, while the second peak is lower compared to the VGR accounts. Furthermore, the decrease of the EVS saving rate during the nineties is not as sharp by far than that of the VGR Accounts. Yet the EVS saving rate continues to fall, while VGR saving displays a rising trend from the beginning of the millennium.

Next, we compare the VGR saving rate to the share of net acquisitions of financial assets in disposable income. The data set to calculate the latter is provided by the Deutsche Bundesbank. The difference between net acquisitions of financial assets and saving follows from factors similar to the case of the difference between FOF saving and FOF net acquisition of financial assets. The path of these two rates is provided by Figure 4. Unlike the U.S. data, the VGR saving rate and the path of net acquisitions of financial assets share more or less the same trends.

The average VGR saving rate for the period between 1950 and 2010 is 10.93 percent, almost identical to the average of the acquisition of financial assets at 10.87 percent. The coefficient of correlation between the two series is as high as 0.86. Contrary to the U.S., indebtedness appears not to play a significant role in Germany, since a sudden boost of household debts drives the two rates away from each other as observed in the U.S. from the mid nineties to 2007.

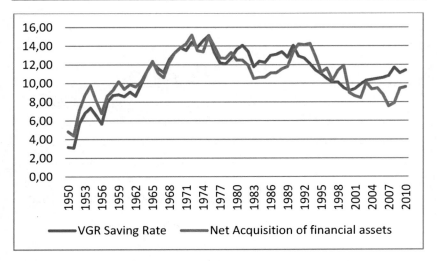

Figure 4. Components of German Saving, Source: VGR, Bundesbank

The Bundesbank provides detailed data about the main components of saving. Until the beginning of the eighties, saving accounts placed with banks were the most important part of household saving. This component then became highly volatile with a shrinking trend. Acquisitions of bonds (which are in the German case primarily public bonds) are also very volatile. Obviously, there exists a substitutional relationship between saving in bonds and saving in bank accounts. Saving with insurances increased permanently.

In comparison to the U.S., the very low level of saving flows directed towards the stock market is striking. Only during the asset bubble of the late nineties do stock purchases by households increase somewhat, then collapsing and remaining negative after the crash. Hence, distortions of the measured saving rate due to saving out of realised capital gains should play a minor role in Germany.

Paragraph 1.3
Stylised Facts at the Macroeconomic Level

1.3.1 Real Income

This section considers the possible determinants of saving at the macroeconomic level, determinants which have been scrutinised in the empirical literature. One of the most frequently tested macroeconomic correlations is that between the saving rate and the disposable income of households, or per capita income. Unfortunately, in this field we are dealing with facts that are far from unanimously accepted. Due to Kuznets' (1953) comprehensive study about saving in the U.S. between the late nineteenth and the mid twentieth century, the so-called absolute income hypothesis—the assumption that the saving rate rises with real income—appeared to have been refuted successfully. Meanwhile, several studies have provided evidence in favour of a positive correlation between saving rates and GDP in a number of countries, some arguing that the U.S. example is no more than an outlier (for instance Maddison (1992)).

Indeed, between the end of World War II and the beginning of the seventies, many OECD-countries appeared to be classic examples confirming the hypothesis that saving rates move in line with real income. In section 1.2.1 we mentioned the upward trend in saving in the OECD, the G7 and the Euro Zone between 1960 and 1974. In almost all OECD countries saving rates were rising during the entire post-war period until the mid-seventies. This was entirely in correspondence to the path of real per capita income. Nevertheless, this relation completely vanished later on: saving rates in most developed countries fell during the eighties and nineties, while income—although at smaller rates—continued to grow.

The different relationship between income and saving in the post-war period compared to the eighties and nineties can be confirmed using econometric techniques. But before we undertake the first regression, it seems necessary to justify the employed estimator. In this book, we test empirical relationships between variables and estimate the respective coefficients using the method of ordinary least squares (OLS).

The appropriateness of the ordinary least square estimator for time-series analyses has been frequently called into question in modern econometrics. Indeed, thoughtlessly calculating coefficients and R-squares between whatever variables and simply interpreting them as proof or rejection of causalities is hardly a convincing procedure. However, we are primarily interested in checking general trends and correlations and we do not intend to interpret significant coefficients—as far as we find some—as immediate confirmation of real relationships. Therefore, we consider the simplest econometric procedure to be the most adequate one, particularly since other methods are also not without shortcomings. Hence, we employ the method of OLS in our empirical calculations. If we qualify a coefficient as significant it always means significant at 0.01 confidence level. If we refer to a different confidence level it is mentioned explicitly. Tables with the detailed outcome of all regressions are freely available on the website http://bit.ly/campus39916.

If we regress the German saving rate on real disposable household income (per head), the dependence of the result on the particular time period is striking. Referring to the years between 1950 and 1975, we obtain a significant positive coefficient and an R-squared of 0.93. If we relate the same variables and choose instead the period between 1976 and 2010, a negative correlation is derived. If we choose the entire half century of German post-war history, a slightly positive correlation remains, but the R-square is reduced to 0.27. Hence, the explanatory power of real income with respect to the personal saving rate is low at best. The regression of the saving rate on log real income per head over the entire period performs hardly better. In fact, the positive coefficient for income in both regressions is dominated by the first 25 years. An analysis of the residuals shows that they are not normally distributed. The rising trend of the error terms seriously questions the derived coefficient. (Detailed regression results are provided in the Annex. See Regressions 1—3.)

If we use U.S. time series data for saving and disposable income, starting in 1929, the absence of any correlation is striking. If we regress the NIPA saving rate upon log real income per head over a period of more than seventy years we obtain an R-square close to zero and an insignificant coefficient. Including 40 additional years to Kuznets calculations does not change the estimation result. If we refer to the post-war period exclusively (starting 1946) the outcome is still the same (Regression 4).

In cross-country comparisons no obvious relationship between GDP per capita and saving rates exists. East-Asian countries for instance have for a long time been achieving much higher saving rates than many wealthier nations. The contrast is salient if we compare China to the United States in terms of income and saving figures.

On the other hand, if the analysis is limited to (or at least dominated by) low-income and middle-income countries, a significant positive correlation between income and saving is evident. Summarising the results from a three-year World Bank project employing about 1800 annual observations for 97 countries, Loayza et al. (2000) find a positive and significant effect of the (log) income level on private saving. The authors estimate that an increase in income by one percentage point raises the long-run private saving rate by 0.15 percentage points.

Another interesting feature was discovered by Masson, Bayoumi and Samiei (1998). The authors estimate the impact of the level of per capita income in developing countries—*measured in relation to per capita income in the United States*—and obtain a significant positive coefficient of that (relative) level but a negative coefficient of its square. This finding indicates that beyond a certain point, higher income stops the boost to saving.

So, the overall picture is ambiguous. There are at best two stylised facts concerning the relation of current disposable income and saving. First, very poor countries tend to have very low saving rates. Second, on average middle-income countries show higher saving rates than low-income countries. With regard to high-income countries, any distinct pattern is missing.

1.3.2 Growth

In contrast to the vague correspondence between saving rates and income levels, a positive effect of income *growth* has been found by almost all studies. The direction of causality may still be a moot point, but most studies agree that it runs from growth to saving and not the other way around. Tests of time series data concerning large samples of countries have been undertaken with similar and convincing results.

Bosworth (1993) infers that the causality from growth to saving is much stronger than that from saving to growth. Edwards (1995) examines data from a panel of 36 countries for the period between 1970 and 1992, confirming that the rate of output growth has a significant positive effect. Carroll and Weil (1994) provide Granger-causality tests for 38 countries in which increases in growth significantly exceed increases in saving. In every regression in Loayza et al. (2000), the growth rate is among the most significant variables determining the national saving rate. They estimate that a one percentage point rise in the growth rate increases the private saving rate by a similar amount, although the effect may be partly transitory. Masson, Bayoumi and Samiei (1998) corroborate a significant positive growth effect, emphasising that it works stronger in developing than in industrialised countries. Yet, developed countries also provide one striking example of this correlation. The productivity and growth slow-down in the OECD area after 1973 was followed by an immediate drop in private saving rates.

Of course, simply including growth in a regression does not solve by far the saving puzzle. In Germany, the regression of household saving upon real income growth as such provides a significant negative coefficient with almost no explanatory power (Regression 5). If we include log real income per head as a second variable, at least the expected positive sign appears on both coefficients. But the R-square is quite low, and the coefficient for growth has no significance (Regression 6).

A more conclusive correlation exists between *changes* in the saving rate and income growth. If we regress these two variables, the coefficient is significantly positive, although the explanatory power indicated by an R-square of 0.28 is not outstanding (Regression 7).

The situation is similar for the U.S. The regression of the FOF saving rate upon income growth alone gives an insignificant positive coefficient (Regression 8). Including log real income does not improve much (Regression 9). Regressing changes of the FOF saving rate upon income growth provides a significant positive coefficient at 0.05 confidence level, but the explanatory power is not relevant (Regression 10). If we use changes of the NIPA saving rate as the dependent variable, the coefficient of income growth is significantly positive and the explanatory power is not negligible (Regression 11).

Based on the previous literature and our own calculations, a positive influence of income growth on saving, particularly on the change of saving, can be stated as a stylised fact. At the macroeconomic level, this indeed seems to be almost the only determinant which is widely accepted.

1.3.3 Real Interest Rates

The effect of real interest rates on saving has been tested in numerous studies. The results, however, are hardly conclusive. Bosworth (1993) finds a positive interest rate coefficient in time-series estimations for individual countries, but a negative coefficient in cross-country estimations. Giovannini (1985) shows that in only five of eighteen developing countries, consumption and saving exhibit any sensitivity with respect to real interest rate changes. In all other countries the elasticity of saving regarding real rate movements is simply zero. Masson, Bayoumi and Samiei (1998) provide evidence for positive interest elasticity in developed countries, but negative (insignificant) elasticity in developing countries. Serres & Pelgrin (2003) in contrast find a significant negative coefficient of real interest rates within a sample of OECD-countries. Other studies confirm very low or completely absent elasticities of saving rates in response to changes in interest rates. Maier (1983) finds evidence of a positive relationship between saving rates and lagged (rather than current) yields for German data. But this is not necessarily evidence in favour of higher interest rates encouraging stronger saving effort. Probably, the correlation is based on amplified interest income as a *consequence* of higher real rates. In this case the link just confirms that the propensity to save out of interest income is higher than out of wage income. This is very plausible, but has nothing to do with the elasticity of saving regarding differentials in the rates of return.

Reviewing the literature dealing with the matter of a possible response of saving to interest rate differentials, Deaton (1992) summarises: "...my own view of the empirical evidence is that saving is little influenced by interest rates."[1] In fact, empirical evidence suggests that not the quantity of money saved but the kind of assets in which it is invested is affected by the rates of return.

If we regress the German saving rate upon the real interest rate (using the yield on German public bonds outstanding as point of reference), the hypothesis of no correlation is confirmed. The coefficient is not significant and the explanatory power is in fact zero (Regression 12). Including log real income and real income growth preserves the insignificant coefficient, while the adjusted R-square remains very low (Regression 13).

---

1 Deaton (1992)

The situation is similar in the U.S. There is a slight correspondence between the peak of real interest rates in the first half of the eighties (the years of Reaganomics) and the peak in the net acquisition of financial assets. The same is true for the increase of the latter in the second half of the nineties that occurred in combination with increasing real rates of return. A relationship between real rates and the saving rate, however, is hard to establish.

The regression of FOF saving on the Fed real effective rate demonstrates the absence of any correlation with an R-square of about zero (Regression 14). If we use the net acquisition of financial assets instead, the coefficient of the real interest rate is significantly positive, although the explanatory power is still very limited (Regression 15).

With respect to the response of saving to differentials in the real interest rate, no stylised facts can be stated.

1.3.4 Inflation

Factors indicating rising uncertainty in the economic environment—such as inflation, unemployment rates or social security standards—have been thoroughly scrutinised in the literature. In this context, extremely high inflation was found to hamper private saving in developing countries. One part of the explanation, however, might simply be the flight of capital due to soaring inflation. While this outflow—often occurring beyond legal limits—is difficult to measure, the statistical effect is a decline in national saving rates.

In the industrialised world, inflation and saving tend to be linked positively. In Germany, for example, some correspondence between the peaks of both rates exists: high inflation seems to encourage saving. This relationship is confirmed if we regress the German saving rate upon the inflation rate. The latter has a positive coefficient that is significant at 0.05 confidence level, but it contributes little to an explanation of saving rate differentials (Regression 16). If we include inflation in addition to log real income and income growth, the adjusted R-square improves to 0.58, compared to 0.39 in the regression without inflation (Regression 17; compared to Regression 6).

Scrutinising the issue in more detail, Maier (1983) finds a different response in different groups of households in Germany. While middle and high income households tend to enhance saving in times of swelling inflation, retirees and unemployed people tend to save less. But in fact, one has to control this result for diverging real income paths of these types of household in case of inflation. A possible explanation could simply be that middle and high income households are better equipped to shield their wealth against losses caused by inflation, while other groups suffer from an (at least temporary) income deficit due to inflation, preventing them from adjusting their saving rates upwards.

For the U.S. there also exists a correlation between inflation and saving. It especially concerns the acquisition of financial assets. If inflation reaches high rates, the acquisition of assets does the same. However, the absolute peak in saving corresponds to a decrease in inflation. If we regress the two FOF saving rates and the rate of net acquisition of assets upon the inflation rate, the result is as expected. In both cases the coefficient for inflation is significant and positive. The explanatory power is higher in the case of net acquisitions of financial assets (Regressions 18 and 19).

Such a positive relationship certainly does not mean that inflation gives an incentive to put money aside. Rather, households attempt to offset losses in financial wealth caused by inflation with a stronger saving effort. Since high inflation is usually connected to high nominal interest rates, the majority of savers are able to do so.

In fact, if we regress the respective saving rates upon *nominal* interest rates, the coefficients are more convincing (Regressions 20, 21 and 22). The coefficient of the nominal interest rate is in all cases significantly positive and the R-square is clearly higher than in the regressions that used the inflation rate as the dependent variable.

Hence, some evidence for a positive relationship between saving and inflation exists, which is most likely caused by the desire to balance losses in financial wealth from inflation. The higher the nominal interest rate, the easier it is to offset such losses. The real source of higher saving in times of soaring inflation appears to be the nominal interest rate.

1.3.5 Unemployment and Social Security Standards

A negative impact of social security standards on saving, although fiercely defended by some economic schools, is not confirmed by empirical evidence. Feldstein (1980) tries to prove a negative influence of public pension schemes on private saving, but his result has been refuted on empirical and theoretical grounds by several subsequent studies. (See for example Koskela & Viren (1983).)

James, Palumbo and Thomas (2006) examine saving data from the pre-1914 era in the U.S. and compare them to current saving behaviour. They find strong evidence that a substantial fraction of low-income households saved nothing during this period, in spite of an absent social security net, while high income households saved a lot. The authors conclude that the cross-sectional patterns of saving are remarkably similar in the time before 1914 and after 1945, despite the vast differences in social security provisions and safety net arrangements.

Kopits & Gotur (1980) find that social security rather encourages saving. Indeed, at least within the OECD-sample, countries with better social security and more generous pension plans tend to display higher saving rates. One may hardly deny that the uncertainties of life—especially for employees—are much more intense in the U.S. than in most European countries, but private saving by U.S.-households is nevertheless remarkably lower. Furthermore, if we analyse saving data for European countries, in which social security has been sharply reduced, and compare them to the decades before, we rarely find examples of increasing household saving.

Probably the most evident indicator of uncertainty, unemployment, lacks a significant coefficient too. As the economic environment became more uncertain in the eighties and nineties with soaring unemployment rates in most OECD-countries, households did not respond with a higher propensity to save, but with the opposite. On the other hand, some examples of recessions, in which private consumption has responded pro-cyclically and saving rates rose, indeed exist. In Germany, that was the case in the downturns of 1974-75 and 1980-82. By and large, however, saving rates tend to drop if real income declines.

Reviewing the literature we have to conclude that concerning the link between social standards or unemployment rates and saving at the macro level, no well-established stylised fact exists.

1.3.6 Demographics

A flood of papers has focused on tests of the effect of demographic parameters on the aggregate saving rate. Unfortunately, the results are as similarly vague as the results concerning uncertainty. Leff (1969), Modigliani (1970), Graham (1987) and others found that higher dependency ratios are associated with lower saving rates. The robustness of the results, however, was called into question by subsequent studies (Koskela, Viren 1983). Loayza et al. (2000) confirm significant negative coefficients of the youth- and the old-dependency ratio. In fact, a negative impact of the former on saving, estimated using cross-sectional panels including developing countries, is not surprising. Since we have the highest fertility rates in the poorest countries, it is quite likely that in this case the crucial hidden determinant is low income. At least within the OECD-sample a negative effect of a higher share of retirees on aggregate saving is hard to confirm. Just those two countries with rather high average and median ages of their population and a fast growing share of elderly people—Germany and Japan—belong to the countries with the highest private saving rates, much higher than comparatively "young" countries like the U.S. or New Zeeland.

Although the ratio of retirement years to lifespan in the U.S. increased by 67 percent from 1890 to 1930, the saving rate displays no rising trend during this period. Thus, concerning demographics we cannot seriously talk about evident stylised facts at macroeconomic level.

1.3.7 Inequality

In many studies, inequality is a factor considered to have a relevant impact on saving. However, econometric estimates of the relationship are quite rare. To a large degree, data problems are responsible for this lack of detailed analyses since estimates of Gini coefficients—as the most common indicator of inequality—are not as reliable by far as time series for per capita income, inflation or growth rates. In fact, regarding inequality, divergent estimates are available for the same countries and periods, differing not only in levels, but also in trends. One is tempted to suspect that political objectives in this field, even more than in many others, influence scientific honesty.

The most commonly used reference point of development research has been the compilation of statistics on household income inequality by Deininger & Squire (1996) of the World Bank. However, the quality of the data is questionable and has been strongly criticised, among others by Atkinson & Brandolini (2001). The authors argue that rather different types of figures are mixed up in the World Bank data set. The University of Texas' Inequality Project (UTIP) has produced an alternative global inequality data set, based on the Industrial Statistics database published annually by the UN Industrial Development Organisation (UNIDO). These data do not measure income inequality in general, but the dispersion of wages in the manufacturing sector. The trends clearly conflict with those derived from the World Bank data set. Galbraith & Kum (2005) strongly confirm the critique of the inequality figures. Using the UNIDO-UTIP results, they provide a broader data set (denoted EHNII) of income inequality based on pay inequality and manufacturing share. The EHNII data appear to be much more in line with empirical evidence than the World Bank calculations. Figure 5 indicates a rising trend in inequality in the developed world since the beginning of the eighties, with a steep increase after 1990. In developing countries the trend is similar, although at higher levels of inequality at each point in time.

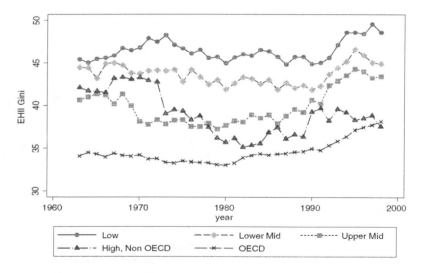

Figure 5. Gini-Coefficient, Source: Galbraith, Kum (2005)

Remembering the historic path of saving rates in the OECD-area considered in section 1.2.1, it is tendentially opposite to the development of inequality. Between World War II and the eighties saving rates in almost all OECD-countries rose, while inequality decreased. After 1980, saving rates in the OECD tended downwards, while inequality reached higher levels than at any time after the Second World War.

The pattern of strongly rising inequality in developed countries is confirmed by panel data. If we compare the respective relative income of certain income deciles in the U.S, the curve clearly shifts downwards after 1976 for low and middle income earners, but upwards for the upper deciles, in particular for the richest one. In Germany, the lowest income groups appear to have experienced the strongest adverse effects of the distributional changes occurring during the eighties. Conversely, and similar to the case of the U.S., groups at the top of the income distribution appear to have benefited the most during the period. (Source: EVS and SCF)

If we refer to the adjusted wage share as another rough indicator of equality, we find a similar trend in the major OECD countries as indicated by the EHNII data set. The wage share had been (strongly or slightly) rising between the beginning of the sixties and the mid-seventies, while it dropped remarkably afterwards. This is exactly the path of the saving rates.

This outcome is astonishing, insofar as saving out of capital income is usually considered to be higher than saving out of wage income. In fact, the historic series do not necessarily contradict this hypothesis. A possible explanation for the strong correspondence of wage share and saving rate might be that the *measured* saving rate overemphasises wage earners saving and reflects not so much the saving by capital owners. This might be particularly true for the NIPA saving rate.

An obvious reason could be the measurement problem considered in Paragraph 1.1. Perhaps, the richest are more eagerly engaged in stock trading and realising and reaccumulating capital gains, while wage earners use mainly traditional banking accounts or save in pension funds. Due to this divergence, saving by the upper class of capital owners might be underreported in the measured saving rate. Since the share of capital gains in total income rises when the wage share goes down, capital owners most likely account for a higher share in total saving under this condition. This could explain why measured saving moves in line with the wage share.

Another interesting feature in this context is that among all considered saving rates in the U.S., the correlation between the rate of net acquisitions of financial assets and the wage share is the lowest. Indeed, rising indebtedness of employees due to falling wages might play an important role in pushing down aggregate saving. Since the FOF's Net Acquisitions of Financial Assets is influenced by dissaving, but not by rising debts, the link to the wage share is less distinct.

Regardless of the above issues, a mainly negative correlation between saving rates and inequality in OECD-countries and a strong positive relationship between (measured) saving rates and the adjusted wage share can soundly be considered stylised facts.

1.3.8 Institutional Environment

A number of other factors such as the impact of the financial system, the wealth effect or the influence of public deficits, have been scrutinised in the literature. With respect to public deficits, the hypothesis of Ricardian Equivalence was widely rejected (among others see Loayza et al. (2000) and Serres & Pelgrin (2003)), but estimation results differ considerably.

Concerning the financial structure, three relationships may be taken as stylised facts. First, countries with market-based financial systems generally display lower saving rates than countries with bank-based financial systems. Second, a striking parallelism between booming stock markets and shrinking saving rates has been discovered in most OECD-countries during the eighties and nineties. Third, financial deregulation reduces private saving rates.

The first two relationships in fact might be explained by the problem of capital gains regarding measured saving. Realising those gains instead of collecting interests plays a serious role in market-based systems, but is only of minor importance in bank-based economies. Moreover, the higher the available wealth (particularly if it is based on stocks), the higher the possible capital gains that could again be realised and accumulated. But this part of saving is not accounted for statistically. Hence, institutional factors appear to have more links to possible distortions of the *measured* saving rate than any real influence on the propensity to save of households.

The negative effect of financial deregulation on saving is different, but not difficult to explain. Deregulation generally eases access to credit, often leading to escalating indebtedness. This could be the main cause of shrinking saving rates and not so much reduced saving efforts of those households who save. In fact, debt to income ratios increased in all OECD countries straight after the liberalisation of financial markets.

1.3.9 Persistency

One last feature has been in the focus of some parts of the literature. Regressions, in which private or household saving is related to its own lagged values, display a high degree of persistency. Saving rates in different countries change over time, but they do so slowly, and a linkage to their own past values seems to be present. Loayza et al. (2000) identify a coefficient of the lagged saving rate term as high as 0.57, suggesting a large degree of persistence. We do not investigate this issue in more detail at this stage.

Instead, we intend to finish our review of the macroeconomic oriented literature here, emphasising that it was not our goal to be exhaustive but to find those macroeconomic variables whose impact on household saving is beyond doubt and which therefore may be called the stylised facts of saving. Our harvest, in fact, has not been abundant.

Paragraph 1.4
Stylised Facts at the Microeconomic Level

1.4.1 Macroeconomic Facts and Microeconomic Distributions

The poor result of our search for stylised facts at the macroeconomic level is not completely surprising. It is a long acknowledged truth that saving decisions are not carried out by a representative consumer bearing in mind the mean values of several aggregated variables, but by millions of individual households deciding on the basis of their own individual constraints and goals. If the relationship between their saving decisions and various determinants cannot be considered to be linear, it becomes blurred by aggregation. Hence, important features are simply not observable at the macro level.

Since we cannot analyse these millions of households separately, discovering the crucial features for forming consistent *groups* of households is the decisive task. The next task then would be to observe the circumstances under which these groups of households act in time. Such circumstances may develop quite differently and this information inevitably vanishes if we deal with aggregated data exclusively. Thus, at the highest level of aggregation we might not be able to identify the *key variables* to which households respond.

In fact, in all countries the income distribution is skewed to the right, and even when the Gini coefficient is comparatively low, the difference between mean and median income is not negligible. If we consider European countries during the previous decade, the mean income of households has exceeded the median in a range between 10 and 20 percent. In most developing countries, the difference is a great deal higher.

Suppose the saving rate (not the absolute amount that is saved) was a linear function of a household's current income. Then, the aggregate saving rate depends crucially on the respective income distribution and not on mean income alone. If we dealt with different countries exhibiting various income distributions, or if we analysed time series data of a single country in which a hidden change in the income distribution occurred, we would never find a clear macroeconomic pattern between income per head and saving rate.

We do not believe that the saving rate is such a simple function. We intend only to illustrate that in a society where the median income differs considerably from the mean, and the difference between mean and median wealth is even more remarkable, the attempt to estimate a saving function using only mean values of income, wealth, etc. may fail to provide an understanding of saving decisions.

1.4.2 Saving Rates in Cross-Section

Passing on to the microeconomic level, patterns indeed become more distinct and a number of stylised facts seem to be available. The most striking feature is the extreme variance in individual saving rates and the high share of households which save virtually nothing. In the German Socio-Economic Panel (SOEP) for 1993, one third of all German households indicated that they are not able to save at all. Two thirds saved less than 200 euros per month. Mean saving per household was about 200 euros, median saving was just 100 euros and the mode was zero. According to opinion polls in Great Britain 45 percent of all parents say that they save nothing at all for their children. A further 28 percent are saving less than 100 pounds a month. Only 11 percent indicate that they save more than 100 pounds.[2]

If we observe this issue in more detail, another pattern becomes evident. The saving rate of an individual household depends crucially on its current position within the income hierarchy. This fact is confirmed by household panels and expenditure surveys in all countries and at any time since the earliest available statistics about household consumption dating back to the nineteenth century. In a comprehensive study on the saving behaviour of households in six OECD-countries—Canada, U.S., Japan, the United Kingdom, Germany and Italy—Poterba et al. (1994) find that saving rates for the lowest quintiles or quartiles are mostly negative, dif-

---

2 The Western Mail. 30.3.05: We're saving more…and still borrowing to much

fering between minus 10 percent (UK, bottom quartile) and minus 1 percent (Canada and Germany, bottom quintile). Certain countries (Japan, bottom quartile) display values around zero for the late eighties and early nineties. Except for Japan, median saving lies below ten percent, while the saving rates of the highest income group ranged between 17 percent (Canada), 24 percent (UK) and 42 percent (Japan).

Referring to German data, Figures 6 and 7 give an overview of the changing curves over time. The striking difference between the saving curves is the complete absence of negative saving figures in the lower income groups up to 1974. This might be a consequence of more strictly regulated financial markets, although other aspects are likely to play a role, too.

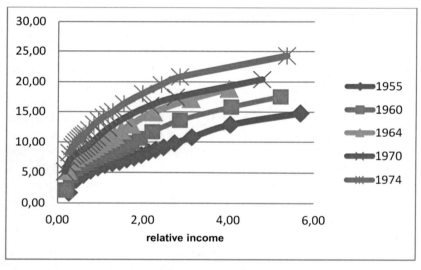

Figure 6. German Saving Rates, Source: DIW (1978)

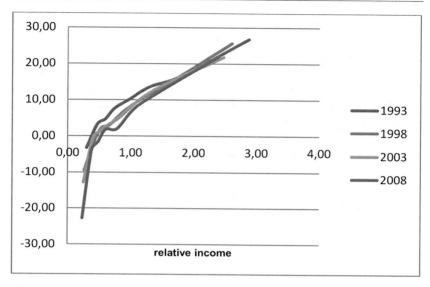

Figure 7. EVS Saving Rates, Source: EVS

If we use data of the U.S. Consumer Expenditure Survey CEX, the overall picture is similar as for other countries. Saving rates rise dramatically with income, starting from minus 230 percent in the lowest quintile to 31 percent in the highest quintile. As mentioned above, the CEX saving rates are not very reliable and the extreme values at the lower end are probably the consequence of a sizeable underreporting of income. According to the Survey of Consumer Finances (SCF), the slope is considerably flatter for the same time period. The saving rate (here measured by change in wealth) rises from minus 2 percent at the bottom up to 27 percent in the top quintile.

The SCF additionally provides detailed information about the propensity to save within the most affluent group. These data show that the saving rate/relative income curve gets much steeper if we reach the upper income categories. We observe a saving rate of 37 percent for those in the top five percent of the income hierarchy and even 49 percent of the top one. Many consumption surveys, unfortunately, do not allow for inferences regarding consumption and saving behaviour of the very rich, as this part of the population is excluded from the panels.

The rise in saving rates with current relative income is in no way a new phenomenon, as can be seen in the data collected by Kuznets for the United States between 1929 and 1950. (Kuznets 1953)

Insofar as survey data from developing countries are available, the pattern is generally the same. According to Attanasio & Székely (1998), more than 70 percent of total household saving in Mexico has been concentrated among the richest 10 percent of the income distribution in 1984, 1989 and 1992, while the poorest 40 percent accounted for a negative proportion.

In all data sets, the saving rate is a strictly increasing function of relative income. In case of scaling by percentiles, the shape of the saving rate curve tends to be convex, while it is mostly concave if we use relative income as the point of reference.

1.4.3 Current Income, Real and Relative

With respect to a particular year, relating saving rates to relative income is in fact the same as using absolute income as a point of reference. In cross-sectional data, saving rates are a strictly rising function of real income, a pattern that might be noted as a stylised fact. However, this is not true for time series comparisons. While in some countries and time periods—for example in Germany from the fifties until the middle of the seventies, as shown in Figure 6—the curves clearly shift upwards while real income rises, the crucial finding from Kuznets, in contrast, was the absence of such a pattern for the U.S. The curves for Germany between 1993 and 2008 plotted in Figure 7 also display a downtrend, which does not correspond to the time path of mean real income.

Using panel data from the German EVS, it can be shown that relative income, indeed, has a stronger effect on saving behaviour than real income. As argued in the first section, the EVS income and, thus, saving figures are more reliable than those of the CEX. Moreover, the time period covered by comparable EVS data is longer, as the first figures date back to 1962/63. Therefore, the EVS is chosen as basis of our calculations. The EVS data strongly confirm the influence of relative income on the saving behaviour.

To approach the data set, first we search for the coefficient of log real income (again using OLS) employing aggregated EVS saving figures for all households for the time period from 1962/63 to 2003. Regression 23 in the Annex provides the estimation results. In fact, it is similar as if we used income data from the German national accounts: because the period is dominated by the time after the mid-seventies, we find no significant coefficient at all.

Instead of using the aggregated real income of all households, in a next step we make use of disaggregated income data of households sorted by social status. The EVS distinguishes six major household groups: self-employed households (including farmers), civil servants, employees, workers, unemployed people and non-working households. The last category covers completely divergent earning groups, ranging from people on the dole to better-off pensioners. Thus we exclude non-working households from our calculations, except for the years 1962—1978, since here the unemployed are also covered by this category. From 1983 onwards, data about the unemployed are provided separately, so we use these data. This way, we have the same number of five observations for each EVS year.

The outcome of the pooled cross-sectional and time-series estimation is shown by Regression 24. As can be seen, cross-sectional income data strongly push up the explanatory power of log real income regarding the saving rate. (If we had regressed to real income as such, the fit would even be slightly better with an R-square of 0.55.)

Next, we undertake the same pooled regression but referring to *relative* instead of absolute real income as the regressor (Regression 25). In fact, the fit is improved decisively with an R-square of 0.71 while the F-value shifts up from 49.9 to 106.95. If we control the residuals for autocorrelation (Durbin-Watson-statistic), the regression using relative income performs better compared to the regressions including real or log real income.

Finally, we regress the same set of pooled cross-sectional and time-series saving rates upon both variables—log real income *and* relative income (Regression 26). The explanatory power of the latter is now even more visible. While relative income still has a significant positive coefficient, log real income has a negative, but completely insignificant coefficient (p-value = 0.73). This shows clearly that relative income contains more information than real income to explain saving rate differentials (irrespective of whether we use its absolute value or its log).

Recent EVS data provide an interesting additional example illustrating the role of relative income. The EVS from 1993 and 1998 provide the saving rate sorted by income groups separately for East and West Germany. Figures 8 and 9 display the paths. According to the graphs, East German households appear to be much more eager savers than West German households at each income position.

However, we have to take into account that the average income in East Germany was (and is) still much lower than in the West. Due to this general divergence, the relative income groups in East Germany stand for population subgroups of different density: the upper income categories represent a significantly smaller part of the population compared to the West, while the vast majority is located in the lower income groups.

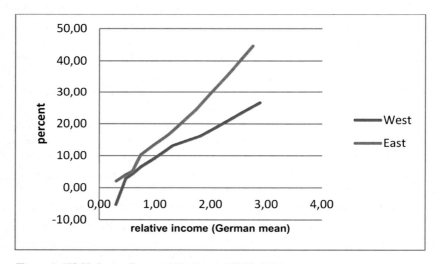

Figure 8. EVS Saving Rates 1993, Source EVS 1993

Our calculation has so far employed the German average income as the reference point for the relative income of all households. It is amazing how any difference between the two saving curves almost completely disappears if we use the East and the West German average income as the reference point for calculating relative income positions instead of referring to the German mean. The results are displayed in Figures 10 and 11.

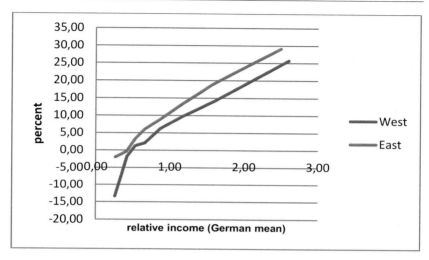

Figure 9. EVS Saving Rates 1998, Source EVS 1998

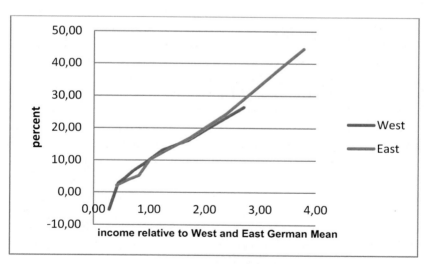

Figure 10. EVS Saving Rates 1993, Source: EVS 1993

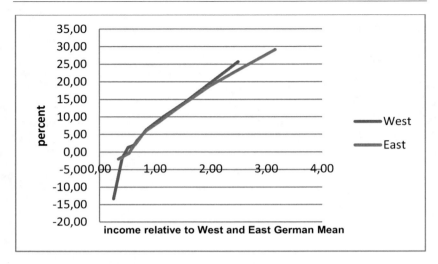

Figure 11. EVS Saving Rates 1998, Source: EVS 1998

Due to the particular German situation of rather dissimilar earning and living conditions, an overall national reference income had not been reached by 1998. This particular example supports the hypothesis, that saving behaviour is more influenced by relative than by absolute income.

Economic research examining the relation between saving rates and relative income, despite the appeal of the topic for the saving debate in the mid-twentieth century, is rather rare. Since relative income is not a crucial variable in the mainstream saving models, the empirical investigation of its link to saving has not been a major concern to the discipline.

General statements about the evolution of the relative income/saving rate curve over time are hardly possible. Bosworth, Burtless, Sabelhaus (1991), examining panel data from the United States, Canada and Japan, find as a general conclusion to their study, that saving rates across population subgroups change in parallel over time. Some authors in Poterba et al. (1994) express a similar observation. However, neither the generality of these results nor the driving forces are evident.

Figure 12 plots the movement of saving rates of different German household types according to the EVS data. We observe some parallelism, but remarkable differences as well. The path of saving by self-employed households is obviously distorted by the upper income limit of the EVS (since the highest income earners that have been excluded in the 1998 and 2003 surveys were probably also the most eager savers). For comparison,

Figure 13 provides the saving rates of similar household types according to data of the national statistics. Except for the self-employed, the saving paths are generally the same as in the EVS. While the self-employed display a rising propensity to save, the saving rates of all other groups of households—as in the EVS—have a downwards trend. The strong decline in the saving rate of unemployed people should be particularly noted, together with the fact that the variance of saving rates of unemployed households over time is higher than of all other households in both datasets; (we exclude the self-employed in the EVS due to the distorted path).

Figure 14 displays the time path of Kuznets' data set and Figure 15 shows the Mexican figures. In both cases saving rates of lower-income households are obviously more volatile over time than saving rates of better-off families. According to Kuznets' data, the standard deviation of saving rates in the lowest income group from 1929 to 1950 is 11.54, that of average income earners is 3.26, and that of the richest is only 2.93. This confirms the intuitive impression from the paths in the figure.

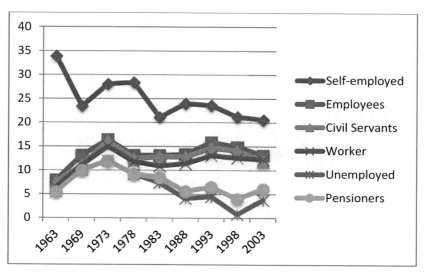

Figure 12. EVS Saving Rates, Source: EVS

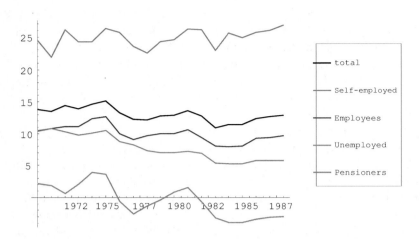

Figure 13. German Saving Rates, Source: Frietsch (1991)

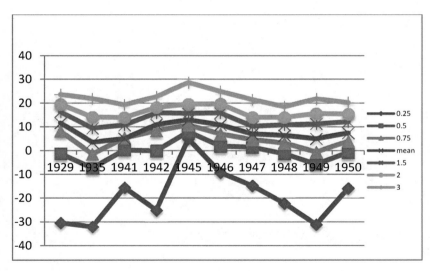

Figure 14. U.S. Saving Rates, Source: Kuznets (1953)

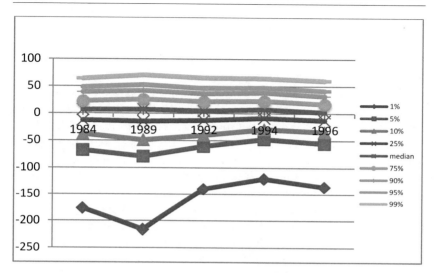

Figure 15. Mexican Saving Rates, Source: Attanasio, Székely (1998)

Another interesting pattern has been discovered by Jung (2001). The author shows for data from the German Income and Expenditure Survey (EVS) 1993 that saving rates in the bottom deciles are not only *on average* much lower than in higher income groups, but display significantly less variance across individual households at a given point of time. While the standard deviation of the ratio of consumption spending in individual income in the lowest income group (annual income below 20 000 DM) was only 0.13, it was 0.15 in the middle-income range and 0.17 in the highest income group.

Hence, we find three soundly confirmed stylised facts. First, the saving rate is a strictly rising function of current relative household income, starting with negative values in the bottom deciles. Second, saving rates of households on the lower end of the earning scale are more volatile over time than saving rates of better-off families. Third, at a given point of time, the variance of saving rates across individual households is smaller in the lower income percentiles.

1.4.4 Permanent Income

The stylised fact of saving rates being a strictly rising function of relative income does not allow for straightforward conclusions regarding the saving behaviour of any single household over time. If households frequently changed their relative income position, being located by chance in the bottom quintile in one period but moving above the median a period later, propositions about the saving rate of distinct quintiles would be of minor interest. Thus, if we want to interpret the observed saving curves adequately, to inquire whether households tend to stay within a certain quintile for most of their "lifetime" or are instead rather mobile entities, unrestrictedly moving up and down the income ladder is a crucial issue.

It is not a trivial task to answer this question by employing usual panel data. Household surveys rarely follow a single household over several periods. They ask a representative panel at one point in time and the next panel (often composed differently) a period later. It is therefore difficult to draw conclusions about past and future earnings of households in a certain decile. But it is not impossible either.

In fact, some surveys are explicitly conducted with the purpose of studying income *dynamics* rather than giving a stationary picture at subsequent points of time. The Panel Study of Income Dynamics (PSID) in the U.S. for example has this objective. The Socio-Economic Panel (SOEP) in Germany, conducted yearly since 1983, is a good base for dynamic inferences, too. Other surveys in other countries with similar focus can surely be found. Based on these and other data, research about the question of income dynamics has been undertaken. The results are surprisingly unanimous. In a detailed analysis of PSID data from 1982 to 1991 Sabelhaus & Groen (2000) find hardly any indicator of sizeable income mobility. Computing permanent income as the average (growth adjusted) annual income of a household over the ten year period covered by the data, they conclude that, "...a family whose permanent income places it in the bottom decile ... has a 69.6 % chance of being in the bottom annual decile... It has a 23.8% chance of being in the second annual decile..., a 4.2% chance of being in the third annual decile"[3] and a much smaller chance of being in any of the fourth through tenth annual deciles. They summarise, "...that families decile rankings are relatively stable, particularly among the very

---

3 Sabelhaus, Groen (2000)

poor and very rich. About 70% of the permanent poor are annual poor, and about 70% of the permanent rich are annual rich. Almost all income variability is restricted to plus or minus one decile. There is almost no overlap between the extremes of the permanent and annual income distribution…"[4]

The assumption of a strong persistency in the income position is confirmed by available income-mobility tables in other countries. Of course, to accept this general proposition does not mean to deny any change in relative income over the life cycle. But empirical evidence suggests that such changes are indeed mostly bounded within the adjacent one or two deciles with a strictly decreasing probability of any further changes.

Under these circumstances, however, the stylised facts concerning the relation between saving rates and current relative income are not snapshots illuminating a short-term relation which individually disappears immediately, but they illustrate a lasting pattern. Low-income households actually save nothing, the median household saves at best a small amount and upper-income households save more the higher their position on the income ladder, or more precisely, the higher their permanent relative income.

This assumption is confirmed by studies explicitly dealing with the link between saving and permanent income. Dynan, Skinner & Zeldes (2004) for example try to answer the question whether the feature of a strong positive relationship between saving rates and current income found in cross-sectional data can be transmitted to the relation between saving rates and permanent or lifetime income. Using data from CEX, SCF and PSID and testing different proxies for permanent income such as education, lagged and future earnings or the value of vehicles purchased etc., they reach similar results. In all cases saving rates rise considerably with permanent income (to be exact: with permanent *relative* income, since what is categorised as *low* or *high* income here is defined relative to the respective average in the U.S. during the period under consideration). The authors estimate that saving rates computed with respect to permanent income range from less than 5 percent for the bottom permanent income quintile to 40 percent for the top 5 percent.

Carroll & Weil (1994) provide additional evidence that saving is positively related to the level of permanent income. In fact, the conclusion that

---

4 Sabelhaus, Groen (2000)

higher lifetime income households save a considerably larger fraction of their income than lower income households, is widely accepted by that part of the literature which has actually scrutinised the relation by means of empirical data. One of the earliest papers engaged in this topic is Mayer (1972). The author estimates permanent income and consumption by five-year averages from annual Swiss budget surveys and finds the elasticity of consumption with respect to permanent income to be notably different from one (0.905) and to be hardly different from the elasticity computed with respect to current income in one year.

If we compare the saving rates for the permanent income position computed by Dynan, Skinner & Zeldes (2004) with those rates reported in surveys referring to current income, we actually notice only one obvious difference: the extreme degree of dissaving at the bottom has disappeared. The figure of minus 230% provided by the CEX is already implausible for the short run; in the long run no one will be allowed to run into new debts as high as 230 percent of his income. Evidence suggests that the negative saving figures in the lowest quintile (which we observe in most survey data, although at more moderate rates) are in fact primarily caused by those households who just moved upwards and still have some reserves and/or access to additional credit.

1.4.5 The Distribution of Financial Wealth

Another empirical fact strongly confirming the assumption of persistency in saving patterns is the distribution of financial wealth, which is exceptionally right-skewed with a huge gap between median and mean. The variance of wealth holdings is still much higher than that of saving rates.

According to the German Income and Consumption Survey (EVS), about 28 percent of households had financial reserves below 5113 euros in 1998. Altogether two thirds of the panel reported assets of less than 25 500 euros. Only 6.6 percent were guessed to possess financial wealth exceeding 102 000 euros, a value roughly corresponding to the mean computed by the Bundesbank. The bulk of wealth is accumulated in deposits far beyond this limit owned by a tiny minority of families. In fact, 50 percent of financial wealth reported in the 1980 German property tax returns was held by just 1.5 percent of all households.

The overall picture is similar in other countries. The median ratio of financial wealth to yearly income in Italy is 0.48, exceeding 1 in the upper income quartile, but falling below 0.15 for the 25 percent of households at the bottom.[5] Median financial wealth in the U.S. in 1998 was about $17 800, but the mean exceeded that amount more than ten times, reaching a value of $212 300. Similar to Germany, the share of the top one percent of richest households in total financial wealth is approaching 50 percent. The concentration of wealth in poorer countries is generally even stronger.

After reviewing international microeconomic evidence concerning saving and household wealth, Coleman (1998) concludes that in a rough approximation "typically the wealthiest ten percent own well over half the non-housing wealth of the economy"[6], which—as we have seen in the given examples—is quite a modest estimation. Moreover, a clear-cut correlation exists between a household's standing in the wealth hierarchy and its current income position, affirming that high and low saving rates are in no way a temporary phenomenon. If we observe, for example, the holdings of financial assets of different household quintiles, we get similar figures regardless of whether households are arranged by income or by net worth. The wealth curve is clearly convex in (relative or real) income, rising steeply towards the upper income groups. The relation is illustrated by Table 1 that uses SCF data from 1998 and 2001 respectively.

The correlation is not surprising since higher saving rates out of higher income not only create more financial wealth, but wealth in turn creates income. Especially at the top, the available assets are likely to bear much higher revenues than labour ever does.

We will not investigate the issue further at this point. Nevertheless, the contradiction between the clearly positive link between saving rates and wealth in cross-section and the apparently negative relationship in the macroeconomic data should be noticed. Cross-sectional data do not provide evidence that higher wealth discourages saving. It is very likely, therefore, that the negative link between saving rates and accumulated wealth at the macro level partly comes from the stronger role of realised and reaccumulated capital gains. Moreover, other factors that simply move in tandem, boosting the wealth holdings of a minority, might be responsible for lower average saving. In any case, to assume that saving efforts cease as a

---

5 Jappelli, Pagano (1994)
6 Coleman (1998)

consequence of prospering wealth holdings clearly conflicts empirical evidence at the microeconomic level.

	Percentage of families holding any financial asset		Median value of holdings for families holding financial assets (thousands of 2001 dollars)	
	1998	2001	1998	2001
All families	**92.9**	**93.1**	**24.5**	**28.0**
Percentile of income				
Less than 20	75.6	74.8	2.0	2.0
20–39.9	93.0	93.0	7.1	8.0
40–59.9	97.1	98.3	17.6	17.1
60–79.9	99.1	99.6	39.8	55.5
80–89.9	99.8	99.8	87.6	97.1
90–100	100.0	99.7	241.1	364.0
Percentile of net worth				
Less than 25	78.0	77.2	1.1	1.3
25–49.9	94.8	96.5	11.4	10.6
50–74.9	99.1	98.9	46.8	53.1
75–89.9	99.9	99.8	157.2	201.7
90–100	100.0	100.0	500.1	707.4

Table 1. Financial Wealth Holdings, Source: SCF 2001

Although the richest save over-proportionally, extremely high levels of wealth are hardly accumulated by a single household alone. Most literature scrutinising the relevance of bequests and intergenerational transfers estimate that a remarkable share of the total private fortune has its sources beyond the households currently holding ownership. The strongest figure was delivered by Kotlikoff & Summers (1981), who infer from a thorough analysis of U.S. wealth and savings data that at least 80 percent of U.S. wealth holdings are based on accumulated intergenerational transfers. In a study on the period between 1962 and 1992 Wolff (1999) estimates that bequests and inter-vivo transfers have each contributed about one third of current wealth, while the remaining third is the result of saving. Atkinson (1971) and Oulton (1976) analyse how much of British wealth inequality could be explained by life-cycle-saving. Their answer: very little. After taking into account the inequality in earning profiles and realized rates of return, Oulton concludes: "The results indicate that none of these factors, neither singly nor in combination are capable of accounting for a substantial proportion of actual wealth inequality."[7]

Other authors (e.g. Modigliani (1988)) provide lower estimates for the role of intergenerational transfers; however, these studies account for wealth accumulation out of revenues from inherited or transferred fortune as part of life-cycle saving, not as part of transfer wealth. Figures differ as do methods, but no one really denies that intergenerational transfer plays an important role in the accumulation of wealth and contributes strongly to the right-skewness in its distribution.

A serious obstacle to clarifying the matter at hand is the lack of data for most countries. Household surveys often exclude the richest one or two percent and herewith just that part of the population that accounts for the mass of financial wealth. While, for instance, the German EVS actually covers wages, salaries and retirement income by more than 99 percent, reported assets account for just 29 percent of what the Deutsche Bundesbank covers.

A remarkable exemption is the US Survey of Consumer Finances which explicitly includes high-income families thus delivering more detailed information about the distribution of private wealth than most other surveys. Employing SCF data, it becomes obvious that the ownership in high-yielding financial assets is even more concentrated than the disposal of financial wealth in general. According to the SCF, the upper 0.5 percent of households, in general disposing around 22.9 percent of financial assets, own about one third of all privately held stocks, a third of the bonds, 41.7 percent of the trusts and the majority of all businesses (54.8 percent). Including the wealthy panel, the SCF does cover approximately 90 percent of the aggregated Flow of Funds wealth data, but still decisively underestimates some treasuries such as U.S. government securities (covering 44.3%) and corporate bonds (21.3%). The over-proportional concentration of traded assets among the very rich is a further indicator backing our assumption that the measured saving rate—particularly the NIPA saving rate that is derived from the residual between income and consumption—does not adequately reflect the saving behaviour of wealthy people. The SCF uncovers that "high income families are much more likely as the whole population to invest in illiquid assets to earn higher returns"[8] and that they

---

7 Oulton (1976)
8 SCF (1986), High-Income Panel

are much more frequently engaged in stock trading. Table 2 provides an overview of the trading behaviour of the different quartiles of the SCF wealthy sample from the mid-eighties. Data from the end of the nineties would probably indicate an even higher propensity to trade for the richest.

Per income group of the wealthy sample (last column: all families of SCF)					
	I.	II.	III.	IV.	All families
Number of publicly traded stocks					
0	53	39	25	10	81
1	20	13	17	8	10
2-4	16	15	15	19	4
5-9	6	12	15	26	2
10-19	4	12	14	19	1
20 or more	2	10	15	18	1
Number of stocks purchased or sold through broker per year					
0	77	53	48	29	94
1	5	5	6	4	1
2-4	11	15	16	17	3
5-9	4	9	9	16	1
10-19	1	10	10	18	1
20 or more	2	8	11	15	*

Table 2. Stock Trading, Source: SCF 1986

While 81 percent of all families did not hold publicly traded stocks and 94 percent reported not to have undertaken any trading, more than 90 percent of the upper quartile of the wealthiest held stocks and more than 70 percent were engaged in stock trading. Above all, one third of them purchased or sold stocks more than ten times a year. Therefore, realised capital gains clearly amount for a larger part of their revenues. At the individual level, reinvesting such gains is not different from reinvesting interest or dividend receipts; the first, however, is statistically not accounted as saving. Furthermore, the richest might carry out more effective strategies to hide their wealth holdings and revenues, for instance for tax reasons. This might further contribute to the situation that the measured aggregate saving rate does not adequately reveal upper class saving.

The most reliable source of figures about private financial wealth appear to be international banks and investment houses specialised in attracting the wealthiest and increasing their financial net worth. According to the Financial Times, the global head of wealth solutions for the JP Morgan Private Bank estimates that so-called Ultra-High Net Worth Individuals—persons who possess net financial assets exceeding $30 million –control 30 to 40 percent of the world's wealth.[9] Only 70 000 persons around the globe belong to this category.

Understanding the saving behaviour of median households therefore fails by far to give an understanding of the mass of wealth creation. In fact, the inquiry into what drives the majority of households to save and by which motives the majority of financial wealth is accumulated, concern distinct questions and will certainly lead to different answers. Nevertheless, saving or dissaving by those 90 percent of the population below the top does matter in a developed country. Whether they contribute half or only twenty to thirty percent to total saving it is a share that is relevant for the path of aggregate saving, particularly, since the measured saving rate is likely to overweigh middle-class saving.

1.4.6 Growth, Income Fluctuations and the Role of Expectations

Considering the question of income mobility, we have already touched another important issue. Are there stylised facts illustrating how households tend to respond to *changes* in income? Does remarkable income growth or a noticeable loss have a significant effect? Is there a crucial difference between the response to transitory income fluctuations compared to the response to changes in income that are expected to last?

Concerning income growth there is strong evidence that the observed correlation between saving and growth at the macroeconomic level can also be found at the individual level. Carroll & Weil (1994) examine the influence of wage income growth using PSID and CEX data. Even when controlling for the positive effect of higher permanent (relative) income, they find a significant positive coefficient of 4.69 for income growth. This

---

9 Financial Times 7.7.04

implies that a 1 percentage point increase in income growth would increase the wealth to income ratio (which due to data problems is used here as an indicator of saving) by almost 5 percent. Deaton, Paxson (2000) find similar evidence for higher income growth being associated with higher household saving for Taiwan.

Concerning short-term income fluctuations, some patterns also appear to be evident. Households tend to save over-proportionally if they receive a sudden income boost. They tend to save much less than before if income abruptly decreases. This insight is almost unanimously accepted in the literature. Friedman (1957) estimates a marginal propensity to save out of transitory income of about one third, while Carroll (1994) finds evidence for a coefficient of approximately 0.2.

The thesis of consumption smoothing out short-term income fluctuations is easily backed by empirical illustration. There are examples in the histories of most countries where groups of households receive abrupt increases in their revenues and respond with higher saving rates. In West-Germany, for instance, retirees received a 26 percent rise in their pensions in 1957. In the same year their saving rate jumped from 1.5 to 7 percent. A similar scenario was observed in 1972. Again, it was retirees who received notable extra revenue due to changes in the treatment of their public health insurance contributions. Again, their saving rate jumped, this time from 5.4 to 8.2 percent. With the repayment of the so-called "Konjunktur-zuschlag", higher income households received a remarkable amount of cash-back from the government in the same year; again, the additional money was mostly saved. However, in both cases household groups that generally display a relative high propensity to save were favoured. Whether people at the bottom of the income ladder would in fact start to save if they receive a sudden income rise rather than expanding their consumption, is a question that cannot be answered by these examples.

Shapiro & Slemrod (1995), studying the effects of the 1992 reduction in income tax withholding, find that those households who expect higher income growth—a group that roughly might be identified with the better-off households in general—are more likely to save out of a temporary increase in income than other households.

Regrettably, such differences have rarely been explored in detail. Nevertheless, we may consider the following stylised facts about the response of saving to income growth and income fluctuations. First, some evidence exists that households with higher income growth display higher saving rates compared to lower income growth households with a similar relative income. Second, consumption tends to smooth out short-term income fluctuation, although the smoothing effect is most likely stronger—thus, the marginal propensity to consume out of transitory income is lower—for better-off households.

Unfortunately, instead of scrutinising those problems, which certainly deserve to receive more attention, an intense effort of economic research has been dedicated to a rather artificial issue. Not the general influence of income growth, but the question how consumption and saving react to *predictable* versus *unexpected* changes in income has been in the focus of a huge amount of papers; especially during the eighties.

Lucas' (1976) critique of the Keynesian consumption function insists that there is no reason to suppose a stable lag structure between consumption and income because of the role of expectations. If saving and consumption are actually determined by income expectations rather than by available income, a correlation between consumption and predictable income growth should not exist. Instead, consumption and saving should react only to new events. So-called orthogonality tests have been undertaken in order to demonstrate that consumption is insensitive to predictable/expected income growth.

Browning & Lusardi (1996), who give an extended overview of one and a half decades of econometric research guided by this major concern, conclude that the results are "deeply ambiguous". In fact, no consensus about the sensitivity of consumption concerning predictable income changes has been reached across different strands of the economic literature. Even by exploiting the same data sets, studies have drawn completely divergent conclusions. Most of them differ considerably in the derivation of what is considered to be the predictable component of income growth. As Browning & Lusardi (1996) emphasise, only very few studies present measures of fit for the auxiliary equation used to predict income growth; those who do report very low R-squares. Authors who took special care to increase the predictive power of their estimation find stronger evidence of excess sensitivity.

However, if relative income is in reality more relevant with respect to saving decisions than absolute income, and if the saving rate is a strictly increasing function of the relative income position, and if, moreover, saving rates are positively related to income growth, consumption actually has to rise slower than income. It may well be that tests for a simple linear relationship between consumption and lagged or current absolute income provide insignificant coefficients. In addition, many studies do not refer to consumption as such, but to food consumption exclusively, such as the PSDI, which allows for the best inferences on individual income dynamics, but reports only data on food consumption. Food, as confirmed by extensive microeconomic research on Engel-curves, displays an income elasticity significantly smaller than unity and makes up a shrinking part of total consumption. From the sixties to the mid-eighties, the period most considered in the respective literature, the share of food in total consumption strongly declines. It is not surprising that such a data set does not confirm a significant response of consumption to income growth.

There is some evidence that the particularly low income elasticity of food consumption plays a role. Some studies have tested whether the response in (food) consumption to predictable changes in earnings is stronger for low income households. Zeldes (1989a), for example, employing PSID data from 1968 to 1982, splits households in two groups: those with high and those with low assets at the beginning of the period, which may be taken as a rough indicator of income differences. The authors find that "excess sensitivity"—i.e. an obvious response of consumption to current changes in income—is only significant for the low asset group. Zeldes (1989a) interprets the result as evidence against the assumption of perfect capital markets in standard models. Although we embrace this critique, it is by far not the only interpretation of this particular finding. Another explanation could be that food consumption is simply too small and too income inelastic for asset-rich households to uncover a significant response to income growth.

Reviewing the mass of papers exploring orthogonality almost unavoidably brings to mind that the results are so ambiguous and poor because tremendous econometric effort has been guided by a wrong question. Studies undertaken in the nineties bolster empirical evidence against the major role of long-term income expectations. Based on an extensive analysis of CEX and PSID data, Carroll (1994) finds "… no evidence that current consumption responds *at all* to long-horizon, predictable changes in income. Conversely, consumption is excessively sensitive to the current level of income, even though this level was predictable in advance."[10] Meanwhile it is evident that the difference between predictable and unex-

---

10 Carroll (1994)

pected income changes is not as crucial as claimed by a large part of the literature.

1.4.7 Uncertainty and Precautionary Saving

Other than long-term income expectations, the degree of uncertainty about the development of income in the future appears to have an impact on current saving decisions. The major problem of economic research exploring the role of uncertainty, however, is to identify an observable and exogenous source of risk that varies sufficiently across the population to analyse this effect. Similar to the case of income expectations, measures of uncertainty used in the regressions differ widely across studies. Consequently, the results diverge as well. Carroll (1994) finds "...that consumption responds strongly to uncertainty in future income" and therefore "consumers with greater income uncertainty, *ceteris paribus*, have lower current consumption."[11] The author estimates that one standard deviation increase in uncertainty decreases consumption by 3 to 5 percent. Skinner (1988) and Kuehlwein (1991), in contrast, using CEX and PSID data, find no evidence of a precautionary motive at all. Guiso, Jappelli, Terlizzese (1992a), employing Italian statistical figures, conclude that 2 percent of the wealth accumulation might be explained by the purpose of precaution. The highest estimate, to the best of our knowledge, is reported by Carroll & Samwick (1997) who find that about 40 percent of the total accumulation of wealth is caused by precautionary saving.

Since Friedman (1957) it is common to use higher income variance and risk to explain higher saving rates of self-employed households relative to employees. But the relative income of self-employed households is on average significantly higher than that of all other types of households, which might be a sufficient explanation of higher saving rates. Furthermore, the correlation between the self-employed status and higher saving rates disappears as soon as data for self-employed households are scrutinised in more detail. Schönig (1996) uses data from the German SOEP panel to emphasise that a strong discrepancy exists between the saving rate of the wealthy and that of middle-income self-employed people. While the

---

11 Carroll (1994)

first save over-proportionally, the latter save at very low rates. However, it is precisely these middle-income self-employed households who have almost no social security net and face the highest risk of ending up with zero wealth and income in a future period. After all, there are thousands of bankruptcies a year in Germany which seldom concern large enterprises. If anything, there is a strong precautionary motive among those self-employed people who are not particularly wealthy.

Additionally, one may consider examples where households, though equipped with the full safety of being able to maintain the given standard of living, save more and not less than others. Civil servants, for instance, typically save at high rates although their jobs are well protected. Or think of a multimillionaire who obviously has no reason to fear the next health bill but nevertheless saves a remarkable share of his large revenues.

Yet, the empirically oriented literature about consumption delivers evidence that the decision whether to buy expensive durables or not has strong connections not only to current income but also to its expected development in the immediate future. In an extensive study about the ability of the consumption climate index to predict the real consumption path, Schnittker-Reiner (1987) cites opinion polls, which indicate that persons purchasing a car or other expensive durables estimate their current and future income situation more optimistically and are more confident about the general economic outlook than the average from the respective panel. Moreover, Schnittker-Reiner (1987) illustrates, that the demand for durables in Germany was more influenced by changes in the real GDP than by changes in disposable household income, supporting the assumption that uncertainty is a vital factor.

One of the conclusions of this study is the proposition that the consumption climate index actually works better in bad times than in good times. Whereas in a business upturn the index exaggerates the real rise in consumption, it predicts the decline around a slowdown quite well. In fact, the role of expectations appears to increase if uncertainty increases. During normal periods, on the other hand, current income is the crucial determinant to purchasing decisions.

One may question whether the measures used to identify uncertainty at the micro level in the literature are reliable and whether consumption as such or only specific parts of it will be substituted by saving in the case of rising uncertainty. Nevertheless, there are indicators at the micro level that uncertainty influences saving decisions, at least regarding the trade-off between durable purchases and keeping money in the account. Emphasising the *ceteris paribus* condition, uncertainty obviously plays role.

1.4.8 Life-Cycle Patterns of Saving

An issue carefully scrutinised in a bulk of papers is the path of life-cycle saving. At the macro level, we found only poor empirical evidence for demographic parameters explaining cross-country or time-series differences in saving rates.

On the microeconomic level one striking feature emerges if we plot average household saving rates against age. For most countries—at least within the developed world—we get a hump-shaped curve, indicating that saving rates rise until a peak around the ages of fifty to sixty, getting flatter after retirement, although often increasing again in higher ages.

To analyse such curves correctly, one has to distinguish between cohort and age effects. A panel contains household heads of different ages; at the same time, these ages represent different generations. Thus, a saving rate/age relation obtained by cross-sectional data does not necessarily prove that age groups behave differently; it could be the year of birth that is the crucial factor. That is why a huge effort was put into constructing synthetic cohort profiles out of data delivered by subsequent panels to gain information about the real age effect. Actually, such synthetic cohorts usually display a hump-shaped saving pattern in relation to age similar to the simple panel of households sorted by age.

But does this confirm that age is the determining factor? If we observe average lifetime income profiles, we obtain just the same hump-shape pattern as in the case of saving. It is rather plausible that saving rates simply follow the income path. A person with a hump-shaped income curve will certainly have a hump-shaped path of saving rates. A person, whose income path is flat is unlikely to display much variance in saving behaviour. The phenomenon of a higher saving rate when lifetime income reaches its peak, and therefore of a flatter consumption path compared to the life-time income path, is fully compatible with the stylised fact about the link between saving rates and relative income. In fact, the average life-time saving curve is satisfactorily explainable by differences in (relative) income at different stages of life.

Such an interpretation is backed by important strands of the literature. Sabelhaus & Groen (2000) emphasise that, although aggregated data middle-aged people (40—60) spend less of their income than the younger and older, this feature disappears within any given income decile. In the top decile, for example, the young spend 65% of their income, the middle-aged 64% and the old 61%. Sabelhaus & Groen (2000) point out, that "…the overall skewness in expenditure-income ratios across income groups holds within any given age group, as well as in the aggregate", concluding, that "age has little explanatory effect"[12]. Takayama & Kitamura (1994), referring to Japanese data notice: "What really matters with the saving rate is income rather than age profile. Variations of saving across different income classes are much wider than those over the age profile within the same income class. Indeed, no stylized pattern in saving rates over the age profile across income classes is found."[13] Other authors in Poterba (1994) almost unanimously confirm this proposition. Poterba summarises, that "…the country studies provide very little evidence that supports the life-cycle model"[14]. Exploring German data, Fachinger (2001) finds that the variance of income shares spent for different kinds of consumption (including the share of income that is not spent but saved) is significantly smaller within income deciles than within age groups.

Moreover, Banks & Blundell (1994), analysing UK data, find the elderly not only continuing to save—this is a common finding in all studies included in Poterba et al. (1994)—but being in fact the only age group displaying positive saving rates in all income quartiles. Danziger et al. (1983) reach a similar result reporting that "…the elderly spend less than the non-elderly at the same level of income and (with) the very oldest of the elderly having the lowest average propensity to consume."[15] If there is a stylised fact concerning saving during the life-cycle, an increasing propensity to save in higher ages may be noted.

12 Sabelhaus, Groen (2000)
13 Takayama, Kitamura (1994)
14 Poterba et al. (1994)
15 Danziger et al. (1983)

1.4.9 Saving Motives

Finally, let us consider the saving motives which are explicitly mentioned in opinion polls. Out of the consumers who participated in the Federal Reserve Board's 1983 Survey of Consumer Finances, 43 percent said that being prepared for emergencies is their most important reason for saving; only 15 percent stated that preparing for retirement is the primary saving goal. Once more in 2001, maintaining liquidity was mentioned as the most important saving motive by 31.2 percent of the respondents. Yet, saving for retirement is the primary purpose for 32.1 percent, a change probably reflecting the deteriorating public pension system in the U.S. 10.9 percent mentioned financing education as their saving aim, 9.5 percent are saving primarily for purchases. Investment—in the sense of the intention to earn a yield—was mentioned by just 1 percent as a major saving motive. German opinion polls display similar results.

Research among people who already possess more than $1 million of net financial assets (so called HNWI), however, has uncovered rather distinct motives. According to the World Wealth Report 2004, 90 percent of those financial net worth millionaires under the age of 50 intend to further build up their wealth rather than simply to preserve it. Furthermore, 50 percent of them beyond the age of 65 have the same purpose. The most frequently mentioned goal of HNWIs (84 percent) underlying the desire of further increasing financial wealth is "maintaining their current standard of living *before* retirement"[16]. 80 percent additionally emphasise the desire to ensure a comfortable standard of living during retirement. Thus, wealth for them is clearly not a buffer-stock protecting against emergencies or a treasure to be used up when labour income ceases, but a crucial source of income before and after retirement.

According to the World Wealth Report 2004, Ultra-HNWIs in particular are moreover highly interested in an intergenerational transfer of wealth. It is usual for them to create '100 year plans', "in which family members are treated as business divisions and emphasis is put on corporate-inspired guidelines"[17]. This actually fuels the demand for specific tax minimisation strategies to facilitate wealth transfer. As stated by Merrill Lynch, 47 percent of HNWIs discussed tax minimisation strategies with their financial advisors in 2003.

---

16 Merrill Lynch, World Wealth Report (2004)
17 Merrill Lynch, World Wealth Report (2004)

In fact, the distribution of assets, considered shortly in the section about the wealth distribution, reflects the different motives quite clearly. While median households primarily save in relatively liquid assets such as checking accounts or put their money in insurances or annuities, the rich first and foremost invest in high-yielding assets, almost exclusively dominating the market for stocks, bonds, trusts and similar assets. This disparity in saving motives and savings behaviour should be noted as a final stylised fact.

Paragraph 1.5
Summary: Stylised Facts of Saving

So what are the most striking features uncovered in our search for stylised facts of saving? At the macro level, we found a general lack of straightforward patterns. The only exceptions are a positive correlation between saving rates and *income growth* and a weaker, somewhat ambiguous, positive correlation between saving rates and *income level*, significant in low- and middle-income countries rather than in the OECD-sample. In developed countries, saving rates tend to increase in periods of higher inflation to balance inflation-caused losses, particularly, if high nominal interest rates guarantee sufficient revenues to do so. No significant link between saving rates and real interest rates could be discovered. Finally, saving rates appear to have a mainly negative correlation on the level of inequality in the developed world and move strongly in line with the wage share. (The latter relationship was partly explained by the fact, that the aggregated saving rate over-proportionally reflects middle-class saving while it does not fully count saving by the very rich).

The outstanding determining factor of saving at the micro level turned out to be the household's *relative income* position. The latter was shown to be quite similar in its current and its permanent level. Even if the exact outline of the saving rate/relative income-curve varies in cross-country comparisons, and the empirical literature provides little knowledge about factors causing shifts or alterations in time, there are some surprisingly common findings whenever saving by different income groups is observed. First, households in the bottom quintile tend to save virtually nothing; a remarkable share of them report negative saving figures at least in short-run. Second, households around the median save, if at all, a very small portion of their income, significantly less than the mean saving rate suggests. Third, the saving rate strictly rises in relative income, shooting steeply upwards for income groups above the median.

These common features arise in situations with highly divergent values of mean income and with remarkably varying real income in each income percentile. Consequently, the relation between saving rates and real income is rather weak also at the microeconomic level.

Confirming a strong persistency in saving behaviour across income groups, the following stylised facts concerning financial wealth can be summarised. First, the bottom quintile has almost no financial wealth, often being indebted instead. Second, the median household has rather small reserves, usually far below one year's income. Third, most of the financial wealth is concentrated within the accounts of a considerably small number of households who are situated at the top of both the income and the wealth distributions and save at high rates. Fourth, a remarkable share of financial wealth is not based on life-cycle saving but on intergenerational transfers.

Generally, we draw the conclusion that two completely distinct types of savers exist. The attitudes, motives and objectives of those savers at the top ends of the wealth and income distributions, who in fact account for a major part of all savings, differ fundamentally from the purposes and the saving behaviour of all other households.

Recapitulating the relevance of other factors, we furthermore note the following stylised facts. First, the positive correlation between saving rates and income growth appears to be confirmed at the microeconomic level. Second, the propensity to save out of transitory income fluctuations tends to be higher than the general propensity to save; nevertheless, it is significantly different from unity and varies with the household's relative income position. Third, rising uncertainty about income in the immediate future, *ceteris paribus*, encourages saving while long-term expectations are of minor relevance. Fourth, the life-cycle pattern of saving turns out to be dominated by the income effect, whereas the propensity to save even rises in ages beyond retirement.

After considering the stylised facts of saving suggested by empirical evidence, we continue by scrutinising the explanatory power and conclusiveness of the most frequently used saving models.

Chapter 2. Do Standard Models of Saving Match the Facts?

Paragraph 2.1
The Standard LCPIH

2.1.1 Basic Ideas of the Standard Approach

Despite serious divergences in detail, the common basis of all strands of contemporary mainstream economics dealing with consumption and saving has been the theory of intertemporal choice. For this approach, the creation of financial wealth—or the accumulation of debt—has one purpose only: to maximise the utility of life-time consumption by balancing the level of consumption in different periods subject to an intertemporal budget constraint. Within this framework the determination of consumption in different time periods is thought to be analogous to the determination of quantities of different goods in a demand system.

The most general way of formalising this approach is to define an intertemporal felicity function $V(c1, c2, ..., cT)$, $t = 1, 2, ..., T$, where ct denotes the consumption of a bundle of goods in period t. The particular shape of V is governed by the utility derived from consuming those goods as well as by preferences regarding the trade-off between current and future consumption. The intertemporal budget constraint corresponds to present wealth plus the present discounted value of all expected future wage income streams.

The model can be developed with either a finite or an infinite time-horizon. In the first case T is limited by the lifespan of a human being, in the second case, T is taken as approaching infinity. One may distinguish these two approaches as the Life-Cycle Hypothesis (LCH) on the one hand and the Permanent Income Hypothesis (PIH) on the other hand. The predictions of these models differ in some respects, but since the common features are much stronger than the divergences, we review their underlying principles together. In both cases, saving or dissaving at time t is determined by the optimal consumption path obtained by maximising V subject to an intertemporal budget constraint. In periods where optimal consumption falls below current income, the consumer saves while he dissaves or searches for credit when the opposite occurs.

Obviously, the utility maximisation problem in this most general form can hardly be confirmed or refuted by empirical data since any individual behaviour can be matched by appropriately specifying the function and the parameters. (Or, stated less approvingly: one can never derive any distinct prediction from this general approach.) In order to evaluate the capability of those models to fit the stylised facts of saving, more structured versions therefore have to be analysed.

The basic ideas of the Permanent Income and the Life-Cycle Hypothesis date back to the middle of the former century and were developed by Friedman (1957) and Modigliani, Brumberg (1954) respectively. The centrepiece of both approaches is that of *forward-looking* households which are concerned about the future insofar as they take into account expected income streams when deciding to spend or to save today.

In the following, the basic assumptions of the two models are summarised: intertemporal utility is strongly separable and additive. One-period utility (u) is a monotonically increasing concave function of the current level of consumption (c), i.e. we have $u'(c) > 0$ and $u''(c) < 0$. Usually, $u'(0) = \infty$ and $u'(\infty) = 0$ has been assumed, too. Preferences are supposed to be homothetic. Future consumption is discounted geometrically by a factor of time preference. There is no uncertainty about future labour income. The same is true for the future path of the real interest rate, which is often assumed to be constant. If the remaining lifespan sets the limit of the planning horizon, its length is known in advance. Capital markets are perfect, i.e. households have access to any desired amount of credit as long as Ponzi games are ruled out.

2.1.2 The Modigliani-Diagram

The basic version of this type of model is represented by the so-called Modigliani-diagram. Here, wage income in the active period of life is assumed to be constant, while income after retirement is assumed to be zero. No financial wealth is available at the beginning of life. The time preference rate as well as the interest rate is assumed to be zero. Under such simplified conditions, life-time collapses into two periods: working life and retirement. Therefore, the life-time optimisation problem can be handled as a two-period problem. The representative household has to solve the following optimisation problem:

$$\max V(c0, c1) = U(c0) + U(c1)$$

(2.1)

s.t.

$$w0 = c0 + c1$$

(2.2)

where $c0$ is consumption during the working age and $c1$ is consumption after retirement. $U(c)$ is the utility of a certain consumption level. Equation (2.2) is the life-time budget constraint with $w0$ being total labour income earned in the working period of life. This optimisation problem can be solved by ordinary Lagrange technique. The Lagrangian under these conditions is:

$$L = U(c0) + U(c1) + \lambda\,[w0 - c0 - c1]$$

(2.3)

This leads to three first order conditions:

$$\frac{\partial L}{\partial c0} = U'(c0) - \lambda = 0$$

(2.4)

$$\frac{\partial L}{\partial c1} = U'(c1) - \lambda = 0$$

(2.5)

$$\frac{\partial L}{\partial \lambda} = w0 - c0 - c1 = 0$$

(2.6)

From (2.4) and (2.5) we get:

$$U'(c0) = U'(c1)$$

(2.7)

Consumers seek to achieve a constant marginal utility of consumption during their entire lifespan, i.e. they try to maintain a constant consumption level. Hence, during working age a constant proportion of labour income is saved; exactly as much as is needed in order to maintain the consumption level in the years after retirement and to die with zero wealth. If both periods are of equal length (which is of course not realistic), the household saves half of the first period's income for the second period. Regardless of the respective length of the two periods, life-time consumption equals life-time income and current consumption is independent from current income.

If positive interest rates $r(t)$ and a positive rate of time preference (δ) are introduced, the intertemporal utility function can be written as follows:

$$\max V(c0, c1) = U(c0) + (1 + \delta)^{-1} U(c1)$$

$$(2.8)$$

And the budget constraint reads:

$$w0 = c0 + (1 + r1)^{-1}c1$$

$$(2.9)$$

From (2.8) and (2.9) we get an optimal consumption path, where the level of consumption in the two periods is linked by:

$$U'(c0) = \frac{(1+r1)}{(1+\delta)} U'(c1)$$

$$(2.10)$$

So, different to the previous model, consumption is not necessarily chosen in a way that marginal consumption is identical in both periods, but a certain positive or negative growth of consumption might be desired. If the interest rate exceeds the rate of time preference, the consumer wants to achieve a higher consumption level in the second period. In the opposite case, he desires shrinking consumption. If the interest rate equals the rate of time preference, he will balance consumption at the same level in both periods as in the basic model. But there is still a difference: if the interest rate is positive, life-time consumption is higher than the first period's labour income, because the consumer additionally obtains a certain amount of interest income. Thus, even if we have $\delta = r1$ and the consumer intends to maintain the same consumption level throughout his lifespan, the level of consumption is higher for both periods compared to the model without interest rates. (Of course, it is not generally true that consumption levels increase with the interest rate; here, it follows from the assumption that all labour income is earned in the first period. This assumption requires saving and excludes running into debts).

With or without a positive real interest rate, the optimal consumption path for the given approaches does not depend on the income path but on life-time income, i.e. the sum of labour income and income received from accumulated wealth.

2.1.3 The Perfect Foresight Model in Discrete Time

The latter conclusion is crucial for all standard models and will be preserved if we generalise to the t-period or the infinite horizon case. Approaches considering optimal consumption across t periods allow for variations in wage income, but assume the income path and total life-time income are subject to perfect foresight. The time preference as well as the interest rate are assumed to differ from zero and can differ from each other. While the rate of time preference is usually assumed to be constant, the real interest rate might change over time. This generalised model can be formalised as follows:

$$\max V = \sum_{t=0}^{T} (1 + \delta)^{-t} u[c(t)]$$

(2.11)

$$s.t.$$

$$c(0) + \sum_{t=1}^{T} \left[\prod_{t=1}^{T} (1 + r(t)) \right]^{-1} c(t) = F(0) + H(0)$$

(2.12)

$$H(0) = w(0) + \sum_{t=1}^{T} \left[\prod_{t=1}^{T} (1 + r(t)) \right]^{-1} w(t)$$

(2.13)

Now, V denotes the T-period felicity function, which is to be maximised, $u[c(t)]$ is the momentary utility function, δ is the rate of time preference and T equals either the remaining number of lifetime periods or infinity. (2.12) and (2.13) specify the budget constraint with $F(0)$ denoting initial financial wealth. $H(0)$ is so-called human wealth corresponding to current income and the present discounted value of all future labour income $w(t)$, $r(t)$ is the real interest rate. Given a constant real interest rate, the model can be reduced to:

$$\max V = \sum_{t=0}^{T} (1 + \delta)^{-t} u[c(t)]$$

(2.14)

s. t.

$$\sum_{t=0}^{T} (1 + r)^{-t} c(t) = F(0) + H(0)$$

(2.15)

$$H(0) = \sum_{t=0}^{T} (1 + r)^{-t} w(t)$$

(2.16)

Since a time-varying real interest rate does not change anything in the basic logic of the model, but requires more complex algebra, we continue with the simpler approach assuming $r(t) = r$ at all points of time.

If we handle this maximisation problem using the same static optimisation technique as in the two-period-case, the Lagrangian is:

$$L = \sum_{t=0}^{T} (1 + \delta)^{-t} u[c(t)]$$

$$+ \lambda \left[F(0) + \sum_{t=0}^{T} (1 + r)^{-t} w(t) \right.$$

$$\left. - \sum_{t=0}^{T} (1 + r)^{-t} c(t) \right]$$

(2.17)

yielding $T + 1$ first order conditions:

$$\frac{\partial L}{\partial c(t)} = (1 + \delta)^{-t} u'[c(t)] - \lambda(1 + r)^{-t} = 0$$

(2.18)

$$\frac{\partial L}{\partial c(t+1)} = (1 + \delta)^{-(t+1)} u'[c(t+1)] - \lambda(1 + r)^{-(t+1)} = 0$$

$$...$$

$$\frac{\partial L}{\partial \lambda} = F(t) + \sum_{i}^{T} (1 + r)^{-i} w(t+i) - \sum_{i}^{T} (1 + r)^{-i} c(t+i) = 0$$

(2.19)

Hence, we have for all periods:

$$u'[c(t)] = \lambda \left[\frac{(1 + \delta)}{(1 + r)} \right]^{t}$$

(2.20)

with λ denoting the marginal utility of lifetime wealth or permanent income respectively.

In the T-period case current consumption depends on preferences and on life-time income exclusively determining the life-time budget constraint. The level of current income has no influence on current consumption at all. An increase of an amount X in today's income has exactly the same impact on current consumption as an increase of an amount $(1 + r)^t X$ occurring t periods in the future. If we have $\delta = r$, consumers seek to balance consumption at the same level in all periods of life and any gain in total life-time income will be distributed equally across life-time consumption. If the rate of time preference exceeds the interest rate, consumers are impatient and the optimal consumption path decreases, while in the case of $r > \delta$ consumers wish to maintain a constant positive rate of consumption growth. As in the two-period case, we have to distinguish two effects of changes in the real interest rates: the substitution effect and the income effect.

The substitution effect concerns the desired rate of consumption growth. The ratio of the real interest rate and the rate of time preference only guides the desired path of *marginal* utilities. The desired growth rate of consumption itself is furthermore determined by the particular shape of the utility function $u(c)$. It is this curvature that decides on the exact response of consumption to divergences between discount factor and interest rate.

If we take the time derivative of equation (2.20), we obtain:

$$u''[c(t)]c'(t) = \lambda \left[\frac{(1+\delta)}{(1+r)}\right]^t \ln \left[\frac{(1+\delta)}{(1+r)}\right]$$

Replacing λ using (2.20) gives:

$$u''[c(t)]c'(t) = u'[c(t)] \ln \left[\frac{(1+\delta)}{(1+r)}\right]$$

Assuming δ and r are sufficiently small and dividing both sides by $c(t)$ we obtain a general schedule guiding desired consumption growth:

$$\frac{c'(t)}{c(t)} = -\frac{u'[c(t)]}{u''[c(t)]\,c(t)} (r - \delta)$$

$$(2.21)$$

Hence, the magnitude of the response of consumption growth to differentials between the real interest rate and the rate of time preference is the reciprocal of the elasticity of the marginal utility of consumption, i.e. the intertemporal elasticity of substitution. The effect of a change in the interest rate on the desired rate of consumption growth, consistently, is called the substitution effect.

The income effect, on the other hand, concerns the level of consumption. Clearly, for a consumer that saves or runs into debt, the entire level of lifetime-consumption changes with the rate of interest. Hence, an increase in the interest rate will increase the desired rate of consumption growth; at the same time, it will change the budget constraint and, hence, the level of consumption the consumer can afford to enjoy. The final effect of a change in the interest rate on consumption and saving is ambiguous since either the income or the substitution effect might dominate. Hence, a rise in the real interest rate may increase or decrease current consumption. But those questions actually become relevant only if we relax our assumption of perfect certainty, as within the framework we are dealing with, that all future changes in the real interest rate are known in advance and included in the budget constraint already.

Linking the first-order conditions for consumption in two subsequent periods, we derive as the optimal solution the Euler equation:

$$u'[c(t)] = \frac{(1 + r)}{(1 + \delta)} u'[c(t + 1)]$$

$$(2.22)$$

which becomes particularly important once we depart from the perfect foresight model.

2.1.4 The Perfect Foresight Model in Continuous Time

Generally, the same results concerning desired consumption growth can be derived, if we deal with a continuous time version of the model and use dynamic optimisation techniques to solve the intertemporal optimisation problem. Using the same notation as before, the life-time felicity function in continuous time with a constant discount factor and a finite horizon can be modelled as follows:

$$V = \int_0^T u[c(t)]e^{-\delta t}\, dt$$

$$(2.23)$$

Under the same assumptions as above (including constant real interest rates), we have the following equation of motion for the state variable that is financial wealth:

$$F'(t) = w(t) + r\, F(t) - c(t)$$

(2.24)

The initial condition is $F(0) = F0$ and the transversality condition is $F(N) \geq 0$, if we exclude dying in debt. The Hamiltonian of this problem is:

$$J = u[c(t)]\, e^{-\delta t} + \mu(t)\, [w(t) + r\, F(t) - c(t)]$$

(2.25)

The following first-order conditions of a maximum can be derived:

$$\frac{\partial J}{\partial c} = u'[c(t)]e^{-\delta t} - \mu(t) = 0$$

(2.26)

$$\frac{\partial J}{\partial F} = -\mu(t)r = \mu'(t)$$

(2.27)

Differentiating (2.26) with respect to time yields:

$$-\delta\, u'[c(t)]e^{-\delta t} + \frac{du'[c(t)]}{dt}\, e^{-\delta t} = \mu'(t)$$

(2.28)

Since $\mu'(t) = -\mu(t)\, r$ from (2.27) and $\mu(t) = u'[c(t)]\, e^{-\delta t}$ from (2.26) we can eliminate the dynamic multiplier to obtain:

$$-\delta\, u'[c(t)]e^{-\delta t} + \frac{du'[c(t)]}{dt}\, e^{-\delta t} = -u'[c(t)]\, e^{-\delta t}\, r$$

(2.29)

Dividing through by $-u'[c(t)]\, e^{-\delta t}$ yields:

$$r - \delta = - \frac{du' \frac{[c(t)]}{dt}}{u'[c(t)]} = - \frac{u''[c(t)]c'(t)}{u'[c(t)]}$$

$$= - \frac{u''[c(t)]c(t)}{u'[c(t)]} \frac{c'(t)}{c(t)}$$

(2.30)

Equation (2.30) is exactly the same condition for optimal consumption growth as the condition derived for the discrete time context by static Lagrange technique (see equation (2.21)). Again, the growth rate of consumption depends on the interest rate, the rate of time preference and the shape of the momentary utility function $u[c(t)]$, but not on the path of life-time income. If $r = \delta$, desired consumption growth $c'(t)/c(t)$ equals zero, as we have already concluded in the discrete time context. Thus, if the rate of time preference corresponds to the interest rate, the consumer seeks to maintain a constant level of consumption through his entire life and the consumption level is determined by available life-time resources of human and non-human wealth.

Since the utility function $u(c)$ is concave and strictly increasing in consumption by design (i.e. $u'[c(t)] > 0$ and $u''[c(t)] < 0$), the ratio $u''[c(t)]/u'[c(t)]$ will be negative and the first term on the right-hand side of (2.30) is positive. Therefore, desired consumption growth has to be positive for $r > \delta$ and negative for $r < \delta$.

As mentioned above, the exact size of the response of consumption to differences between r and δ depends on the assumptions about the shape of the momentary utility function $u(c)$. In this context, it is common to employ a constant elasticity of substitution (CES) specification:

$$u(c) = \frac{c^{1-\rho}}{1 - \rho}$$

(2.31)

The first derivative of (2.31) with respect to consumption, i.e. the marginal utility of consumption, is $c^{-\rho}$. The second derivative is $-\rho c^{-\rho-1}$. The term on the right-hand side of equation (2.30) determining consumption growth thus becomes:

$$-\frac{u''(c)c}{u'(c)} = \frac{\rho\, c^{-\rho-1}\, c}{c^{-\rho}} = \rho$$

(2.32)

The convenience of the CES-function is that it leads to a constant inter-temporal elasticity of substitution $- u'(c)/[u''(c)c] = 1/\rho$. The optimality condition for consumption growth consistently simplifies to:

$$\frac{c'(t)}{c(t)} = \rho^{-1}\,(r - \delta)$$

(2.33)

Since δ and r are assumed to be constant, life-time consumption follows a strictly determined path:

$$c(t) = c0\, e^{\left(\frac{1}{\rho}\right)(r-\delta)t}$$

(2.34)

Hence, the following conclusions are straightforward: the lower ρ (with $\rho > 0$), i.e. the higher the intertemporal elasticity of substitution, the stronger is the response of consumption growth to differences between the interest rate and the rate of time preference. Conversely, a higher value of ρ implies a lower willingness to substitute consumption intertemporally and, therefore, a smaller reaction of consumption growth to a gap between r and δ. For $\rho = 1$ we have logarithmic utility and consumption growth responds directly to the difference between r and δ, at the same time the income effect exactly offsets the substitution effect. Usually, higher values of ρ (3 up to 5) are assumed in the literature.

2.1.5 The Certainty Equivalent Model

The models reviewed so far fundamentally rest on the assumption that there is no uncertainty about income. This implies the proposition that every consumer knows the exact amount of his total life-time income (from labour as well as from wealth) at the beginning of his life, which is certainly far from reality. Alternatively, the absence of uncertainty implies that financial markets are perfect and complete, allowing everybody to fully ensure against random income shocks by purchasing state-contingent claims for all eventualities that could ever occur. Obviously, this is hardly realistic either.

Therefore, mainstream economics has attempted to overcome the perfect foresight approach, seeking models capable of including uncertainty. It has nevertheless tried to preserve the crucial conclusions of the standard approach, in particular the predicted independence of current income and consumption. One of the first economists focusing on the implications of forward-looking behaviour under uncertainty was Hall (1978), who developed the so-called certainty equivalence model. In fact, he didn't introduce true uncertainty, but risk. Risk supposes that not the exact future value but the probability distribution of a variable in the future is known. In the case of true uncertainty, even this information is not available and one cannot calculate the expected value.

If labour income is assumed to be stochastic, the discrete time consumption optimisation problem becomes:

$$\max V = E_0 \left\{ \sum_{t=0}^{T} (1 + \delta)^{-t} u[c(t)] \right\}$$

(2.35)

s. t.

$$E_0 \left\{ \sum_{t=0}^{T} (1 + r)^{-t} c(t) \right\} = F(0) + H(0)$$

(2.36)

$$H(0) = E_0 \left\{ \sum_{t=0}^{T} (1 + r)^{-t} w(t) \right\}$$

(2.37)

To avoid dealing with two stochastic variables, the model assumes a constant interest rate, which is in fact similarly unrealistic as supposing perfect foresight with respect to the income process.

From this system of equations (2.35–2.37), Hall defined the Euler equation as the first order intertemporal optimising equation linking marginal consumption in two subsequent periods. Under uncertainty the Euler equation becomes:

$$E_t \{ u'[c(t+1)] \} = \frac{(1+\delta)}{(1+r)} \, u'[c(t)]$$

(2.38)

Equation (2.38) indicates that, under the given conditions, marginal consumption evolves as a random walk. It is a walk with trend if time preference and interest rate differ, and a trendless walk if they are equal. In the latter case—including appropriate assumptions about the error distribution—the stochastic process governing marginal utility is a martingale: this period's expectation of the next period's marginal utility is equal to the current value of marginal utility. If the expectation is fulfilled, consumption remains constant otherwise current consumption, and hence expectations of the next period's consumption, will be adjusted according to modified expectations of life-time wealth.

An important special case occurs when we deal with quadratic instead of CES-utility, as marginal utility derived from a quadratic function is linear in consumption. The introduction and exploration of this particular case has been the main legacy of Hall's (1978) paper.

A possible quadratic utility function is:

$$u[c(t)] = A \, c(t) - B \, c(t)^2 \qquad A > 0, \qquad B > 0$$

(2.39)

Then marginal utility is $A - 2B \, c(t)$, and the Euler equation implies:

$$E_t \{ c(t+1) \} = a0 + a1 \, c(t) + e(t+1)$$

(2.40)

Equation (2.40) appears to be easily testable using ordinary econometric techniques. If we have $r = \delta$, a0 should be zero and a1 should equal unity. If r and δ differ, a0 is increasing and a1 decreasing in the difference.

Thus, if we additionally assume $E_t \{e(t+1)\} = 0$, not only marginal utility but consumption follows a random walk with or without drift.

The model with quadratic momentary utility functions has become known as the *certainty-equivalent model* (CEQ) because its implications for the intertemporal consumption path correspond exactly to those of models excluding uncertainty. The only difference is that within the CEQ-model unpredicted transitory or persistent income shocks do occur, in the latter case causing the expected permanent income to be revised upwards or downwards. Planned consumption then must be revised in order to be constant at the new permanent income level.

However, the general hypothesis of the standard model of consumption, i.e. current consumption not tracking current income but depending on permanent or life-time income alone, is preserved in any respect. If we observe a change in the level of consumption, it has to be caused by unexpected events under the CEQ assumptions.

Paragraph 2.2
The Empirical Failure of the Standard Models

2.2.1 Excess Sensitivity and Excess Smoothness— Ambiguous Results

Hall's (1978) approach triggered a large empirical research programme aimed at testing the prediction that consumption does not respond to expected current changes in income, while unpredicted income shocks cause consumers to revise their consumption by an amount equal to the permanent income value of that change.

But in fact this thesis was not as easy to confirm or to reject as it appeared to be since the empirical results depend critically on the assumptions about the income process. If those unexpected changes in income are supposed to be quickly reversed, their permanent income value is small and consumption should hardly alter. If, in contrast, unexpected changes are assumed to be long-lasting, consumption should change roughly in line with the income shock. Due to divergences in the modelling of the income process, empirical research led to quite contradictory results.

The earliest tests of Hall's model (Flavin 1981) conclude that consumption is excessively sensitive to income, i.e. consumption changes by more than the permanent income value of an income shock. Some later work, e.g. Campbell & Deaton (1989), however, suggests the opposite: consumption is too smooth in relation to the income process. Actually, these contradictions do not have much to do with the empirical data, but arise directly from different models of the income process. Flavin suggests that income follows an autoregressive process, whereby a rise of X in current income implies a rise of less than X in permanent income. By contrast, Campbell & Deaton suggest that the growth rate—not the level—of income is autoregressive, whereby a rise of X in current income implies a rise of more than X in permanent income. This led to different results for the response of consumption to a shock in income and, hence, was responsible for the contradictory conclusions.

2.2.2 MPC and Income Growth—Wrong Predictions

Since the early nineties the literature increasingly acknowledges that the prediction of the standard models are in many respects at odds with the facts. In the empirical literature a number of cases can be found where changes in income have been predictable in advance and the response of consumers and households can be scrutinised. None of these studies find that consumers respond to expected future income changes in the same way as if they occurred (at discounted value) presently. Instead, overwhelming empirical evidence suggests that consumption tracks income over the life-cycle, while it displays almost no response to long-term expectations.

With respect to transitory income fluctuations, the standard model hardly matches the facts either. Although a tendency to smooth high-frequency short-term income shocks certainly exists, the empirical estimates of the marginal propensity to consume out of transitory income fluctuations are much higher than those close to zero as predicted by the standard approach.

Regarding the response to income growth, the model also fails, predicting that households expecting a considerable income boost will run into debts, while in the case of expected low growth or decline in income they save particularly diligently. As shown, the empirical facts just lean towards the opposite direction. Households appear not to be willing to borrow unlimitedly against expected future income, utterly shrugging off the degree of uncertainty of that expectation. Even if households would like to borrow without limits, they would hardly be allowed to do so by the financial markets.

Finally, there is no empirical evidence to suggest that consumption and saving react significantly to changes in real interest rates, even though model predictions about the exact outcome are ambiguous due to the contrary income and substitution effect. The absence of a consistent response of saving to real interest rate movements might simply be caused by the fact that it is even harder to form expectations about real interest rates than about labour income. Knowing only the current real interest rate requires exact knowledge of the current rate of inflation, which is only available ex post. The real interest rates of the next decade are simply unknown. All this suggests that consumption and saving behaviour follow motives different from the ones contained in the mainstream approach.

These deficiencies have been criticised in a number of papers expressing rising dissatisfaction with the results of one and a half decades of economic research on consumption and saving primarily focused on estimating the parameters of Euler equations.

2.2.3 Incapability to Explain Saving Rate Differentials

There is another essential malfunction of the standard models that has been in the focus more seldom. That is the prediction that saving rates have to be independent from the level of permanent income or lifetime wealth, a prediction directly implied by the assumption of consumer optimisation under homothetic preferences. As a consequence, standard approaches are generally not able to explain the extreme variance of saving rates across relative income groups.

Of course, the standard models do provide justifications for cross-sectional saving rate differentials. However, they are hardly convincing. One major strand of the literature claims that the income of an individual household varies strongly enough in time to explain the phenomenon of rising saving rates across income groups. Since Friedman (1957), economists have repeatedly referred to the alleged over representation of high-transitory-income households in the upper deciles and low-transitory-income groups in the bottom deciles of the distribution. Within a life-cycle approach this has often been identified with an over representation of middle-age-households in the top-quintiles saving at the highest rates while preparing for retirement. But as shown above, neither the general income mobility nor the income variance over the life-cycle is strong enough to explain the enormous divergences between individual saving rates. Such an explanation, in addition, fails to explain the even more extreme variance in the wealth distribution: the very limited wealth of the median household remains as equally incomprehensible as the huge assets of the rich.

A different approach to saving rate differentials compatible with the premises of the standard models argues that social security programs offer dramatically different returns to households with different earning levels, thereby discouraging saving in the lower quintiles[1]. However, this explanation implies saving rate differentials being much smaller, and average saving being significantly higher in countries with poorer social security systems. This prediction, as we have seen, is not backed by the facts either.

A third strand of the literature considers different discount factors of different types of households to give reasons for diverging saving behaviour. Since discount factors are simply not observable, this approach is widely protected against empirical refutation. Lacking a powerful explanation for low or completely absent saving in lower-income households, these theories *conclude* that this behaviour must be caused by impatience. In a next step, dispelling where the 'insight' has originally been derived from, they *'explain'* lower saving by higher discount rates. At this point, the reasoning becomes circular.

There are even more bizarre examples in the literature. E.g. lower saving by poorer people indeed has been justified by their statistically shorter lifespan compared to more affluent people. These approaches are more cynical than scientific and they are not worth any further discussion here.

Reviewing the literature, standard models appear to be completely incapable of providing satisfying explanations for the divergent saving behaviour of different (permanent) income groups.

---

1 E.g. Feldstein (1980)

Paragraph 2.3
Refinements: Allowing for Precautionary Saving, Liquidity Constraints and Habit Formation

2.3.1 Convex Marginal Utility and the Precautionary Motive

As mentioned above, one strand of critique on the CEQ-approach has been focused on the unrealistic prediction that the degree of expected income variance has no influence on current saving decisions. This outcome follows exclusively from the use of quadratic utility functions yielding linear marginal utility. If, in contrast, models including uncertainty employ CES-utility, they lead to rather different conclusions. Supposing CES-utility and taking uncertainty of future income streams into account, the Euler equation can be written as follows:

$$c(t)^{-\rho} = \frac{(1 + r)}{(1 + \delta)} E_t \{ c(t + 1)^{-\rho} \}$$

$$(2.41)$$

The main difference to the approaches considered earlier is that now, mathematically, the mean expectation of the first derivatives deviates from the first derivative of the expected mean. The expected future marginal utility $E_t\{u'[c(t + 1)]\}$ is higher than the marginal utility of expected future consumption $u'[E_t\{c(t + 1)\}]$. The reason is that CES-utility has *convex* instead of linear marginal functions, i.e. the third derivatives governing the curvature of the first derivatives are positive. A mean preserving spread in the probability distribution of future income, is thus no longer irrelevant for the consumer's choice between spending and saving. Rather, the marginal utility of future consumption increases if the expected variance of future income rises. That is why a model with convex marginal utility predicts a drop in current consumption and a higher saving rate for the case of a soaring lack of confidence. Generally, for a given pattern of income uncertainty, CES preferences lead to lower current consumption and higher planned future consumption compared to the certainty equivalence case. This extra saving is usually called *precautionary saving*.

In the CES-case, the intertemporal elasticity of substitution and the risk aversion are controlled by the same parameter ρ. Since the standard measure of absolute risk aversion is $-u''(c)/u'(c)$, which equals $\rho/c(t)$ for CES-utility, relative risk aversion is constant at ρ. This kind of utility function is often referred to as Constant-Relative-Risk-Aversion (CRRA) utility in models including stochastic variables. While *risk aversion* generally shows how much a consumer dislikes uncertainty, Kimball (1990) introduces a measure of absolute *prudence* defined as $-u'''(c)/u''(c)$, indicating the propensity of a consumer to prepare itself in the face of uncertainty.

While in the case of quadratic utility functions prudence is zero, it becomes positive if we deal with CRRA-utility since we have:

$$\frac{-u'''(c)}{u''(c)} = \frac{(\rho + 1)}{c}$$

$$(2.42)$$

Generally, prudence is positive, if the third derivatives of the utility function are positive. It is higher, the lower the intertemporal elasticity of substitution (i.e. the higher ρ) and it decreases in the level of expected future consumption. If prudence is positive, consumption and saving respond not only to the expected mean of permanent income, but also to its expected variance.

2.3.2 The Technique of Stochastic Dynamic Programming

Despite the fact that models including precautionary saving motives are obviously more realistic than Perfect Forecast or CEQ-assumptions, no systematic work exploring the idea of precautionary saving had been done until the early nineties. This lack of research was caused, first and foremost, by the substantial technical difficulties in extending the two-period example into a multi-period context. In this case, an analytical solution determining the optimal consumption path is no longer available. The only way to solve such a model is by backward recursion, beginning with the last period of life, in which wealth, by assumption, has to be used up. Then the previous stages can be determined one after another using the first-order optimality conditions.

This is due to the fact that the Euler equation determines only the relation between marginal utility in two subsequent periods, but does not provide a self-contained solution for the case of uncertainty and CRRA-utility unless the second period is also the final period—otherwise the second-period solution depends on a further Euler equation relating periods two and three, and so on. Stochastic dynamic programming is a technique capable of solving this problem. However, until the beginning of the nineties the computing power required to find the numerical solutions of those problems was simply not available.

The procedure applying stochastic dynamic programming to multi-period life cycle consumption problems is as follows: The basic aim is to find a function which determines optimal consumption $c(t)$ in relation to current available resources, i.e. labour income and accumulated wealth. Following Deaton (1992), the liquidity available in period t is usually termed *cash on hand* denoted by the symbol $x(t)$ with $x(t) = F(t) + w(t)$. Hence, the sought function is: $c(t) = f[x(t)]$.

At first, a final period of life T is defined, in which all remaining recourses are to be consumed. Thus, in this latest period of life the optimal rule is simply:

$$c(T) = x(T)$$

$$(2.43)$$

Considering period $(T - 1)$, assuming $r = \delta$ and logarithmic utility as the simplest case, the Euler equation is:

$$c(T - 1)^{-1} = E_{T-1}\{ c(T)^{-1} \}$$

$$(2.44)$$

Substituting the one-period budget constraint for $c(T)$ we obtain:

$$c(T-1)^{-1} = E_{T-1}\left\{\left((1+r)(x(T-1)-c(T-1))+w(T)\right)^{-1}\right\}$$

$$= \sum_i \left((1+r)(x(T-1)-c(T-1))+w_i(T)\right)^{-1}$$

$$(2.45)$$

The proposed stochastic variable is labour income, while the real interest rate is again taken as known and fixed. Since (2.45) cannot be solved analytically, numerical solutions have to be found. The usual way to search for them is to formulate a grid of discrete values for $x(T)$, based on distributions of possible values for $w(T)$ and current cash on hand $x(T-1)$. Then for each point on the grid, the value of $c(T-1)$ which solves (2.44) can be calculated numerically. The entire grid of results gives the function $c(T-1) = f[x(T-1)]$ defining optimal consumption as a function of current cash on hand in period $(T-1)$. Proceeding to period $(T-2)$, the same procedure has to be repeated but becomes even more complicated. We now search for $c(T-2) = f[x(T-2)]$ and have to use the already available function $c(T-1) = f[x(T-1)]$. So we have to solve:

$$f[x(T-2)]^{-1} = \sum_i f[(1+r)(x(T-2)-f[x(T-2)])$$
$$+ w_i(T-1)]^{-1}$$

$$(2.46)$$

Again, this equation has to be solved over a grid of values, which is more complex since two functions are involved now instead of one.

If $c(T-2) = f[x(T-2)]$ has been calculated, we have to proceed to $(T-3)$, and so on. For any income process with a reasonable range of possible stochastic outcomes, and for a life-cycle of a significant number of periods, the total size of grid rapidly escalates, requiring a huge amount of computing memory.

Thanks to powerful modern processors, those computations are feasible and have been carried out by several economists leading to predictions different from those of the Modigliani/Hall framework. Of course, the details depend on the exact function and on the parameter values that have been used, but general results are: 1) The marginal propensity to consume out of an increase in current income is considerably larger than out of an increase of equal present value in the expected future income. 2) This disparity is particularly important for households at the lower end of the wealth hierarchy. Conversely, households with a high level of financial resources appear to behave similar to Modigliani consumers. 3) A household's planned rate of future consumption growth is negatively related to its current asset holdings. 4) A systematic relationship between the marginal propensity to consume out of a current unexpected income shock and the latter's permanent income equivalent does not exist. 5) The path of lifetime consumption is closely linked to the path of lifetime income.

2.3.3 The Buffer-Stock Model

A comprehensive application of stochastic programming techniques to the problem of intertemporal optimisation has been provided by Carroll (1997) based on the ideas of Deaton (1991) and Carroll (1992). Because of the model's predictions about desired wealth holdings of households, it is named the *buffer-stock model*. Carroll deals with the usual intertemporal additive felicity function and CRRA utility (2.31). The income process and budget constraints are specified as follows:

$$x(t+1) = (1+r)[x(t) - c(t)] + E_t\{w(t+1)\}$$

(2.47)

$$E_t\{w(t+1)\} = E_t\{p(t+1)v(t+1)\}$$

(2.48)

$$E_t\{p(t+1)\} = (1+g)p(t)E_t\{n(t+1)\}$$

(2.49)

$$v(t) = \begin{cases} 0 & \textit{with probability } q \\ z & \textit{with probability } (1-q) \end{cases}$$

(2.50)

$$\ln z \sim TN\left(\frac{-\sigma^2{}_{\ln z}}{2}, \sigma^2{}_{\ln z}\right)$$

$$(2.51)$$

$$\ln n \ \sim \ TN\left(\frac{-\sigma^2{}_{\ln n}}{2}, \sigma^2{}_{\ln n}\right)$$

$$(2.52)$$

Labour income has a persistent and a transitory component. The transitory component contains a certain probability of zero income, which Carroll assumes to be 0.5 percent per year. Persistent income grows at a constant rate g, but is also stochastic. TN signifies a truncated normal distribution with expected values of z as well as of n equalling unity. The rate of return is supposed to be constant. Carroll then rewrites the entire problem by dividing all variables by the level of persistent labour income $p(t)$, specifying the optimal consumption rule for period t in terms of these normalised variables:

$$\left[\frac{c(t)}{p(t)}\right] = f\left[\frac{x(t)}{p(t)}\right]$$

$$(2.53)$$

Carroll focuses on cases in which the discount rate exceeds the interest rate, i.e. consumers are impatient. In a CEQ model this parameter combination, together with positive labour income growth, generates strong initial borrowing against future income and a negative growth rate of consumption over life. Within the buffer-stock model, however, the positive probability of zero income in future periods causes consumers to fear for zero consumption if they do not accumulate a buffer stock of wealth.

Formally, the marginal utility in the case of zero consumption is infinite under CRRA-utility. Hence, the desire to smooth marginal utilities in the optimal path causes a strong wish to exclude such events. Consumers will always choose to hold some positive wealth in order to insure themselves against this possibility of total destitution. Nevertheless, the consumer's impatience $(\delta > r)$ conflicts with his prudence. The model thus predicts a compromise: the household decides to accumulate some but not too much wealth. As soon as the household has attained its target level of wealth relative to normal income, further income growth leads to approximately proportionate growth in consumption. In contrast to the CEQ model, however, a change of the expected value of income in the future has little impact on current consumption since it does not affect the ratio $x(t)/p(t)$.

Carroll shows that the function $c(t) = f[x(t)]$ converges if the following impatience condition holds:

$$\rho^{-1}(r - \delta) + \left(\frac{\rho}{2}\right) \sigma^2{}_{\ln n} < g - \frac{\sigma^2{}_{\ln n}}{2}$$

(2.54)

If there is no income uncertainty ($\sigma^2{}_{\ln n} = 0$), the condition simplifies to $\rho^{-1}(r - \delta) < g$, which is the convergence condition in a Modigliani life cycle framework.

The basic logic of the buffer-stock model becomes even clearer if we consider the second-order log-linearized Euler equation:

$$E_t\{\Delta \ln c(t + 1)\}$$
$$\approx \rho^{-1}(r - \delta) + \frac{\rho}{2}\, var_t\,(\Delta \ln c(t + 1)) + e(t + 1)$$

(2.55)

where $var_t\,(\Delta \ln c(t + 1))$ is the expected variance in future income growth.

Carroll uses this equation to show that in the case of buffer-stock savers the usual procedure of Euler equation estimation cannot uncover undistorted parameter values. Yet, previous econometric work had mostly dealt with a first-order approximation of the Euler equation for which only the first term on the right-hand side matters. But neglecting the probability spread of expected future income is only appropriate in a certainty equivalent context or if uncertainty is ruled out at all. Given these circumstances, the expected variance of future consumption growth is either zero or has no influence on the expected marginal utility of future consumption. In the case of CRRA-utility, however, the second-order variance term in the Euler equation cannot be ignored as it is not a constant but endogenous and positively correlated with planned consumption growth.

The reason is the following: the lower the wealth to income ratio of a consumer, the higher the expected future variance of consumption growth. A consumer with few assets has fewer possibilities to insure himself against a negative income shock, particularly against zero income. Such a possibility of zero income, for the rest of his life, does occur in the model with low but certain probability. In the extreme case of no wealth and a long-lasting zero-income shock, cash on hand is zero and there is no possibility to borrow since dying indebted is excluded by the budget constraint. But if expected consumption is zero with some probability in at least one period, expected consumption growth goes to infinity at the same probability and becomes completely independent from the parameters ρ, r and δ. If, in contrast, cash on hand approaches infinity due to large amounts of accumulated wealth, the expected growth rate of consumption approaches the desired rate $\rho^{-1}(r - \delta)$ since consumption becomes almost completely independent from negative income shocks. Hence, the larger the available assets, the smaller is the expected variance of future consumption growth. Therefore, as Carroll stresses repeatedly, econometric estimates of the parameters using the first-order approximation of the Euler equation provide erroneous results since the error term is not normally distributed but heteroskedastic.

Independent from these econometric issues, the behavioural predictions of the buffer-stock model can easily be understood from equation (2.55). Planned optimal consumption growth is positively related to the variance of future consumption growth. The value of the latter, in turn, is partly determined by the variance of future labour income, but also by the relation of labour income to financial wealth. Available wealth increases cash on hand and the return on wealth is per assumption not subject to uncertainty. Consumption growth can only be expected to be high if current consumption is relatively low compared to the present discounted value of future labour income and to available wealth. Therefore, the second-order log linearised Euler equation indicates that when wealth is low relative to labour income, consumers seek to accumulate wealth by lowering current consumption while planned consumption growth is high. If the expected variance of future labour income increases—particularly if the probability of zero income shocks is expected to rise—consumers with relatively little wealth will respond with stronger efforts to save while the response of wealthier households is much weaker. This kind of model is therefore called a buffer-stock model: wealth acts as a buffer stock shielding against negative income shocks.

The buffer-stock model provides an explanation why the median household typically holds only small but positive amounts of financial wealth over the entire working life-time and why increasing income uncertainty might cause households to strengthen their effort to save.

2.3.4 Liquidity Constrained Consumers

A different approach to overcome the unrealistic predictions of the Modigliani/Hall models questions the assumption of perfect capital markets. It has been argued that liquidity constraints are a crucial issue preventing groups of households from borrowing in spite of expected income growth[2]. These consumers are not allowed to decide optimally if their desired level of consumption exceeds their current level of cash on hand. Thus, the intertemporal budget constraint is modified: saving and dissaving continue to be guided by the long-run perspective. The predictions correspond to those of the standard models as long as the optimal level of consumption is lower than available cash. If, in contrast, optimality requires borrowing against future income, liquidity constraint consumers have to deviate from the predictions of the standard models, spending their income exactly in every period. Taking this restriction into account, the Euler equation takes the following form:

$$u'[c(t)] = \max\left\{ u'[x(t)], \frac{1 + r}{1 + \delta} E_t \{u'[c(t + 1)]\}\right\}$$
(2.56)

Obviously, if cash on hand is lower than planned consumption, the first term on the right-hand side exceeds the second and the constraint is binding. If, in contrast, planned consumption can be financed out of cash on hand, the second term is larger and the optimal path has the standard form.

The existence of liquidity constraints strongly boosts the precautionary motive since consumers without any assets and no access to credit are threatened by zero consumption even in the case of a single period of zero income. Several models have been developed combining both approaches. Generally, the predictions from liquidity constrained models are similar but somewhat stronger compared to a pure buffer-stock model. Whereas in the latter the precautionary motive restrains the desire to borrow, the liquidity constrained consumer wishes to borrow but has no opportunity at all to do so.

---

2 Carroll & Kimbal (2001); Deaton (1991); Ludvigson (1999); Runkle (1991)

2.3.5 Models Including Habit Formation

Another major line of criticism has attempted to overcome the strong separability condition of the life-time felicity function. It has been emphasised that the influence of past consumption on the utility yielded by current consumption must no longer be neglected, as in reality undeniable links exist. One may think about durable purchases, such as cars, which influence preferences about non-durables (fuel, repair service etc.) in subsequent periods. But even if the link is not technically required, it has been a long acknowledged phenomenon that consumers get accustomed to goods or services and attempt to maintain a certain standard of living. Duesenberry (1949) questions the realism of the separability assumptions, emphasising that the desired level of current consumption is influenced by the consumption level achieved in the past.

One way to overcome simple additivity is to allow the one-period utility functions to depend not only on current consumption, but also on consumption in prior periods. A general form of the resulting life-time felicity function is:

$$V = \sum_{t=0}^{T} u(t)[c(t), c(t-1), \ldots, c(t-n)]$$

(2.57)

where n is the number of lags to be included. An example of the latter would be to model momentary utility as a function of the excess of consumption over some familiar level carried over from the past. Assuming usual CRRA-utility and discounting future income, the life-time felicity function is then structured as follows:

$$V = \sum_{t=0}^{T} (1 + \delta)^{-t} \frac{[c(t) - a\,c(t-1)]^{1-\rho}}{1 - \rho}$$

(2.58)

This kind of function has been the base of simulations provided by Carroll & Weil (1994). Their finding is that introducing habit formation can explain the positive relation between saving and income growth but only if rather implausible parameter assumptions are used. Normally, the human wealth effect prevails over the habit-stock effect, strongly damping the desire to save. This is particularly so because in the employed model the effects of uncertainty are excluded. Therefore, Carroll & Weil suggest combining habit formation with liquidity constraints and precautionary motives to achieve more reasonable results.

An alternative way to model the evolution of habits and to introduce them into the general model is given by Deaton (1992). In this approach utility depends directly on a stock variable, which might be a psychological stock of habits or simply a stock of durable goods, both affecting the utility obtained from current consumption. Such a model could look like:

$$V = \sum_{t=0}^{T} u(t)[\alpha\, c(t) - \beta\, S(t)]$$

$$(2.59)$$

where the state variable $S(t)$ itself evolves with current consumption, governed by the rule:

$$S(t+1) = (1 - \theta)S(t) + c(t+1)$$

$$(2.60)$$

Here, θ can be thought of as a depreciation parameter. The parameter α has to exceed zero, while β should be positive if we deal with habits reducing the utility of a certain consumption level, and negative if durable goods are modelled, increasing utility by their flow of service.

A rigorous formal model based on the idea of the evolution of a habit stock influencing the intertemporal problem of consumption optimisation has been provided by Carroll, Overland, Weil (2000). Their approach is modelled in continuous time and, for simplicity, is non-stochastic. The employed instantaneous utility function is:

$$u(c, h) = \frac{\left(\frac{c}{h^{\gamma}}\right)^{1-\rho}}{1 - \rho}$$

$$(2.61)$$

where c is the instantaneous flow of consumption, h denotes the stock of habits and γ indexes the importance of habits. If $\gamma = 0$, only the level of consumption is important as in the standard CRRA model, while if $\gamma = 1$, consumption relative to the habit stock is all that matters. Realistically, values between the two extremes should be used.

The stock of habits is assumed to evolve according to the equation of motion:

$$h' = \alpha(c - h)$$

(2.62)

So, the habit stock is a weighted average of past consumption with α determining the relative weights of consumption at different times.

The infinite horizon felicity function, based on (2.61), is:

$$V = \int_0^\infty u(c, h)e^{-\delta t}$$

(2.63)

If, additionally, a budget constraint is included, the problem can be solved analytically. The outcome differs considerably from the usual Euler equation determining consumption growth. Now, the optimal *rate of change* of consumption growth is determined as a function of the taste parameters and the real rate of return r. This result arises because the consumer's utility is now affected not only by the level of current consumption, as in the standard framework, but also by the growth rate of consumption due to its effect on c/h^γ. Therefore, the intertemporal evolution of the *growth rate* of consumption as such must satisfy an optimality condition. Hence, habit-forming consumers will have a desire to smooth consumption growth rates for the same reasons that Modigliani/Hall-consumers have a desire to smooth the level of consumption.

Consequently, the model predicts a different response of saving rates to growth than the standard framework. In the latter, higher income growth leads to lower saving or higher borrowing due to the human wealth effect. Carrol, on the other hand, provides simulations of his model indicating that saving could respond positively to higher expected income growth under reasonable parameter values. The strength of the effect depends on the value of γ.

Other approaches to overcome the strong and implausible assumption of additivity can be found in the literature. Uzawa (1989) and Obstfeld

(1990) suggest making the rate at which utility is discounted through time a function of past consumption behaviour.

These are by far not all the refinements introduced by mainstream economics to gain realism, but are the most widely cited and debated ones. The general problem in any case is the more complicated the assumed utility function, the more difficult or almost impossible it is to derive the optimal consumption path. Particularly numerical simulations, which are the only solution procedure in most of these cases, quickly reach the limits even of modern computer capacity. If uncertainty is included and marginal utility is convex, models including a more complex felicity function become almost unmanageable.

Paragraph 2.4
Do the Elaborated Models Perform Better?

2.4.1 Gain in Realism at the Cost of Predictive Power

Due to either a different structure of the utility function or amended assumptions about the intertemporal budget constraint, the predictions derived from the models considered in the previous section differ remarkably from the conclusions of the Perfect Foresight and the CEQ-approach. More precisely, those models are compatible with a much richer variety of short-run and long-run consumption patterns, including those predicted by the standard models. Actually, we are able to predict almost everything by appropriately specifying the parameters. This capacity has often been taken as an advantage of the elaborated models, but it might be questioned whether this is really a gain. After all, the downside is a considerable loss in explanatory and predictive power.

Take the CRRA-model under uncertainty: if the marginal utility functions are assumed to be flat (i.e. the intertemporal elasticity of substitution is high) and the expected future variance in income and wealth is assumed to be small, the model predicts almost the same behaviour as the standard Modigliani/Hall model. In the case of a lower elasticity of substitution and a certain probability (even if it is very small) of zero income in the future, the model, in contrast, predicts a strong reluctance to borrow against expected future income and an attempt to save, even if income growth is anticipated. If this is combined with impatience (a discount rate exceeding the real interest rate), the model simulates a consumption path that closely tracks the path of income. The same combination of parameters also explains why most households build relatively limited wealth. According to this model, consumers are eager to save, because the convex marginal utility requires minimising the risk of zero future consumption. However, as soon as a buffer-stock of wealth exists that protects against such an event, impatience drives the households to stop saving and to consume the bulk of their income. Consistently, such a model of buffer-stock savers also justifies why the marginal propensity to consume out of transitory income is significantly different from zero.

Three empirical findings, which the standard approach cannot account for, appear to be explainable within a CRRA-model that includes uncertainty. First, it provides reasons why consumption tracks income closely over a lifespan. Second, it provides an explanation why the marginal propensity to consume out of transitory income is relatively high. Third, it suggests a rationale why median wealth holdings are low.

Nevertheless, it has been questioned in the literature whether such a strong precautionary motive is really justified by empirical evidence. Considering the stylised facts of saving, we also come to the conclusion that although the fact of precautionary saving is supported, a strong pattern is not discernible.

2.4.2 Remaining Deficiencies

However, there are still important empirical facts not covered by this approach. Buffer-stock savers might be more reserved in responding to persistent income growth with indebtedness, but they have no reason to save more intensely in that case. The strong divergences in saving rates across income groups also remain unexplained. According to the model, the bottom quintiles, where households with an over-proportional risk of negative income shocks caused by unemployment or poor paid jobs are concentrated, should face particularly strong incentives to build a buffer-stock. The huge assets held by households at the top end of the income hierarchy remain equally mysterious.

The effect of the assumption of liquidity constraints is in fact similar to that of a strong precautionary saving motive. Models including liquidity constraints provide explanations why consumption might track current income closely. In this case such a path is backed by the proposition that the non-saving consumers in the bottom deciles actually wish to borrow, but are not allowed to do so. However, this assumption seems to lack empirical evidence. Most households in the bottom income groups—at least today—have little reason to expect strong income growth in the future to justify their desire to borrow under optimality conditions. In addition, if households are asked about their reason for abstaining from saving, they mostly report that they cannot afford to save.

Furthermore, if the assumption of liquidity constraints is the only amendment to the standard framework, households which do save, even if only a small amount, should behave exactly according to the standard predictions. But as we have seen, in many respects they do not.

Finally, similar to the precautionary motive, liquidity constraints might explain why consumers show almost no response to predictable income growth; however, it does not explain, why persistent income growth actually triggers higher saving rates. Thus, although the assumption of liquidity constraints is undeniably realistic, the predictive power of models adjusted just by this specification remains limited.

Models including habit formation perform better than all other approaches in one respect: they are able to explain the positive relation between income growth and saving rates. But in fact, this is the only crucial difference. Saving rate disparity across permanent income groups and divergences in wealth holdings continue to be incomprehensible if they are not attributable to different growths rates in income. But the growth rates hardly differ sufficiently to justify such an approach.

Moreover, elaborated models further complicate the possibility of deriving testable implications. Expected income variance is hardly measurable, and the same is true for liquidity constraints or habit formation. In any attempt to estimate the parameters of those models, the assumptions about the income process or about the structure of the utility function have an overwhelming effect on the estimation results. Hence, different approaches will inevitably reach divergent conclusions which can barely be used to verify the models in turn.

Consequently, combining all these elaborated versions is certainly not the breakthrough solution. Even in dealing with models built on more realistic notions, one still faces a serious lack of explanatory power and can derive at best only vague and unsatisfactory predictions, not to mention the difficulties to even find the optimal path.

Paragraph 2.5
The Optimal Consumption Path—
General Remarks

2.5.1 Hidden Assumptions and Fundamental Flaws

All models of saving and consumption which have been at the centre of mainstream economics for decades—the standard approach as well as the refined versions—share the same underlying principles. The most fundamental one is the hypothesis that one can consistently model a society's saving behaviour in time as if private households—often even grasped as a single representative consumer—try to solve an intertemporal utility maximisation problem guided by the purpose of deriving an optimal lifetime consumption path. Although one can simulate almost any behaviour within this general approach, there are a number of hidden assumptions behind it which are far from being undisputable.

A first objection refers to the fact that saving is nothing than a by-product of *an intertemporal consumption plan.* It is in no way self-evident that the purpose of all savings is future consumption. Second, one should seriously question whether the *time horizon* for which a human being is planning actually refers to the remainder of his life, to say nothing of infinity. Third, two problems of aggregation are involved in the approaches considered. One concerns the issue whether analysing the behaviour of a *representative household* equipped with mean income and mean wealth allows statements to be made about the outcome of decisions of heterogeneous households each equipped with different assets and flows of income. This is the question of the appropriateness of the representative consumer approach, still used by most of the literature. The other aggregation problem concerns the argument of the utility function. All models reviewed above assume that the bundle of consumption goods the consumer uses up in every period can be grasped as a *single unity*, and as such providing utility. Fourth, it is rather dubious whether categories that might appropriately describe preferences in a static demand system are at all applicable to the matter of *intertemporal* choice. Finally, even if all these assumptions could be proven to be adequate, one is tempted to doubt whether a consumer will ever be able to discover his current optimal consumption level before starving and dying. From the mathematical point of view, the solvability of the respective models depends on extremely simplifying assumptions. If, for instance, the interest rate was introduced as a second stochastic variable into a standard buffer-stock model, even the most modern computer software—not to mention an ordinary consumer—would fail to provide a numerical solution. Yet no one is able to perfectly foresee the path of future interest rates. Even information about the probability distribution of certain variables in a far-away future is not available in a world of true uncertainty. Hence, the highly complicated solution procedure presupposes information that is simply not at hand.

2.5.2 Arguments of the Utility Function—Wealth as an End in Itself

Let us start with the first hidden assumption regarding the commonly used utility function and the entity it refers to. Although it may appear to be a trivial statement that financial wealth is devoted to being used up at some point, such an approach, at best, adequately describes the saving purposes of about 90 or 95 percent of the population. The primary interest of families who already possess enormous amounts of financial wealth and still try to enlarge their assets, being much more eager to invest in high-yielding assets than the average saver (see the section about saving motives in Chapter 1), is certainly different. But just these wealthy households account for the bulk of savings. Darby (1977) uses data on U.S. private wealth holding and subsequent labour income and consumption to conclude that at most 29 percent of U.S. private net worth is dedicated to future consumption.

This contradiction has been widely neglected in the recent saving literature. One of the exemptions is Carroll (2000c), who acknowledges "that the saving behaviour of the richest households cannot be explained by models in which the only purpose of wealth accumulation is to finance future consumption, either their own or that of heirs."[3] Carroll, proposing a "Capitalist Spirit"-model, suggests including wealth as such in the utility function. Wealth is considered a luxury good, only becoming relevant if high levels are already reached.

As private wealth creation is the source as well as the outcome of capital accumulation in the current economic system, the volume of financial wealth must definitely not be restricted to the purpose of being eaten up in a later lifespan since under these circumstances it would never reach the level required to meet the capital needs of a modern economy. But financial wealth beyond a certain limit is a scarce good: only a few households command it and hardly anyone will be able to join this league by means of life-cycle saving out of labour income. Thus, those few families who, by whatever sources, own huge financial assets, control one of the most fundamental monopolies in a capitalist society and are in fact enormously served by it.

As Carroll (2000c) points out, wealth beyond a certain level creates power, social status, safety, leisure or duties, whatever one prefers; and not to forget, it generates a stream of income that is never available to labour, even for the most capable, hardworking and best skilled persons. That is why these richest households, although usually not able to consume only the earnings out of their wealth, heavily resist whenever someone attempts to distribute parts of their fortune to less satiated consumers. Since capitalist economies desperately depend on those huge private assets, their owners are accustomed to being successful in pushing through their desires.

It is really amazing that generations of economists have been creating models of saving behaviour in which the central agents of wealth creation of the current economic system have simply been ignored. In fact, long ago the Keynesian economist Nicholas Kaldor already pointed out that two essentially different types of savers exist. He distinguished saving by wage earners from capitalist saving. Today, it is probably more appropriate to differentiate middle-class saving (including saving by wage earners as well as saving by the majority of self-employed people who are not exceptionally rich) from the wealth accumulation of capitalists. The fundamental difference between these two types of savers and between their motives and goals is confirmed by the stylised facts. Hence, models trying to ex-

---

3 Carroll (2000c)

plain the saving behaviour of all private households by the uniform motive of consumption smoothing are hardly convincing.

2.5.3 A Realistic Time-Horizon

Even if we limit our scope to those 95 percent of households below the top, the traditional models are hardly convincing. Let us begin with the realism of the time horizon assumed to be relevant for planning decisions. As the cited opinion polls of Merrill Lynch have shown, so-called Ultra-HNWIs are in fact used to creating 100 year plans treating family members as business divisions. The common saver, however, rarely considers his purchase and saving decisions with extended horizons in mind, be it the remainder of his life or even longer. Probably no-one has ever been observed planning his life-time consumption. Except for some consumption decisions that actually refer to decades—such as the decision to buy a house and to take a large mortgage—households will take into account expectations for just the next two or three years even in the case of expensive durables.

Of course, one can specify the models under consideration in a way that only a limited period matters. But the particular intention of these approaches is that the long-run has explanatory power—e.g. for the buffer-stock model the complicated solution procedure by backwards recursion would not make sense otherwise.

Realistically, the time horizon human beings plan for hardly exceeds a decade, being much shorter in most cases. This is not only a problem of psychology but, even more vitally, a problem of information. It is simply impossible for any consumer to obtain a sensible estimate of his income flows for the next twenty or thirty years; or of the most likely values of nominal interest rate and inflation one or two decades into the future—not to mention the desired consumption path in far-off periods since many consumption goods that will then be customary are probably not even known today. We shall come back to the information problem later. To sum up with respect to the horizon of saving decisions, a consumer guided by rational expectations in the literal meaning will never be tempted to plan his annual consumption expenditure far into the future.

2.5.4 The Representative Consumer

Next, let us analyse the two aggregation problems noted above, considering first aggregation across consumers or households. The theoretical conditions are very stringent for an economy composed of many heterogeneous individuals to behave exactly as if the decisions were carried out a by a single representative agent equipped with mean income and wealth. The crucial condition guaranteeing aggregation is linearity: the optimal individual consumption and saving path has to be linear in the relevant variables. Under this condition one can model aggregate dynamics using the representative consumer approach.

In fact, if we deal with CRRA-utility under perfect foresight conditions, current consumption is a linear function of lifetime-income with the same being true for saving. For the simplest model that deals with only two periods (one with and one without labour income) and no initial wealth, this is easy to show. Under these conditions the lifetime budget constraint was:

$$w1 \ = \ c1 \ + \ (1 \ + \ r2)^{-1}c2$$

$$(2.64)$$

and the Euler equation, linking consumption in the two periods, was:

$$c1 \ = \ \left[\frac{1 \ + \ r2}{1 \ + \ \delta}\right]^{-\frac{1}{\rho}} c2$$

$$(2.65)$$

Using (2.65), $c2$ could be consistently expressed as a function of $c1$, too. Inserting the latter equation into the budget constraint gives:

$$c1 \ + \ (1 \ + \ r2)^{-1}\left[\frac{1 \ + \ r2}{1 \ + \ \delta}\right]^{\frac{1}{\rho}} c1 \ = \ w1$$

$$(2.66)$$

Rearranging terms leads to:

$$\left(1 + \frac{(1 + r2)^{\frac{1-\rho}{\rho}}}{(1 + \delta)^{\frac{1}{\rho}}}\right) c1 \;=\; w1$$

$$\frac{(1 + \delta)^{\frac{1}{\rho}} + (1 + r2)^{\frac{1-\rho}{\rho}}}{(1 + \delta)^{\frac{1}{\rho}}} \Big) c1 \;=\; w1$$

$$c1 \;=\; \frac{(1 + \delta)^{\frac{1}{\rho}}}{(1 + \delta)^{\frac{1}{\rho}} + (1 + r2)^{\frac{1-\rho}{\rho}}} \; w1$$

$$(2.67)$$

Therefore, saving in the first period equals $s1 \;=\; w1 - c1$:

$$s1 \;=\; w1 - \frac{(1 + \delta)^{\frac{1}{\rho}}}{(1 + \delta)^{\frac{1}{\rho}} + (1 + r2)^{\frac{1-\rho}{\rho}}} \; w1$$

$$=\; \frac{(1 + r2)^{\frac{1-\rho}{\rho}}}{(1 + \delta)^{\frac{1}{\rho}} + (1 + r2)^{\frac{1-\rho}{\rho}}} \; w1$$

$$(2.68)$$

The coefficient of labour income $w1$ is a constant that depends on three parameters (ρ, δ and $r2$) and covers the substitution as well as the income effect. Hence, whatever the relationship between the real interest rate and the rate of time preference, and whatever the intertemporal elasticity of substitution $1/\rho$, the first period's consumption and saving depend linearly on the first period's labour income. Since we have $c2 = (1 + r2) s1$, the same is true for consumption in the second period. Therefore, if the real interest rate and the rate of time preference can be assumed to be identical for all consumers, the representative agent approach gives the same consumption path as an aggregate of n heterogeneous households.

This result can easily be generalised for the T period case. In this case, as we have seen, the budget constraint was:

$$\sum_{t=0}^{T} (1 + r)^{-t} c(t) = F(0) + H(0)$$

(2.69)

The Euler equation linking consumption in two subsequent periods was:

$$c(t) = \left[\frac{1 + r}{1 + \delta}\right]^{-\frac{1}{\rho}} c(t + 1)$$

(2.70)

Iterating this equation, one can represent each level of consumption as a function of the first period's consumption (for simplicity of the algebraic expression, we again assume a constant real interest rate):

$$c(t) = \left[\frac{1 + r}{1 + \delta}\right]^{t/\rho} c(0)$$

(2.71)

Inserting this into the budget constraint gives:

$$\sum_{t=0}^{T} (1 + r)^{-t} \left[\frac{1 + r}{1 + \delta}\right]^{\frac{t}{\rho}} c(0) = F(0) + H(0)$$

(2.72)

Solving for $c(0)$ leads to:

$$c(0) = \left[\sum_{t=0}^{T} \frac{(1 + r)^{\frac{t - t\rho}{\rho}}}{(1 + \delta)^{\frac{t}{\rho}}}\right]^{-1} \left(F(0) + H(0)\right)$$

(2.73)

Again, consumption in the first period of life (and the same could be derived for consumption in any period) is a linear function of permanent income or life-time wealth, respectively.

Moreover, since

$$H(0) = w(0) + \sum_{t=1}^{T} (1 + r)^{-t} w(t)$$

we can also write:

$$c(0) = \xi\, w(0) + \xi \left[F(0) + \sum_{t=1}^{T} (1 + r)^{-t} w(t) \right]$$

(2.74)

with:

$$\xi = \left[\sum_{t=0}^{T} \frac{(1 + r)^{\frac{t - t\rho}{\rho}}}{(1 + \delta)^{\frac{t}{\rho}}} \right]^{-1}$$

Therefore, in the multi-period case as well, current consumption is a linear function of current labour income and of life-time wealth. Hence, if we deal with CES-utility under perfect foresight conditions, aggregation of individual consumption paths is not a problem. (See also Bertola, Foellmi & Zweimüller (2006))

However, this outcome follows exclusively from the homotheticity property of CES-utility. If preferences display a constant and therefore income-independent elasticity of substitution, the income-expansion path is linear. In the case of *intratemporal* optimisation this means that the composition of optimal consumption does not depend on total expenditure, but that the proportions of the certain goods and services remain constant. In the case of intertemporal optimisation, homothetic preferences imply that saving increases linearly with permanent income, while the saving rate is exactly the same for all permanent income groups. Under those conditions distributional parameters do not play a role and aggregation using mean values is possible.

However, the assumption of income-independent saving rates is as unrealistic as is the assumption of unit income elasticity of certain goods and services in a demand system. Hence, although the homotheticity assumption is of undeniable convenience, realism strongly suggests a departing from it.

Bertola, Foellmi & Zweimüller (2006) show that the mentioned result concerning the possibility of aggregation is not only true for homothetic CES-utility, but for a more general class of "quasi-homothetic" or "hyperbolic absolute risk aversion" (HARA) preferences. The perfect foresight assumption, of course, has to be preserved.

The general structure of marginal utility under HARA-preferences is:

$$u'(c) = \left(\frac{\beta c}{\sigma} - c^*\right)^{-\sigma}$$

(2.75)

This functional form includes CRRA-preferences where $c^* = 0$ and $\beta = \sigma > 0$, quadratic utility with $\sigma = -1$, and constant absolute risk aversion (CARA) utility with $\sigma = -\infty$ and $c^* = -1$.

The important property of HARA-preferences is a linear relationship between current and future consumption. This can be shown as follows: if marginal utility has the form of equation (2.75), we can write $u'(c) = f(g(c))$, where $f(.)$ is a power function and $g(.)$ is an affine (constant slope) function. Therefore, the Euler equation can be written as:

$$g(c(t)) = f^{-1}\left[\frac{1 + r(t+1)}{1 + \rho} f\left(g(c(t+1))\right)\right]$$

(2.76)

Rearranging terms gives:

$$c(t) = g^{-1}\left[f^{-1}\left[\frac{1 + r(t+1)}{1 + \rho}\right] g(c(t+1))\right]$$

(2.77)

The function on the right-hand side of this expression is linear in $c(t+1)$, since the slope of $g(.)$ and of its inverse $g^{-1}(.)$ is constant. Hence, individual consumption levels in adjoining periods are linked in a linear way. If additionally $r(t+1)$ and ρ are assumed to be equal for all individuals, the Euler equation can simply be aggregated by replacing individual consumption by aggregate consumption. The same is true with respect to lifetime-income.

Bertola, Foellmi & Zweimüller (2006) prove that the link between current consumption and life-time income is linear under HARA-preferences. HARA-preferences are called quasi-homothetic, since they generally guarantee a linear income expansion path, although—other than in the constant elasticity of substitution case—this path does not go through the origin. In this case utility is perhaps not well defined below a certain level of individual income, but if everybody reaches at least that level, macroeconomic dynamics can be interpreted in terms of representative agent saving choices even when the economy features persistent and variable heterogeneity of individual consumption paths.

Hence, if all households have the same HARA-preferences, face the same real interest rate (that is known in advance) and maximise utility intertemporally under perfect foresight or certainty equivalent conditions, the distribution of income and wealth has no effect on aggregate consumption and saving.

Yet as soon as we accept that individual income paths are uncertain, that consumers cannot fully ensure themselves against idiosyncratic risks and utility is not quadratic, the likely outcome is a nonlinear consumption function. As Carroll (2000b) points out, even within the framework of a buffer-stock model the ratio of consumption to permanent labour income is a concave function of the ratio of cash on hand to permanent labour income. Hence, under such circumstances the distribution of wealth affects the level of aggregate consumption and the average marginal propensity to consume. If wealth is distributed very unequally, the results derived for a representative consumer will differ considerably from the behaviour of the real aggregate. Since in reality the distribution of wealth is extremely right-skewed, Carroll (2000b) concludes, that a model with uninsurable idiosyncratic risk and realistic wealth distribution produces behaviour very different from that produced by a representative agent economy. Therefore, he suggests that the representative consumer model should be abandoned in favour of a model that matches key microeconomic facts.

If one assumes non-homothetic preferences, aggregation of preferences is essentially impossible and the pretensions to build a macroeconomic model by straight-forward aggregation of microeconomic relationships are generally made on feet of clay.

As a consequence, dealing with heterogeneous agents has recently become more popular. The most commonly used approach in this context is to distinguish between employed and unemployed consumers while the individual employment state is assumed to follow a first-order Markov chain according to a transition matrix with known probabilities. With only a few exceptions, such dynamic heterogeneous agent general equilibrium models do not have an analytical solution or allow for the derivation of analytical results. Even to handle them numerically becomes more difficult, the more heterogeneity is assumed or the more structure in the intertemporal utility function is introduced.

Attempts have been made using those models to derive the business cycle dynamics of the income distribution or the unequal distribution of wealth holdings. But, especially in the latter case, they mostly failed because all the models predict a much more equal spread of wealth across agents than is found in real societies.

To summarise, one main condition is required in order to obtain adequate results from the representative consumer approach: the marginal propensity to consume has to be independent from individual income as well as from individual wealth holdings. Only under this restrictive condition does the distribution of either of these variables play no role, and the path of aggregate consumption be assumed to be exclusively determined by mean values. Empirical evidence, however, suggests a marginal propensity to consume that is clearly linked to the level of income and possibly to the wealth level.

2.5.5 Per-period Consumption as a Single Entity

The next question refers to the aggregate consumption level, which is the crucial argument of the utility function. In the standard approach, $c(t)$ simply stands for the price-adjusted total consumption expenditure in period t. To what extent intertemporal consumer optimisation can actually be captured in terms of this variable is questionable.

The real level of consumption in every period obviously consists of a long list of goods and services. To actually grasp this situation, one has to reformulate the life-time utility function by replacing the consumption level $c(t)$ with vectors $q(t)$ of a dimension large enough to capture all the richness of variety and product differentiation that exists in reality. Assuming weak separability, one would get a life-time felicity function of following structure: $V(u1(q1), u2(q2), ..., uT(qT))$.

These consumption vectors, however, can be translated into money values by replacing each one-period utility function $u(t)(q(n))$ by the corresponding *indirect subutility function*, defined by:

$$\Psi(t)[y(t), p(t)] = \max q(t) \{u(t)[q(t)]; \quad s.t. p(t)q(t) = y(t)\}$$

(2.78)

where $p(t)$ is the price level in t and $y(t)$ is total expenditure in that period. Substituting (2.79) into the life-time felicity function, provides a formula of life-time utility as a function of prices and expenditure levels in each of the t periods. Assuming intertemporal additive preferences and a constant discount factor as before, this function appears as follows:

$$V = \sum_{t}^{T} (1 + \delta)^{-t} \Psi[y(t), p(t)]$$

(2.79)

If one additionally assumes homothetic preferences regarding the different goods consumed in a certain period, the indirect utility functions have indeed one single argument that is total expenditure deflated by a price index, as Deaton & Muellbauer (1980) have already shown. Thus, if homothetic preferences were backed by empirical evidence, dealing with consumption aggregates as a single argument entering the one-period subutility functions would be justified. We then had:

$$\Psi(t)[y(t), p(t)] = u \left[\frac{y(t)}{\pi(t)} \right]$$

(2.80)

Here, $\pi(t)$ is the consumer price index defined over the optimal composition of consumption in period t. Hence, if $\pi(t)$ is available and the consumption aggregate $c(t)$ is defined as $y(t)/\pi(t)$, the sought intertemporal utility function referring to consumption aggregates has been derived.

However, two problems that are involved in this approach have been emphasised by Deaton (1992). The first is that the consumer price index provided by official statistics does not correspond to the index required here. The second and much more serious objection is that again homothetic preferences are strongly rejected by empirical evidence.

In fact, if homothetic preferences cannot be assumed, the situation becomes much more complex. Aggregating across consumption goods in the given way will no longer be possible since under non-homothetic preferences the proportions in which consumption expenditure is spread across goods and services depend on the level of total expenditure. A common price index for optimal consumption no longer exists, and the indirect subutility functions do not therefore have a single argument.

One way to escape this difficulty, as proposed by Deaton (1992), is to split the indirect utility functions into two parts, yielding:

$$\Psi(t)[y(t),p(t)] = u(t)\left[\frac{y(t)}{\pi(t)}\right] + \gamma(t)[p(t)]$$

$$(2.81)$$

where $\gamma(t)[p(t)]$ is a concave, linearly homogeneous function, which can be thought of as an aggregate of basic consumption goods and $y(t)$ is total outlay minus expenditure for those basic needs. This approach is backed by the assumption that choice referring to some necessities is guided by principles other than those defined by the utility function $u(.)$. In fact, this approach means assumption of quasi-homothetic preferences: Beyond a certain outlay the expenditure expansion path is supposed to be linear, although it no longer passes the origin.

If intertemporal utility is additive and we define $c(t)$ as $y(t)/\pi(t)$, the intertemporal utility function can be written:

$$V = \sum_{t}^{T}(1 + \delta)^{-t}u[c(t)] + \sum_{t}^{T}\gamma(t)[p(t)]$$

$$(2.82)$$

Since the second term on the right-hand side appears additively, it has no consequence for the choice of the path of consumption $c(t)$. Therefore, intertemporal optimisation generates the same result as maximisation of the first term alone. However, the additive second term certainly influences current cash on hand. Strictly speaking, it determines which part of cash is actually available for expenditures in t. Under this condition, optimal consumption no longer depends alone on real income and intertemporal considerations.

In fact, a wide range of non-linear Engel curves might be approximated by this approach. Nevertheless, how $\gamma(t)$ should be determined and what part of consumption can be assumed to correspond to each of these terms remains an open question. If, for instance, the second term exceeds the first, the huge effort to find the optimal consumption path would only determine the development of a minor part of total expenditure while changes in $\gamma(t)[p(t)]$ would influence consumption and saving behaviour much more significantly.

2.5.6 The Elasticity of Intertemporal Substitution

There are even more fundamental questions to be raised. Although generations of economists have been used to adopting the method, it is not self-evident that the assumptions developed to describe preferences referring to certain goods in a demand system are at all properly applicable to the matter of *intertemporal* choice across levels of consumption. At this point, we are not going to debate whether it is actually inevitable to translate demand curves related to single goods in utility functions and to talk about marginal rates of substitution, compensated demand and related issues. Maybe an ordering of goods or bundles at the basis of observable own-price-, cross-price- and income-elasticities would do. This question has been put forward from time to time in the literature. Becker's (1962) model of "irrational choice" might be mentioned in this context. More distinctly, Joan Robinson (1962: Chap. 3) dismisses the entire approach stating: "Utility maximisation is a metaphysical concept of impregnable circularity". It is possible to construct a utility function to justify any conceivable behaviour, she argued, just by assuming that the behaviour in question yields more utility than its alternatives.

However, in the field of single goods we are at least able to clearly identify relationships such as substitutability or complementarity. Categories such as the elasticity of substitution correspond to observable issues. Also, the distinction between substitution effects and income effects has an empirical background.

If we deal with bundles of goods sorted by major characteristics—such as food, clothes, furniture etc.—the situation becomes different. It is one of the findings of the empirical consumption literature that in the case of groups of goods the elasticity of substitution approaches zero. Almost the only effect that matters in this case, determining own- and cross-price-elasticities, is the income effect. Therefore, demand responds quite inelastically if prices of most goods within such a group change in parallel.

In fact, substitutability in its original meaning takes place within bundles of goods, not across bundles. It appears reasonable to assume the existence of a compensated demand curve, for household devices for instance, for a certain supplier because of the opportunity to switch to another one. The same is true for clothes of a certain brand, for asparagus harvested in a particular area or for holiday trips to a specific city.

All these goods might be replaced by similar ones if relative price differentials exceed a certain limit. Since individual preferences differ, as does the limit, at the aggregated level, a curve will appear. But there is no comparable trade-off between holiday trips and energy expenses or between asparagus and purchases of shoes or shirts. The overwhelming effect by which changes in the relative price of those groups of goods influence each other is the income effect, depending on the respective income elasticities and the income share of those expenditures. Compensated cross-price elasticities across bundles of goods can soundly assumed to be close to zero.

In empirical consumption research it has often been attempted to eliminate the income effect by using deflated values of the monetary variables. The remaining price effects were supposed to be compensated effects, but they were always found to violate the homogeneity and symmetry restrictions required for compensated demand. It is in fact very likely that the identified coefficients were not compensated price elasticities. Rather, they were dominated by hidden income effects since what was usually used for deflation was not a group specific but the general consumption price index. Such an index, however, does not cover changes in the *relative* price of the respective groups of goods.

If, for instance, the relative price of energy increases, causing an increasing energy share in consumption expenditure, while demand for, say, expensive wine shrinks, the latter occurs not due to cross-price effects, but rather because a hidden income effect is at work.

We do not intend to treat this issue in more detail at this point but will come back to the question of sectoral price indices and their divergence from the general CPI later on. The main point of this excursion was to provide evidence that even in the case of within-period choice, empirical evidence suggests that the elasticity of substitution between groups of goods is not significantly different from zero.

Even more questionable is the immediate transmission of categories covering choice between single goods towards the area of intertemporal decisions about consumption *levels*. Indeed households probably do weight up to consume a certain amount today or tomorrow. It seems to be extremely doubtful, however, whether real interest rates are the crucial variables guiding such decisions. Even in the case of durable purchases, where intertemporal considerations are more natural, it is probably not the interest rate but the expected future development of the relative price that primarily matters.

Certainly, expectations about inflation and interest play a role regarding the choice to put money aside or to run into debt. But they are at best one factor among others otherwise it is inexplicable why neither at the macro nor at the micro level a significant response of consumption to changes in real rates has been observed. If interest rates were indeed an intertemporal counterpart of individual prices, the pattern should be much stronger. In the light of empirical evidence, it is rather doubtful that the relationship between interest rate and discount factor is the crucial parameter guiding saving decisions.

However, if we mull over the underlying logic of the traditional models, the devotion to the interest rate becomes understandable. To identify an "intertemporal price" of consumption is in fact the precondition for modelling inter-goods and inter-temporal choice by immediate analogy. The adjustments of the elaborated models mainly consist in reducing the unrealistic conclusions from such an approach. However, the principle is maintained.

Yet another indicator suggests that the orthodox models are badly designed. This is the striking incapability of economic research to uncover conclusive estimates of just the most fundamental parameter: the intertemporal elasticity of substitution. Huge econometric efforts have been dedicated to this issue; however, the results of almost three decades of Euler equation estimations are poor. Different studies have produced completely divergent results and in many cases the estimated coefficients have not been significantly different from zero.

Carroll (2001a) shows that the frequently used log-linearized Euler equation would not uncover the real parameter even if consumers behaved exactly according to the model predictions. This is because the higher order terms are endogenous with respect to the first and second-order terms and therefore cannot be omitted. Nonetheless, the original nonlinear equation was not a basis of conclusive estimates either.

It is our belief, that it is not the wrong approximation technique that is primarily responsible for the scanty results of the decade-long struggle with consumption Euler equations, but the focus on the wrong variables. If there is simply no serious correlation between consumption growth and the interest rate, the attempt to estimate any parameter governing this relation is impractical. In fact, in the first-order log-linearized Euler equation, this parameter appears only as the coefficient of the real interest rate. Estimates close to zero are therefore not surprising.

However, using the original non-linear equation would not solve the problem. If the elasticity of substitution between bundles of goods at a given point of time has to be assumed to approach zero, the supposition of a distinct elasticity of substitution between consuming today or two years later is simply a fiction.

In fact, the category 'intertemporal elasticity of substitution' can at best be used as a metaphor for the general willingness or ability of a consumer not to consume parts of his income today. A poor and starving person, for instance, is hardly able to abstain from consuming every coin he gets, while a wealthy entrepreneur easily puts additional money into his bank account. Thus, if tax incentives rewarding higher saving efforts are introduced, the latter will most likely respond with a stronger saving effort while the former definitely will not. In this sense, one can talk about a different elasticity of intertemporal substitution. Yet more clearly one can point out that saving is not entirely a matter of choice but of ability: only households in which basic needs are satisfied are free to abstain from consuming their entire income today and to save parts of it.

2.5.7 The Optimising Procedure—Benefits and Costs

Even supposing that consumers are willing to make detailed consumption and saving plans far into the future, and that they know the probability distribution of all relevant variables several decades ahead, one problem is not resolved: who has taught them how to undertake the necessary calculations?

While the ordinary Perfect Foresight Model is already quite unsolvable for the consumer who is not exceptionally educated, stochastic dynamic programming techniques contain an extremely complex decision making process. We have to bear in mind that the computing power to solve fairly simple models on that basis did not exist until the late eighties. As soon as we deal with somewhat more realistic, and hence, even more complicated models, they are still likely to go beyond the limits of the most modern processors. Thus, how sensible is the assumption that the alleged optimal consumption path, which is invisible without advanced mathematical knowledge and the support of powerful technical equipment, governs the behaviour of any real consumer?

The traditional Keynesian macroeconomic approach has often been accused for a lack of *explanatory* power. A macroeconomic consumption function composed of certain variables certainly does not as such provide insights into underlying motives and intentions and is therefore indeed at risk of misspecification and spurious relations. From this understanding, the call for microeconomic foundations has never been denied by Keynesian economists.

But one should ask even more: what is the explanatory power of a model of consumer behaviour which is only solvable by mathematically high-skilled experts employing high-level computer technology and assisted by modern Kassandras able to forecast the development of crucial variables in the far-off future?

This obvious question has triggered the search for rules of thumb to guide the day-to-day decisions of real consumers. One approach to solve the problem has been put forward by Allen & Carroll (2001) seeking to specify a learning mechanism which leads to similar results as stochastic dynamic programming. From their point of view, the optimal solution of a buffer-stock model can be approximated by a seemingly simple rule of thumb:

$$\frac{c(t)}{p(t)} = \min\left\{\frac{x(t)}{p(t)}, \quad \left(\frac{x}{p}\right)^* + h\left[\frac{x(t)}{p(t)} - \left(\frac{x}{p}\right)^*\right]\right\}$$

$$0 < h < 1$$

$$(2.83)$$

Here, $(x/p)^*$ denotes the desired cash on hand relative to the level of permanent income determining the target stock of assets. The term h is a constant. The intuition behind this formula corresponds to a straightforward rule: to save when times are good (the second term in brackets matters), and to spend all cash on hand when times are bad (the first term is binding). This is easy to handle but the real problem for the consumer is to identify what are 'good times' and 'bad times' and which share of income should be saved during the former. In other words: he has to find reasonable parameter values for the target cash on hand to permanent income ratio $(x/p)^*$ and for h, since these parameters are crucial for approximating the results of the stochastic dynamic programming procedure.

Allen & Carroll (2001) specify a learning procedure to approach the optimal values. The procedure consists of selecting initial parameters, observing the results, updating the values, observing again etc. This is generally feasible, but the authors conclude that for an individual consumer it would require at least one million years of observations to be confident of approaching sensible results.

Some recent papers reveal a growing interest in identifying rules of thumb of saving decisions, motivated by the view that stochastic dynamic programming is too complex to be a plausible decision-making process. Moreover, there is another argument against the complicated optimisation procedures put forward by Pemberton (2003): if possible, decision-making models are evaluated not only from the viewpoint of their benefits in terms of a stream of consumption outcomes, but also under the aspect of their learning and operating costs, no reason exists to accept the stochastic dynamic programming technique as ideal. Rather, there is an array of possible models each offering benefits but also involving costs in terms of time and effort needed to learn and operate them. The optimal model then is the one with the most favourable benefit/cost ratio. Using this criterion, approaches requiring a huge amount of information and demanding extremely complicated procedures to solve them are rarely promising candidates. Such models appear to be even less reasonable if we reconsider the approach given by Deaton to solve the aggregation problem, implying that possibly only a minor part of total consumption is subject to optimising rules at all, while the rest is guided by other principles.

Instead, Hey (1983) and Pemberton (1993, 1995) suggest present-future trade-off models. Here, saving decisions are derived from an elementary trade-off between present and future; trading 'future consumption' as a single entity. Those models convert the multi-period life-cycle problem into a two-period problem; households are assumed to take the future seriously, but they do not try to make precise plans for each individual sub-period of that future.

Hence, no one can deny the role of intertemporal considerations regarding saving and spending decisions. However, theoretical reasoning as well as empirical evidence strongly supports the conclusion that the underlying principles of those decisions are not uncovered by the models that have dominated mainstream economics over the previous decades.

Chapter 3. A New Approach to Saving Behaviour

Paragraph 3.1
Basic Needs and Saving

3.1.1 The Relative-Income Hypothesis

Let us briefly recapitulate the outstanding stylised facts of household saving: the individual saving rate rises with relative income, is ambiguous concerning real income, but pushed up in the case of stronger income growth. An approach assuming habit formation can explain the last phenomenon and also the ambiguity with respect to real income, but it is at a loss with the strong positive correlation between the propensity to save and permanent (relative) income.

If we assume, however, that the process of habit formation occurs not individually but socially, the connection between saving rates and relative income might lose its myth. This intention is expressed by Duesenberry (1949), whose relative-income hypothesis is based on the assumption that preferences are interdependent. According to Duesenberry, the better-off households in a society define a standard of living which constitutes a benchmark for all other households. To move towards the desired level, households neglect saving, and the lower the income position, the higher the required share of income that has to be spent for consumption to keep pace.

Duesenberrys approach is more plausible than many of the models elaborated later, but it is also not satisfying. Living standards, even within developed countries, differ extensively and particular brands of clothes or cars might be a must among some social classes. On the other hand, a middle-income employee will probably not empty his checking account for an up-to-date Armani twin set or a luxury limousine. What in fact is socially set with respect to the standard of living appears to be much more elementary, and "habit" is perhaps not an adequate expression to cover it. People in developed countries are used to living in solid houses with a fresh water supply and heating system; they are accustomed to using certain electronic devices, to communicating via phone and email and to travelling either by public transport or their own car.

These features are not actually a matter of choice, unless one wants to exclude oneself from the entire economic and social life; in fact, a considerable minority *is* excluded. To pay for the satisfaction of those basic needs is clearly not a habit in the sense of the habit to eat fish on Fridays, to wear clothes of a particular fashion, or to enjoy a fine tea in the afternoon. Models with habit formation are right to assume that habits are fixed only in the short-run, but almost completely flexible in the long-run. But a considerable amount of everybody's income is spent on satisfying needs, which are as such not flexible at all. To live in a modest apartment or in a luxury villa with a view of the lake might be a matter of choice (and of income, of course), but to live either in a building or on the street are not serious alternatives at all. No one would give up his home to be able to maintain monthly payments on a savings account. The same is true for food and drinks or, in a modern society for essential transport needs and communication expenses. Expenditures to satisfy such requests should realistically not be taken as being guided by habits but acknowledged as a subsistence need that has to be satisfied before individual choices about consumption starts.

3.1.2 Subsistence Consumption in Developing Countries

Models including subsistence points are nothing new. Usually, they are employed exclusively to developing countries, at least in that part of the literature which is concerned with the issue of saving. In some papers the very low saving rates of poor countries have been explained by appealing to the fact that below a certain subsistence level saving is strictly impossible. The reference to subsistence points has also been used to justify the positive correlation between saving rates and income in those countries, or the zero elasticity of saving with respect to interest rates.

One of the first to analyse the role of subsistence consumption with respect to saving and growth was Rebelo (1992). His starting point is the implausible prediction of the standard intertemporal utility function that the optimal saving rate is identical for two countries with the same real interest rate but different income levels. Rebelo provides a model based on a simple extension of standard preferences assuming that within-period utility has Stone-Geary-form. Hence, momentary utility is supposed to be derived not from the entire level of consumption, but from the difference between total consumption and a certain subsistence level. Using the same formulation as usual, within-period utility under these conditions becomes:

$$u[c(t)] = \frac{(c(t) - c^*)^{1-\rho}}{1 - \rho}$$

$$c(t) \geq c^*$$

$$(3.1)$$

with c^* denoting a certain basket of subsistence consumption assumed to be constant over time. Obviously, this kind of utility belongs to the class of HARA-preferences considered above.

The intertemporal felicity function under these conditions is:

$$V = \sum_{t=0}^{T} (1 + \delta)^{-t} \frac{(c(t) - c^*)^{1-\rho}}{1 - \rho}$$

$$c(t) \geq c^*$$

$$(3.2)$$

The budget constraint is the usual one:

$$\sum_{t=0}^{T} (1 + r)^{-t} c(t) = F(0) + \sum_{t=0}^{T} (1 + r)^{-t} w(t)$$

$$(3.3)$$

This leads to the following first-order conditions:

$$(c(t) - c^*)^{-\rho} = \lambda \left[\frac{1 + \delta}{1 + r} \right]^{t}$$

$$\rho > 0$$

$$(3.4)$$

which gives for consumption growth:

$$\frac{c'(t)}{c(t)} = \left(\frac{1}{\rho}\right)\left(1 - \frac{c^*}{c(t)}\right)(r - \delta)$$

(3.5)

It is the term $\left(1 - \frac{c^*}{c(t)}\right)$ which distinguishes the subsistence consumption model from the standard CES-approach. Obviously, the factor $\left(1 - \frac{c^*}{c(t)}\right)$ reduces the intertemporal elasticity of substitution the more the closer the actual level of consumption approaches the subsistence basket. If $c(t)$ exceeds c^* many times, the intertemporal elasticity of substitution almost equals $1/\rho$, which is the value derived in the standard models. In contrast, if we have $c(t) = c^*$, the elasticity to substitute consumption intertemporally is simply zero. (For $c(t) < c^*$ the model is not defined.)

Yet a near to zero intertemporal elasticity of substitution does not only imply that consumption is not responding to changes in real interest rates, but that there is almost no planned consumption growth in general. Under such circumstances we consistently observe very low saving rates or even no saving at all. Hence, in contrast to the predictions of the standard model, this kind of preferences implies that the rate of saving should be lower in poorer countries compared to richer ones. Moreover, it gives reasons why, at least in developing countries, pushing up the real interest rate is by no means an appropriate tool to encourage saving.

The plausible intuition behind this approach is that people definitely do not care about intertemporal consumption smoothing and an optimal consumption path, as long as their most elementary needs are not satisfied. Beyond the subsistence point, intertemporal reflections might be undertaken while when close to the survival level, other considerations are incomparably more urgent.

Confirming such an assumption, Kraay (2000) finds that in Chinese rural districts the share of food consumption in total consumption, which can be taken as a proxy for the importance of subsistence effects, "…is a robust predictor of saving rates in a panel of provincial saving rates."

An even more comprehensive test of a model of saving that takes note of subsistence requirements has been offered by Ogaki, Ostry & Reinhart (1996). The authors consider the hypothesis that consumption in developing countries "may be more related to subsistence considerations (…) than to intertemporal consumption smoothing. If households must first achieve a subsistence consumption level, letting intertemporal considerations guide their decisions only for that portion of their budget left after subsistence has been satisfied, then the intertemporal elasticity of substitution and the interest rate sensitivity of private saving will be close to zero for countries at or near subsistence consumption levels (...)".[1]

Moreover, the authors consider the possibility that different parts of consumption may display a differing intertemporal elasticity of substitution, so that consumption smoothing actually does not occur with regard to the level of expenditures as such, but to certain goods and services separately. Hence, they argue that a second reason for the low intertemporal elasticity of substitution in developing countries is possibly the relatively high share of necessities in the budget of poor households: "If necessities (for example, food) are less substitutable through time than other goods, then the intertemporal elasticity of substitution will be lower for households with a larger proportion of necessities in their budgets (...)"[2]

Stone-Geary preferences replace the usual assumption of homothetic preferences that has been refuted by empirical research. While non-homothetic preferences in general are difficult to check at the macroeconomic level, Stone-Geary preferences are quasi-homothetic, i.e. the expenditure expansion path is a straight line, although not going through the origin. Hence, given the condition that all households reach at least the subsistence level, the macro-level outcome does not depend on the distribution of income. Such a model can be tested referring to mean values of consumption and saving in the respective countries.

Estimating the parameters of an intertemporal utility function with subsistence consumption employing annual time-series data for thirteen countries, Ogaki, Ostry & Reinhart (1996) conclude, "that a model, in which the intertemporal elasticity of substitution is an increasing function of the gap between permanent income and the subsistence consumption level cannot be rejected"[3].

---

1 Ogaki, Ostry, Reinhart (1996)
2 Ogaki, Ostry, Reinhart (1996)
3 Ogaki, Ostry, Reinhart (1996)

3.1.3 Necessities in Developed Countries

In the debate about saving and consumption in developed countries, subsistence needs are typically not regarded to be crucial since subsistence in a biological sense of naked survival is not a major concern. However, subsistence needs which determine the minimum level required for social survival in current societies appear to be almost equally important. No one even thinks about saving as long as the basic requirements of a modern live are not being satisfied. It is fully consistent with such an approach that those families who do not save almost always report in opinion polls that they simply cannot afford saving because all their money is used paying for the basics of living. Those households almost never answer that they find it unimportant or irrelevant to build up savings.

Moreover, the saving rates in the bottom quintiles are not only *on average* either negative or much lower than in higher quintiles. As noted in Chapter 1, there is evidence that at a given point in time the individual variance of saving rates across households is significantly lower in the lower quintiles (Jung 2001). This supports the assumption that neglecting saving by these income groups is not primarily the outcome of individual choice.

One of the exemptions in the debate about the relevance of subsistence consumption in developed countries are Ravn, Schmitt-Grohe & Uribe (2008), who analyse the impact of good-specific subsistence points on the price elasticity of demand, concluding that such an approach gives rise to a theory of countercyclical mark-ups due to a shrinking price-elasticity of demand when income declines. The authors explicitly support a "broader interpretation of necessities"[4], including those dictated by social norms. They emphasise: "A luxury in a poor society, such as tap water, inside plumbing, and health care are considered necessities in developed countries."[5]

One may add that even within the history of developed countries, some former luxuries, such as colour TV, personal computers or mobile phones, have become rather elementary equipment, which people taking part in social live can hardly do without anymore. Thus, a theoretical approach defining momentary utility as a positive function of the difference between

---

4 Ravn, Schmitt-Grohe, Uribe (2008)
5 Ravn, Schmitt-Grohe, Uribe (2008)

actual consumption and a basic level of consumption does not appear to be unjustified in the case of developed countries either.

Ravn, Schmitt-Grohe & Uribe (2008) suggest that "subsistence points might be appropriately modelled as an increasing function of long-run measures of output."[6] Indeed, it seems to be adequate not to assume a fixed subsistence *level* as in the Rebelo model considered above. Instead, those expenditures that are devoted to satisfying basic needs according to the common standard of living, will most likely increase with this standard. A telephone or a car was still a luxury in the mid twentieth century, but is hardly avoidable for most households today. The same has occurred with many household devices. Mobile phones, personal computers and internet connections have just recently transformed into the basic equipment of many professional groups. The same is true for possessing a banking account, a credit card or certain insurances. Fees for those services are nowadays mainly unavoidable. Hence, the necessity basket which a consumer almost inevitably has to pay for, changes in time and across countries depending on the general standard of living. Income growth also leads to a rising amount of expenditure directed into purchases, which are not really a matter of choice.

This is not meant to imply that income and basic needs simply grow in parallel. Some indicators suggest that the weight of the necessity share varies over time. The relative income position, for instance, at which saving becomes positive is rather diverse for different periods and countries. According to Kuznets' (1953) data, the relative income of the lowest saving decile ranges between 0.4 in 1946 and 0.8 in 1935. In 1945 all income groups saved. Bearing in mind that we are dealing with years of crisis and war with highly volatile income, the variance is not surprising. On average, Kuznets' data suggest a saving minimum of about 0.75 percent of mean income.

However, since we intend to find driving forces for saving rate *differentials* across countries or in time, we are not primarily interested in long run averages but rather in analysing the path of the necessity share over time. We have to search for those economic factors responsible for *changes* in subsistence expenditure. Thus, a reasonable approach to saving behaviour from our point of view has to go into the details of consumption and its

---

6 Ravn, Schmitt-Grohe, Uribe (2008)

development, while the standard models deal with optimising the path of consumption *as such*.

Under Stone-Geary preferences, the life-time budget-constraint no longer equals permanent income but is limited in each period by the *free* income share after all basic needs have been satisfied. If only this free income share matters for the decision to spend or to save, measuring its extent becomes crucial for explaining the motion of saving.

Not all groups of goods are possible candidates of subsistence consumption; those which are match that feature to a different degree and at different relative prices that change over time. Hence, the essential problem is to identify conclusive criteria for the part of expenditure that is inevitable for households in a certain period.

Certainly, saving does not equal an *immutable portion* of the free income share. Variables measuring uncertainty, inflation, interest rates— in other words: the usual suspects explaining saving behaviour— might continue to have an influence. Defining the free share in income therefore will not solve the entire saving puzzle. But if the necessity share covers a relevant part of income and changes significantly over time, analysing its development will decode a substantial part of the saving mystery. Parameters covering the influence of other factors can be reintroduced later on.

The approach suggested here is in any case much more easily testable than the standard models. While the latter are based on a number of parameters that are simply not observable, the time path of the necessity share can be reproduced as soon as the necessity basket is soundly defined. Then its link to the development of saving can be checked by ordinary regressions. Depending on whether there are significant correlations or not, our approach is supported or has to be rejected. However, provided our hypothesis finds backing by empirical evidence, it allows for rather distinct predictions.

Hence, to achieve sensible hypotheses about forces and restrictions of saving, we have to depart from talking about consumption *levels* and have to start investigating the details of consumption. Before we analyse the stylised facts of consumption patterns in cross-section and in time, we will develop our model of saving behaviour in a formally satisfying manner.

Paragraph 3.2
Basic Needs in Standard Models

3.2.1 Introducing Good-specific Subsistence Points into a Standard Dixit-Stiglitz framework

As a first step, we include basic needs into a traditional model of disaggregated consumption demand. The main purpose of the following section is to clarify the consequences concerning the elasticity of demand, the appropriate price index and the variation of a given welfare level when prices change. To formalise such an approach, we follow Ravn, Schmitt-Grohe &, Uribe (2008), who introduce the assumption of good-specific subsistence points into a standard Dixit-Stiglitz framework (Dixit, Stiglitz (1977)).

The momentary utility function shall be composed of a continuum of differentiated goods indexed by $i \in [0, 1]$:

$$X = \left[\int_0^1 (c_i - c_i^*)^{\frac{\varepsilon - 1}{\varepsilon}} \, di \right]^{\frac{\varepsilon}{\varepsilon - 1}}$$

$$c_i \geq c_i^*, \qquad 0 \leq i \leq 1$$

$$(3.6)$$

Each c_i^* denotes the subsistence point of good i, in other words, the amount of good i that has to be consumed and that is not substitutable by any other good. This point exceeds zero for some goods and is zero for others. X is the aggregated consumption level defined by the utility provided by a certain basket of goods c_i.

The within-period budget constraint of each consumer is:

$$C = \int_0^1 p_i\, c_i\, di$$

$$(3.7)$$

where C is total consumption expenditure. At this point, we are not concerned with the question by what rule this expenditure is determined.

The nominal value of the necessity basket will be denoted by the symbol C^* defined as:

$$C^* = \int_0^1 p_i\, c_i^*\, di$$

$$(3.8)$$

Insofar as total consumption outlay exceeds the necessity basket, the consumer has to solve a standard static optimisation problem. If, in contrast, total consumption just equals the basic requirements C^*, no room for optimisation exists. Instead, goods and services have to be purchased in a composition that is determined by the proportion of the various subsistence points c_i^*.

The model is not defined for the case that consumption expenditure falls below subsistence needs. Actually, one could assume hierarchic preferences concerning the composition of the subsistence basket. This would allow for a defined outcome in cases where total expenditure is not sufficient to purchase the entire necessity basket.

The Lagrangian for static optimisation within the given framework is:

$$L = \left[\int_0^1 (c_i - c_i^*)^{\frac{\varepsilon-1}{\varepsilon}}\, di \right]^{\frac{\varepsilon}{\varepsilon-1}} + \lambda \left(C - \int_0^1 p_i\, c_i\, di \right)$$

$$C \geq \int_0^1 p_i\, c_i^*\, di$$

$$(3.9)$$

The first-order conditions are:

$$\frac{\partial L}{\partial c_i} = (c_i - c_i^*)^{-\frac{1}{\varepsilon}} \left[\int_0^1 (c_i - c_i^*)^{\frac{\varepsilon-1}{\varepsilon}} \, di \right]^{\frac{1}{\varepsilon-1}} - \lambda \, p_i = 0$$

$$(3.10)$$

This leads to following relative demand functions regarding demand for each good i (i ≠ j):

$$c_i \quad = \quad p_i^{-\varepsilon} \, p_j^{\varepsilon} \left(c_j - c_j^* \right) + c_i^*$$

Substituting these relations into the budget constraint gives:

$$\int_0^1 p_i \, c_i \, di = \int_0^1 p_i \left(p_i^{-\varepsilon} \, p_j^{\varepsilon} \left(c_j - c_j^* \right) + c_i^* \right) di$$

$$= \int_0^1 p_i^{1-\varepsilon} \, p_j^{\varepsilon} \left(c_j - c_j^* \right) + p_i \, c_i^* \, di$$

$$= p_j^{\varepsilon} \left(c_j - c_j^* \right) \int_0^1 p_i^{1-\varepsilon} \, di \, + \, \int_0^1 p_i \, c_i^* \, di$$

So we have for each good j:

$$c_j = p_j^{-\varepsilon} \frac{C - C^*}{\int_0^1 p_i^{1-\varepsilon} \, di} + c_j^*$$

$$(3.11)$$

As usual in the Dixit-Stiglitz framework, we define the nominal price index for the optimally composed consumption good X by:

$$P = \left[\int_0^1 p_i^{1-\varepsilon} \, di \right]^{\frac{1}{1-\varepsilon}}$$

$$(3.12)$$

We have to bear in mind, however, that within the model provided here we do not deal with PX = C as usual, but:

$$PX = C - C^*$$

The reason is that the composed consumption good X refers only to that part of consumption, which is subject to optimisation. The nominal price index P in turn reflects just the optimal proportion of the various varieties in X.

Employing the price index, we can rewrite the demand equation (3.11) as:

$$c_j = \left(\frac{p_j}{P}\right)^{-\varepsilon} \frac{C - C^*}{P} + c_j^* = \left(\frac{p_j}{P}\right)^{-\varepsilon} X + c_j^*$$

$$(3.13)$$

The formula on the very right-hand side looks like the usual demand equation in a Dixit-Stiglitz model with X being real income available for optimising decisions, $\frac{p_j}{P}$ being the relative price of good j, and ε being the own-price elasticity of demand. Apparently, the only two modifications are that real income or consumption outlay (in the static framework, we can use these terms synonymously) is reduced by the amount spent for the basic basket and that the subsistence quantity of the respective good appears additively.

Yet, there are serious differences between this approach and the original Dixit-Stiglitz framework. One consequence of the introduction of subsistence points has been analysed by Ravn, Schmitt-Grohe & Uribe (2008). It concerns the own-price elasticity of demand which no longer equals ε, but is smaller than ε for all goods and services with positive subsistence points. Clearly, the higher the subsistence consumption of a certain good c_j^* compared to its total consumption c_j, the smaller the price elasticity of demand, approaching zero if c_j approaches c_j^*. Hence, if goods and services have unequal subsistence points, the mark-ups, and therefore the prices, will also be unequal. Additionally, the mark-ups behave counter-cyclically under these conditions since fluctuations in income change the proportion between subsistence and optimised consumption and this way boost or reduce the elasticity of demand. Thus, even if we assume identical c_i^*'s for all goods and services, the model predicts that mark-ups (and as a consequence the functional income distribution) depend on fluctuations in real income.

This can be formally shown as follows. The elasticity of demand with respect to changes in the relative price can be derived from equation (3.13).

To avoid confusion between price and income effects, the general price level shall be assumed to remain constant. Thus, we can normalise it to unity. (In fact, this simply means using the deflated values of all variables). So we have:

$$c_i = p_i^{-\varepsilon} (C - C^*) + c_i^*$$

$$(3.14)$$

Hence, for the own-price elasticity of demand we get:

$$\varepsilon_{ipi} = \frac{-\dfrac{\partial c_i}{\partial p_i}}{\dfrac{c_i}{p_i}} = - \frac{\varepsilon \, p_i^{-\varepsilon} (C - C^*)}{p_i^{-\varepsilon} (C - C^*) + c_i^*} = \frac{-\varepsilon}{\left(1 + \dfrac{p_i^{\varepsilon} \, c_i^*}{C - C^*}\right)}$$

$$(3.15)$$

Obviously, the own-price elasticity depends on two determinants: first, the size of the subsistence point of the respective good c_i^* and, second, the amount at which the entire consumption expenditure exceeds basic needs C^*. If either subsistence consumption of a certain good is close to zero or consumption outlay by far exceeds subsistence requirements, the own-price elasticity of demand approaches ε. In contrast, the elasticity of demand is significantly smaller than ε for all goods with a substantial amount of subsistence expenditure, and this elasticity varies with fluctuations in total outlay C. The model with good-specific subsistence points thus overcomes the symmetry property of the standard Dixit-Stiglitz approach with all goods being substitutable by each other in exactly the same way.

A second difference to the standard approach, which is closely related to the non-symmetric price elasticities, concerns the income (or total expenditure) elasticity of consumption. In fact, a model with good-specific subsistence points departs from the standard framework by abandoning the assumption of homothetic preferences. The model provided here is of course somewhat artificial, too, since beyond subsistence needs all goods have the same marginal income elasticity, equalling unity. Consequently, any additional amount of consumption outlay will be spread across goods in exactly the same way which certainly does not describe real consumption patterns in their complexity. Nevertheless, other than the standard Dixit-Stiglitz approach, this model allows for the crucial distinction between necessities and luxuries: while the income elasticity of some goods exceeds unity, that of others falls below unity.

The difference between these two categories is determined by the size of their subsistence points. The only condition for this distinction is that total consumption outlay does not exceed the sum of subsistence purchases by a huge amount since the income elasticity of consumption of every c_i will approach unity if total consumption spending is far beyond the subsistence level. In this case, a one percentage change in income approximately leads to a one percentage change in consumption of every good. However, this simply means departing from a model with significant good-specific subsistence points and moving towards the standard Dixit-Stiglitz approach that presupposes homothetic preferences. The crucial idea of a model with good-specific subsistence points is just that those points are negligibly not small.

As long as C^* is not marginal compared to C, an additional unit of consumption outlay (exceeding the subsistence basket) leads to a less-than-unit percentage change in the consumption of those goods which predominate in the subsistence basket (i.e. displaying a high c_i^*). For goods which are proportionally underrepresented, or not at all, in the subsistence basket, the percentage increase in consumption exceeds unity when total outlay rises by one percent.

This can easily be shown. The elasticity of expenditure for each good c_i in relation to changes in total consumption outlay C is defined as:

$$\varepsilon_{ic} = \frac{\frac{\partial c_i}{\partial C}}{\frac{c_i}{C}} = \frac{\partial c_i}{\partial C} \frac{C}{c_i}$$

We can split total consumption outlay into a part spent for purchasing subsistence goods C^* and a residual part $C - C^*$. The same can be done with the consumption expenditure for each consumption good individually. This leads to:

$$\varepsilon_{ic} = \frac{\partial c_i \left((C - C^*) + C^* \right)}{\partial C \left((c_i - c_i^*) + c_i^* \right)}$$

$$(3.16)$$

The expenditure expansion path beyond C^*, as mentioned, is linear, i.e. the marginal elasticity of purchases to total outlay beyond C^* equals unity. This directly follows from equation (3.14):

$$\frac{\partial c_i / \partial C}{(c_i - c_i^*)/ (C - C^*)} = \frac{p_j^{-\varepsilon}}{(p_j^{-\varepsilon} (C - C^*))/(C - C^*)} = 1$$

$$\text{all } c_i > c_i^*$$

(3.17)

Hence, we have:

$$\partial c_i (C - C^*) = \partial C (c_i - c_i^*)$$

(3.18)

Therefore, we can divide the numerator of (3.16) by $\partial c_i (C - C^*)$ and the denominator by $\partial C (c_i - c_i^*)$. This gives:

$$\varepsilon_{ic} = \frac{1 + \dfrac{C^*}{C - C^*}}{1 + \dfrac{c_i^*}{c_i - c_i^*}}$$

(3.19)

$$= \frac{C/(C - C^*)}{c_i/(c_i - c_i^*)}$$

$$= \frac{1/(1 - \dfrac{C^*}{C})}{1/(1 - \dfrac{c_i^*}{c_i})}$$

Therefore:

$$\varepsilon_{ic} = \frac{\left(1 - \dfrac{c_i^*}{c_i}\right)}{\left(1 - \dfrac{C^*}{C}\right)}$$

(3.20)

Equation (3.20) confirms that for goods with a relation between subsistence point and total consumption c_i^*/c_i exceeding the average relation between subsistence consumption and total consumption C^*/C, the income (or outlay) elasticity is smaller than unity, while for goods with small or no subsistence points, the income elasticity exceeds unity. Therefore, goods with a relatively high c_i^* can be referred to as necessities, while the others are appropriately named luxuries.

Although X is certainly not exclusively composed by luxuries and, in turn, some goods with small subsistence point might appear in C^*, it seems to be natural to understand C^* as basic consumption outlay, while PX stands for the luxury part of nominal consumption spending. The categorisation by income elasticities generally corresponds to the categorisation by the extent of choice. In this respect, the model covers some realistic and important features of the structure of real consumption.

There is a third vital difference between a model with good-specific subsistence points and the standard Dixit-Stiglitz approach. It concerns the appropriateness of the general price index P and is a direct consequence of the non-symmetric properties.

The price index P, usually employed in Dixit-Stiglitz-like models, is homogenous of degree one in prices. Hence, an identical percentage change of all prices by, say, a rate i changes P by the same rate, while the imputed proportions of the consumption basket remain constant. However, if only some prices change, P mirrors not only those price changes, but at the same time the changing composition of optimal consumption. If some prices increase by a given factor, P increases by less than this factor times the weight of the respective goods in the previous consumption bundle. Instead, P reflects the demand shift away from those more expensive goods. Therefore, the latter are less represented in the composition of the new optimal consumption basket that underlies the new P. In fact, the higher the elasticity of demand ε, the stronger the presumed willingness to substitute expensive goods by cheaper ones and, accordingly, the smaller the change in P due to price changes of some goods. (Since $\varepsilon > 1$ is required in a standard Dixit-Stiglitz model, all varieties are considered substitutes).

If agents are compensated for the price boost by an increase in income just equalling the change in P, they are able to maintain their previous standard of living, expressed in the utility level X, although they will purchase a different bundle of goods. In the standard Dixit-Stiglitz approach,

P indicates exactly the amount by which consumers have to be compensated for price changes to hold utility constant. It is due to this property that P is the appropriate price index in a Dixit-Stiglitz model.

To show how P works, let us assume that all prices of goods $i \leq n$ change by an identical inflation rate, while all prices of goods $i > n$ remain constant. So, we can split the price index into two parts:

$$P = \left[\int_0^1 p_i^{1-\varepsilon}\, di \right]^{\frac{1}{1-\varepsilon}} = \left[\int_0^n p_i^{1-\varepsilon}\, di + \int_n^1 p_i^{1-\varepsilon}\, di \right]^{\frac{1}{1-\varepsilon}}$$

(3.21)

The first term in brackets consistently increases due to the change in prices p_i, $0 \leq i \leq n$, while the second term is constant. Hence, the new price index P^{new} corresponds to:

$$P^{new} = \left[\int_0^n ((1 + \text{infl})p_i)^{1-\varepsilon} di + \int_n^1 p_i^{1-\varepsilon}\, di \right]^{\frac{1}{1-\varepsilon}}$$

$$= \left[(1 + \text{infl})^{1-\varepsilon} \int_0^n p_i^{1-\varepsilon}\, di + \int_n^1 p_i^{1-\varepsilon}\, di \right]^{\frac{1}{1-\varepsilon}}$$

(3.22)

Assuming all prices being equal before the change (which is not an equilibrium assumption in the case of differing good-specific subsistence points, but for the standard approach), we obtain:

$$P^{new} = [(1 + \text{infl})^{1-\varepsilon} n p^{1-\varepsilon} + (1 - n)p^{1-\varepsilon}]^{\frac{1}{1-\varepsilon}}$$

$$= [((1 + \text{infl})^{1-\varepsilon} n + (1 - n))p^{1-\varepsilon}]^{\frac{1}{1-\varepsilon}}$$

(3.23)

Denoting the percentage increase in P by θ, we have:

$$\frac{P^{new}}{P} = (1 + \theta) = \frac{[((1 + \text{infl})^{1-\varepsilon} n + (1 - n))p^{1-\varepsilon}]^{\frac{1}{1-\varepsilon}}}{[(n + (1 - n))p^{1-\varepsilon}]^{\frac{1}{1-\varepsilon}}}$$

(3.24)

$$= \left[\frac{((1 + \text{infl})^{1-\varepsilon} n + (1 - n))p^{1-\varepsilon}}{(n + (1 - n))p^{1-\varepsilon}}\right]^{\frac{1}{1-\varepsilon}}$$

Hence:

$$\frac{P^{new}}{P} = (1 + \theta) = [n(1 + \text{infl})^{1-\varepsilon} + (1 - n)]^{\frac{1}{1-\varepsilon}}$$

(3.25)

For $n = 1$, the second term in brackets disappears and we obtain $\theta = \text{infl}$. This is the outcome of the homogeneity property of P. If all prices change by the same rate, P changes by this rate, too. For every $n < 1$, however, the deviation of θ from infl is guided not only by n, but crucially by ε. With increasing ε, the influence of infl immediately disappears. Even if n is relatively high, $(1 + \text{infl})^{1-\varepsilon}$ approaches zero for higher ε. Thus, the increase in the price level comes close to zero since $(1 + \theta)$ approaches $(1 - n)^{1/(1-\varepsilon)}$, which moves towards unity. Hence, the price index remains more or less constant although some prices might have changed significantly.

Let us consider the extreme case of $\text{infl} = 1$ and $n = 0.9$. In other words: the prices of ninety percent of goods double. If the elasticity of demand is assumed to equal, say, 10, such tremendous price inflation will enlarge P by a factor of just 0.28. Hence, an increase in income of 28 percent is assumed to be sufficient to enable every consumer to maintain his standard of living despite exploding prices for almost all goods. Thanks to the proposed elasticity of substitution, model consumers would simply shift the major part of their demand towards the 10 percent of goods with stable prices. If the elasticity of demand reached $\varepsilon = 100$ under the same circumstances, even an increase in income of 2 percent would compensate the consumers for all losses. If, in contrast, the elasticity of demand is only 2, general price inflation would be calculated at 81 percent.

However, even this might be too low if some goods or services with exploding prices are not substitutable. At least across the borders of the major groups of consumption expenditure, a very low elasticity of substitution actually has to be assumed. In view of this fact alone, the assumption of a subsistence basket beyond which substitution starts at all is certainly realistic.

Indeed, within a model with good-specific subsistence points, P is no longer the appropriate price index to indicate the welfare loss caused by price changes. This can easily be shown. Suppose again, that some prices change, while total consumption outlay deflated by the price index P remains constant. Hence, we have:

$$\frac{C + C'}{P + P'} = \frac{C}{P}$$

(3.26)

Under standard conditions this would imply a constant utility or welfare level.

Since $C = PX + C^*$, and therefore $C' = P'X + PX' + C^{*'}$, we can reformulate (3.26) by:

$$\frac{PX + C^* + P'X + PX' + C^{*'}}{P + P'} = \frac{PX + C^*}{P}$$

(3.27)

Normalising the initial price level P at unity, leads us to:

$$\frac{X + C^* + P'X + X' + C^{*'}}{(1 + P')} = X + C^*$$

(3.28)

Hence:

$$X' = P'C^* - C^{*'}$$

(3.29)

In fact, if nominal basic expenditure had changed exactly in line with general inflation, i.e. if we had $C^{*'} = P'C^*$, the welfare loss would be zero and P would remain the adequate index. But this is very unlikely, since P' does not only reflect price changes but simultaneously changes in demand induced by price changes under a price elasticity of demand of ε. The composition of the necessity basket, however, does not depend on price changes since within C^* the price elasticity of demand is zero. Therefore, the change in nominal basic expenditure $C^{*\prime}$ will most likely exceed $P'C^*$. The higher the elasticity of demand ε beyond the subsistence point the larger the difference. The only exception is either a proportional change of all prices leaving relative prices unchanged, or a price inflation that mainly concerns goods with low or zero subsistence points. While $C^{*\prime}$ will exactly correspond to $P'C^*$ in the first case, it is probably even lower in the latter.

In all other cases, the consumer might suffer from a considerable welfare loss although consumption expenditure, deflated by the price index, remains constant. The damage is stronger, the higher the consumer's necessity share. Consumers will therefore not be fully compensated by an increase in nominal income equalling the inflation rate, and low-income consumers will particularly suffer. Hence, in a model with good-specific subsistence points, the change in P is no longer an appropriate indicator of the extent the consumer has to be remunerated for price changes in order to hold his utility or his welfare level constant.

Of course, the usual consumer price index as provided by statistics differs from P used in a Dixit-Stiglitz framework since the weights of the different groups of goods do not immediately change when relative prices change. This reflects the low elasticity of substitution between those major groups of goods and services. The general conclusion from (3.29), however, does not depend on the special price index used here. It is true for all cases in which subsistence goods exist and prices of those goods do not move absolutely in parallel to general price inflation. Given these conditions, we always have: $C^{*\prime} \neq P'C^*$. In all such cases a constant real income does not prevent losses (or possibly gains) in the standard of living due to changing prices. The exact loss (or gain) differs across consumers depending on the individual income level.

Of course, if all prices moved more or less in parallel, i.e. the general price index approximately corresponds to the price inflation of basic goods, the relation emphasised here will have little explanatory power. However, if there is a significant divergence, the issue becomes relevant.

3.2.2 Intertemporal Optimisation with Moving Subsistence Consumption

In the previous chapter we examined the approach of intertemporal utility optimisation and concluded for a number of reasons that it is generally not an appropriate tool to explain consumption and saving behaviour. We will therefore ultimately provide a model of saving based on a new fundament. Yet before we develop our own model, we intend to show that the inclusion of moving subsistence consumption into a standard intertemporal optimisation model already changes its predictions in a fundamental way. So even if one believes in the standard approach of intertemporal utility maximisation, but is realistic enough not to dismiss the fact of necessity consumption, one has to depart from the usual reasoning and focus on very different variables to explain saving decisions. To confirm this statement, and to clarify the consequences, is the purpose of this section.

As a first point, we have to consider whether a model with good-specific subsistence points allows for two-stage budgeting, i.e. for separating within-period optimisation of the consumption basket according to relative prices as developed in the previous section from intertemporal optimisation of the path of consumption. The general condition for two-stage-budgeting is that utility is separable, i.e. that the conditional ordering of goods within a group is independent from consumption levels outside the group. Hence, a separation of intertemporal choice from intratemporal choice requires that the composition of consumption in each period does not depend on consumption in other periods.

Generally, in cases of non-homothetic preferences the composition of consumption depends on the entire outlay, hence, it is not independent from the time path of expenditure. Moreover, the intertemporal elasticity of substitution certainly differs across goods in the case of different subsistence points. A good with a relatively high subsistence point is clearly less substitutable than a good with a low subsistence point since a larger amount of the former has to be consumed in each period.

Nevertheless, for the part of consumption that is subject to choice, i.e. the part that exceeds basic needs, the expenditure expansion path is linear and the marginal intertemporal elasticity of substitution does not depend on the amount of the respective good consumed in each period. Hence, $X(t)$ can be balanced intertemporally, while $C^*(t)$ has to be consumed in fixed proportions in each period.

As a consequence, the optimal saving rate (calculated as share of total income) directly depends on the extent of income exceeding $C^*(t)$ and the development of the relationship between $C^*(t)$ and total current income over time. This relationship, as we have seen, is crucially influenced by the difference between the price index for basic goods and general inflation.

So we are dealing with an intertemporal optimisation problem that neither refers to the amount of consumption of each single good c_{it} nor to the entire consumption level $C(t)$ but to the optimally composed consumption aggregate $X(t) = (C(t) - C^*(t))/P(t)$.

To simplify notation, we use the bold symbols $\mathbf{C}(t)$ and $\mathbf{C}^*(t)$ to denote total consumption outlay $C(t)$ and basic consumption expenditure $C^*(t)$, deflated by the general price index $P(t)$ (hence, bold symbols do not denote vectors or matrices here, but scalars):

$$\mathbf{C}(t) = \frac{C(t)}{P(t)}, \quad \mathbf{C}^*(t) = \frac{C^*(t)}{P(t)}$$

$$(3.30)$$

We have to bear in mind that $P(t)$ is not the adequate index to correct $C^*(t)$ for the influence of price changes. Hence, a varying amount of $\mathbf{C}^*(t)$ does not necessarily mean varying quantities of c_{it}^*. Rather, $\mathbf{C}^*(t)$ will change not only due to quantity changes of some c_{it}^*, but also due to divergences in the development of prices for basic goods and the general price index. Consequently, the deflated value of $C^*(t)$ is not identical with its "real" value in the strict sense of being unaffected by the monetary level.

Assuming CES-utility and perfect foresight leads to an intertemporal utility function in the following form:

$$V = \sum_{t=0}^{T} (1 + \delta)^{-t} \frac{\left(\mathbf{C}(t) - \mathbf{C}^*(t)\right)^{1-\rho}}{(1 - \rho)}$$

$$(3.31)$$

The intertemporal budget constraint for total consumption outlay is as usual:

$$\sum_{t=0}^{T} (1 + r)^{-t} C(t) = F(0) + \sum_{t=0}^{T} (1 + r)^{-t} w(t)$$

(3.32)

Again, r is the real interest rate, $F(0)$ denotes initial wealth and $w(t)$ the real wage.

This leads to following first order conditions for the time path of $C(t)$:

$$\left(C(t) - C^*(t)\right)^{-\rho} = \lambda \left[\frac{1 + \delta}{1 + r}\right]^t$$

(3.33)

Taking the time derivative and replacing λ gives:

$$-\rho \left(C(t) - C^*(t)\right)^{-\rho-1} \left(C'(t) - C'^*(t)\right) = \left(C(t) - C^*(t)\right)^{-\rho} (\delta - r)$$

Hence, we obtain for optimal consumption growth:

$$\frac{C'(t)}{C(t)} = \frac{1}{\rho}(r - \delta) \left(1 - \frac{C^*(t)}{C(t)}\right) + \frac{C'^*(t)}{C(t)}$$

(3.34)

The first term on the right-hand side of equation (3.34) corresponds to the equation guiding optimal consumption in a model with fixed subsistence level as considered in section 3.2. But since in our approach $C^*(t)$ appeared with a time script, a second term influencing optimal consumption growth has to be added in order to capture variations in necessity spending. On the one hand, such changes in $C^*(t)$ might happen due to quantity changes in the necessity basket and, on the other hand, they might be caused by differences between the CPI and basic price inflation.

To clarify the consequences of equation (3.34), we have to introduce some additional variables. While general consumer price inflation $P'(t)/P(t)$ is denoted now by the term $i(t)$, the inflation rate of basic consumption goods will be denoted by $i^*(t)$. It is defined as:

$$i^*(t) = \frac{\int_0^1 p_{it}' \, c_{it}^* di}{\int_0^1 p_{it} \, c_{it}^* di}$$

(3.35)

In order to derive $i^*(t)$, price changes are weighted by the quantity at which each subsistence good enters the subsistence basket in the current period t. Basic price inflation might exceed the inflation rate of the general price index or fall below it. The divergence between the two variables shall be called the rate of excess basic inflation, denoted by $i^{**}(t)$. Hence, $i^{**}(t)$ is defined by:

$$i^{**}(t) = i^*(t) - i(t)$$

(3.36)

The expression $i^{**}(t)$ is positive if subsistence good prices move quicker than general inflation and negative in the opposite case.

The quantitative change in the subsistence basket shall be measured by the rate $g^*(t)$ that is defined as:

$$g^*(t) = \frac{\int_0^1 p_{it} \, c_{it}^{*'} di}{\int_0^1 p_{it} \, c_{it}^* di}$$

(3.37)

It appears plausible to assume subsistence points increase according to long-term trends in real income growth. This does not only mean assuming the respective c_{it}^*s becomes extended over time, but goods or services that originally did not belong to the subsistence basket might be introduced with income growth. Moreover, technological innovations may essentially change the basket in its proportions. We will attempt to empirically operationalize the variable $g^*(t)$ in a later chapter.

The nominal value of the subsistence point moves according to:

$$C^{*'}(t) = \big(g^*(t) + i^*(t)\big)C^*(t)$$

(3.38)

which yields for deflated $\mathbf{C^{*'}(t)}$:

$$\mathbf{C}^{*'}(t) = \big(g^*(t) + i^*(t) - i(t)\big)\mathbf{C}^*(t) = \big(g^*(t) + i^{**}(t)\big)\mathbf{C}^*(t)$$

$$(3.39)$$

Denoting the necessity share in total consumption outlay the lower-case letter $c^*(t)$ is used. Hence, we have:

$$c^*(t) = \frac{C^*(t)}{C(t)} = \frac{\mathbf{C}^*(t)}{\mathbf{C}(t)}$$

$$(3.40)$$

The growth rate of total real consumption outlay $\mathbf{C}(t)$ will be denoted by $g_c(t)$. Using these variables, the equation for optimal consumption expenditure growth can be rewritten as:

$$g_c(t) = \frac{1}{\rho}\big(1 - c^*(t)\big)(r - \delta) + \big(g^*(t) + i^{**}(t)\big)c^*(t)$$

$$(3.41)$$

If the necessity share $c^*(t)$ is negligibly small, the first term on the right-hand side dominates and one has to focus on the usual variables to explain saving behaviour. If the real interest rate r equals the rate of time preference δ, the desired consumption growth is simply zero. If the two rates differ, the intertemporal elasticity of substitution $1/\rho$ governs the response.

However, as soon as a relevant part of expenditure is devoted to satisfying basic needs, the intertemporal elasticity of substitution is lowered by the factor $(1 - c^*(t))$. Hence, the response of the consumer to interest differentials depends on the necessity share in consumption. If the necessity share varies, the elasticity of intertemporal substitution will also vary.

Moreover, two additional variables, which are usually not considered to be relevant for saving behaviour, appear in the equation. These are the rate of quantitative growth of the necessity basket and the difference between general and basic price inflation. The two variables are likely to become crucial in determining desired consumption growth if the necessity share is relatively high.

Therefore, if a relevant part of consumption spending is committed to satisfying basic needs, one has to focus on rather different variables to understand saving behaviour even within the framework of the standard model of intertemporal utility maximisation. One has to analyse the deviation between the general price index and the price inflation of basic goods, and one has to analyse the growth rate of the necessity basket that possibly follows long-term trends of income growth.

Consider the simplest case of constant real wage income in every period and a factor of time discounting δ equalling the real interest rate r. Given these conditions, the standard model predicts that in every period all income is consumed, desired consumption growth is zero and saving is zero. This is remarkably different from the prediction derived from (3.41). For $r = \delta$ the first term on the right-hand side completely disappears. However, the consumer does not desire constant consumption, but consumption growth that exactly follows the sum of $g^*(t)$ and $i^{**}(t)$ times $c^*(t)$. Even if we suppose $C^*(t)$ being quantitatively unchanged, a development of basic good prices deviating from the general price index unavoidably leads to changes in desired consumption outlay. In other words, the consumer has to save or dissave rather than spending his entire revenue in every period. If the two rates guiding basic consumption expenditure are excluded from the analysis, consumption outlay might appear to change randomly, although it is determined by the motion of basic spending.

A second example supposes the standard equation determines a desired annual growth rate of consumption of 2 percent and the growth rate of real income also equals 2 percent. There is no initial wealth. According to the standard model, the consumer will again not save but spend his revenue in each period. Yet an initial necessity share of 0.5 exists. The necessity basket grows at the same rate as income but basic price inflation exceeds general price inflation by 1 percent each year. If there is perfect foresight, the desired consumption expenditure growth has to be higher than income growth reaching 2.5 percent. Hence, to maintain this rate of consumption growth, the consumer has to save a considerable amount in the first part of his life and will dissave later on.

Of course, the perfect foresight case is as unrealistic in a model with basic consumption as in the standard framework. If we suppose the rate of excess basic inflation as well as the rate of necessity growth to be subject to stochastic shocks, consumption in two subsequent periods has to be balanced according to:

$$\frac{1 + r}{1 + \delta} \; E(t) \left[\frac{\left(C(t + 1) - C^*(t + 1) \right)^{-\rho}}{\left(C(t) - C^*(t) \right)^{-\rho}} \right] = 1$$

$$(3.42)$$

The behaviour of a consumer solving this kind of optimisation problem is different from the buffer-stock saver— the outcome of the standard model including CRRA-utility and uncertainty— in two respects. First, not the expected variance of future consumption as such, but the expected variance of the difference between total consumption and basic needs matters. The latter depends not only on income shocks but on two additional stochastic variables. Second and even more crucial, an unexpected deviation between general price inflation and basic good inflation directly influences saving leading to an upward or downward adjustment of real consumption expenditure, even if real income remains constant. In periods of $g^*(t)$ and/or $i^{**}(t)$ being positive, consumption expenditure has to be adjusted upwards, hence, saving will be lower or negative. The opposite case will push saving.

Hence, intertemporal optimisation under the condition of basic needs leads to considerably different predictions compared to the traditional models. Notably, two additional variables appear in the Euler equation: first, the growth rate of the necessity basket, possibly equalling long-term trends of income growth and, second, the rate of excess basic price inflation defined as the difference between a particular price index gauging basic goods inflation and the general consumer price index.

Thus, even if one believes in the approach of intertemporal utility maximisation, an analysis of consumption and saving that excludes variables governing the development of the necessity share turns out to be biased and incapable of revealing the driving forces of saving decisions.

Paragraph 3.3
Modelling Saving Decisions by a Simple Rule of Thumb

In the previous section, we applied the standard procedure of intertemporal optimisation, suggesting a number of additional (certainly realistic) assumptions concerning the structure of momentary and intertemporal utility. We have seen that the hypothesis of good-specific subsistence points introduced into a standard framework of intertemporal choice substantially changes the predictions of the model. As shown, additional variables, which are usually not considered to have any influence on saving decisions, appear in the Euler equation. Moreover, if the hypothesis of a significant necessity share is true, the impact of those variables is likely to be much stronger than the effect of the determinants of saving considered by traditional analysis.

Despite the use of standard tools in the previous passage, we of course maintain our critique of this approach as expressed in section 2.5. The optimisation problem already in the original buffer-stock model was hardly solvable due to the complicated structure and lack of information, and so supports even more the case for the approach now provided. To take into account, at minimum, three stochastic variables and to acquire information about their probability distribution far into the future is an absurd task that presumably no one in real day-to-day life will attempt to solve. Even if the required information were available, to find the optimal consumption path by iteration will definitely overstrain the capacity of even advanced computer processors.

As mentioned before, the complexity of the Stochastic Dynamic Programming procedure and the vital information problem has already induced a search for rules of thumb to allow for the formulation of an optimal solution by consumers with realistic capabilities in an environment of low information.

We will consider an extremely simple rule of thumb that guides saving behaviour: when income exceeds the necessity basket, the consumer saves, and dissaves (or runs into debt) when income falls below basic needs. In the simplest version one could suppose the consumer saves a constant proportion of his free income share, which in the case of basic consumption exceeding income, implies he dissaves a certain amount. Additionally, one could consider the propensity to save out of free income and the propensity to dissave to both be a function of standard variables such as the rate of inflation, the real interest rate, uncertainty, or the level of already available wealth. Moreover, the propensity to dissave is most likely influenced by institutional conditions determining access to credit. Financial deregulation, for instance, can be assumed to ease getting into debt and will certainly strengthen the propensity to dissave.

Hence, if $S_j(t)$ denotes nominal saving by consumer j, we will expect him to behave according to following ordinary rule:

$$S_j(t) = \begin{cases} \alpha 1(t)\big(Y_j(t) - C^*(t)\big), & \quad if \quad Y_j(t) \geq C^*(t) \\ \alpha 2(t)\big(Y_j(t) - C^*(t)\big), & \quad if \quad Y_j(t) < C^*(t) \end{cases}$$

$$0 \leq \alpha 1(t), \alpha 2(t) \leq 1$$

(3.43)

$Y_j(t)$ is the consumer's personal nominal income. $C^*(t)$ is still the sum of basic goods valued at current prices. $C^*(t)$ does not appear with subscript j, since necessities are assumed to be identical for all consumers in a given period. This is of course an over-simplification of reality since for a middle-class family, certainly other purchases are required than for a young single person. Nevertheless, we will use this approach since our hypothesis is that at least an essential part of basic needs is connected to the average standard of living. (Group-specific necessity baskets— influenced by family status, age or social status— may be tested as a refinement in more advanced versions as far as the required detailed survey data are available).

$\alpha 1(t)$ denotes the propensity to save out of free income, while $\alpha 2(t)$ stands for the propensity to dissave out of the difference between income and basic expenditure. We refer to these two variables as the propensities to save and to dissave, although this does not exactly correspond to the usual understanding of these categories since the propensities do not refer to income as a whole.

All variables and parameters appear with a time script since neither individual income $Y_j(t)$, nor necessity consumption $C^*(t)$, nor the respective propensities to save and to dissave are regarded to be constant over time.

3.3.1 The Necessity Share in Outlay and in Income

Consumers following the provided rule of thumb do not explicitly aim at a certain amount of total consumption expenditure, saving being merely the by-product; instead they decide on the amount of saving out of free income while total consumption outlay is simultaneously determined. The result in this case is also a smoothing of consumption over time; however, the decision process is different.

So far we have defined the necessity share as the share of necessity purchases *in total consumption outlay*, $c^*(t)$. However, given $C^*(t)$, the necessity share $c^*(t)$ is not determined before saving but rather simultaneously, what is determined ahead of any saving decision is the free income share, or its opposite, i.e. the share of required basic spending in *income*.

In the following, we use the symbol $cc^*(t)$ to denote the mean necessity share in the sense of the share of basic purchases $C^*(t)$ in mean income $Y(t)$ at time t. The double c serves to distinguish this share from the necessity share defined as the share of necessity purchases *in total consumption outlay*. The individual necessity share in income is consistently denoted by $cc_j^*(t)$. Hence, in the following we deal with:

$$cc^*(t) = \frac{C^*(t)}{Y(t)}$$

and

$$cc_j^*(t) = \frac{C^*(t)}{Y_j(t)}$$

(3.44)

with $Y(t)$ denoting mean nominal income and $Y_j(t)$ individual nominal income in the respective period.

Empirically, total consumption outlay and total income tend to move in a similar direction. Therefore, $cc^*(t)$ and $c^*(t)$ can safely be assumed to be strongly linked. Since we have $C(t) = (1 - s(t)) Y(t)$, the correct relationship is:

$$cc^*(t) = (1 - s(t))c^*(t)$$

$$(3.45)$$

Hence, only in the case of a very volatile saving rate might a significant difference in the time path of $c^*(t)$ and $cc^*(t)$ occur. Generally, a boost in $C^*(t)$ will increase $c^*(t)$ as well as $cc^*(t)$. Therefore, when we check our model in the last chapter, we will mainly consider $c^*(t)$, the necessity share in consumption outlay instead of income, to exclude any influence of saving on a variable that is used to explain saving rate differentials. Although according to *our* model $C^*(t)/Y(t)$ is determined by spending for necessities and independent from saving, the share of any part of consumption in total income is generally smaller, the higher the saving. Therefore, to prove a negative relationship between the saving rate and the proportion of a certain part of consumption spending *in income* might appear to be a tautology. We will come back to these questions later on.

3.3.2 Determinants of Saving under the Proposed Rule of Thumb

In the next paragraphs we ignore the time subscript for a better understanding of the basic structure of our model. This is possible because the rule of thumb as such does not include any reference to variables from the past or the future. Nevertheless, we have to bear in mind that all variables refer to a specific point in time and are not considered to be constant.

Derived from the rule above, the individual saving rate of consumer j is:

$$s_j = \frac{S_j}{Y_j} = \begin{cases} \alpha 1 \left(1 - cc_j^*\right), & \text{if} \quad cc_j^* \leq 1 \\ \alpha 2 \left(1 - cc_j^*\right), & \text{if} \quad cc_j^* > 1 \end{cases}$$

$$(3.46)$$

We can express the individual saving rate also with respect to the consumer's relative income y_j, defined as the ratio of the consumer's nominal income and mean nominal income in the respective period:

$$y_j = \frac{Y_j}{Y}$$

(3.47)

Since C^*/Y_j is identical to cc^*/y_j, the saving rule referring to y_j is:

$$s_j = \begin{cases} \alpha 1 \left(1 - \dfrac{cc^*}{y_j} \right), & \textit{if} \quad y_j \geq cc^* \\[4mm] \alpha 2 \left(1 - \dfrac{cc^*}{y_j} \right), & \textit{if} \quad y_j < cc^* \end{cases}$$

(3.48)

The first derivatives of the individual saving rate with respect to the mean necessity share, the individual relative income and the individual necessity share are:

$$\partial s_j / \partial cc^* = -\alpha 1/y_j \quad \text{resp.} \quad -\alpha 2/y_j \qquad < 0 \qquad (3.49)$$

$$\partial s_j / \partial y_j = \alpha 1 cc^*/y_j^2 \quad \text{resp.} \quad \alpha 2 \, cc^*/y_j^2 \qquad > 0 \qquad (3.50)$$

$$\partial s_j / \partial cc_j^* = -\alpha 1 \qquad \text{resp.} \quad -\alpha 2 \qquad < 0 \qquad (3.51)$$

Hence, the individual saving rate is a linearly decreasing function of the individual necessity share cc_j^*. It is also linearly decreasing in the mean necessity share, while the slope in this case depends inversely on the consumer's relative income. Consequently, a change in the mean necessity share changes the saving behaviour of low-income consumers much more than that of wealthier households. Moreover, the individual saving rate is a strictly increasing concave function of relative income. Hence, a change in a consumer's individual income position changes his saving behaviour the more lower his relative income before the change and the higher the mean necessity share.

Under the given rule of thumb, the individual necessity share— determined by the mean necessity share and current individual relative income— is the crucial variable explaining a household's saving behaviour. Let us therefore consider the driving forces of the time path of this individual necessity share.

As argued above, changes in nominal necessity spending C^* over time depend on two parameters: first, the quantitative growth rate of the necessity basket g^* and, second, the price inflation for necessities i^*:

$$C^{*\prime} = (g^* + i^*)C^*$$

Changes in mean nominal income, in turn, depend on the general rate of price inflation i and the growth rate of real income g:

$$Y' = (g + i)Y$$

$$(3.52)$$

Consistently, the mean necessity share moves according to:

$$cc^{*\prime} = \frac{C^{*\prime}}{Y} - \frac{C^* Y'}{Y^2}$$

$$= (g^* - g + i^{**})cc^*$$

$$(3.53)$$

Individual nominal income changes due to inflation and real growth:

$$Y_j' = (g_j + i)Y_j$$

$$(3.54)$$

Here, g_j denotes the growth rate of individual real income of consumer j, while i stands for general inflation.

Hence, for the time change in individual relative income y_j' we have:

$$y_j' = \frac{Y_j'}{Y} - \frac{Y_j \, Y'^2}{Y}$$

$$= (g_j - g)y_j$$

$$(3.55)$$

For the change in the individual necessity share cc_j^* we consistently obtain:

$$cc_j^{*'} = \frac{cc^{*'}}{y_j} - \frac{cc^* y_j'}{y_j^2} = \frac{cc^{*'} - cc_j^* y_j'}{y_j}$$

$$= \frac{(g^* - g + i^{**})cc^* - cc_j^*(g_j - g)y_j}{y_j}$$

$$= (g^* + i^{**} - g_j)cc_j^*$$

$$(3.56)$$

Since the first derivative of the individual saving rate with respect to the individual necessity share is linear and negative, changes in the individual saving rate should, *ceteris paribus*, be positively correlated to individual income growth g_j and negatively correlated to the growth rate of the necessity basket g^* as well as the rate of excess basic inflation i^{**}.

Hence, the predictions of our rule of thumb for individual saving behaviour are: an increase in the necessity share decreases saving by all income groups; the strongest effect, however, occurs with low-income households. The individual saving rate increases when individual income growth exceeds the general growth rate of the necessity basket or when basic price inflation is lower than general price inflation. While individual income growth differs across households, the rate of growth of the necessity basket and the rate of excess basic price inflation are assumed to be the same for all consumers.

3.3.3 The Aggregated Saving Rate under the Given Rule of Thumb

Applying these insights to the macroeconomic level, one can conclude that changes in the aggregate saving rate, *inter alia*, depend on three factors: the rate of excess basic inflation, the growth rate of the necessity basket and the *mean* (instead of individual) income growth.

In fact, one can merge the influence of the two latter rates by introducing one additional variable. Above, we defined excess inflation of subsistence expenditure by the extent at which basic good inflation exceeds general price inflation. Similar to this definition, one can grasp the extent at which the growth rate of the necessity basket exceeds the current growth rate of real income by the term excess growth of subsistence expenditure, or shortened, excess basic growth. This variable shall is denoted by g^{**}. Hence, we have:

$$g^{**} = g^* - g$$

$$(3.57)$$

Like Ravn, Schmitt-Grohe & Uribe (2008) we will assume subsistence points grow according to long-term trends in real income. Thus, the difference between the growth rate of the subsistence basket g^* and the growth rate of real income g in period t is assumed to be positive when average income growth falls below its long run trend; conversely, it is negative in periods of over-proportional income growth compared to the years before.

Using this variable, the time path of the mean necessity share is guided by only two factors:

$$cc^{*'} = (g^{**} + i^{**})cc^*$$

$$(3.58)$$

Hence, as the individual saving rate is determined first by the rate of excess basic inflation and, second, by the difference between the growth rate of the necessity basket and individual real income growth, changes of the aggregated saving rate should be negatively correlated with the rate of excess basic inflation and the rate of excess basic growth.

However, this is not the whole story, since aggregate saving is additionally influenced by the distribution of income. If one could assume everyone to be equipped with current income covering at least his or her basic needs, the average saving rate would be independent from the distribution of income and one could directly transmit the predictions from the micro to the macro level by using the mean values of all variables in order to determine the aggregate saving rate.

Actually, the same is true if we assume the propensity to save $\alpha 1$ to be identical to the propensity to dissave $\alpha 2$. In this case, the aggregated saving rate could also be derived directly from the mean necessity share; a redistribution of income would have no influence.

However, if we depart from the assumption of identical propensities to save and to dissave, and if we assume some households to be at relative income positions below the mean necessity share, the distribution of income has to be taken into account.

To derive the exact formula for the aggregate saving rate, let us assume a continuum of households of mass 1. Let S stand for aggregate nominal saving and s denote the aggregate saving rate. If individual saving behaviour follows the rule considered above, aggregate saving in a certain period will be:

$$S = \int_0^1 S_j \, dj = \int_0^1 s_j \, Y_j \, dj = \int_0^1 s_j \, y_j \, Y \, dj = Y \int_0^1 s_j \, y_j \, dj$$

$$(3.59)$$

The aggregate saving rate can be consistently derived by:

$$s = \frac{S}{Y} = \int_0^1 s_j \, y_j \, dj$$

$$(3.60)$$

Let us assume that households are ordered by their relative income position, beginning with the poorest and ending with the richest. Hence, we can divide households into two groups:

Households $0 < j \le k$ with: $y_j \le y_k = cc^*$
Households $k < j < 1$ with: $y_j > y_k = cc^*$

For k, we consistently have:

$0 < k < 1$ if cc^* is within the range of the relative income distribution,
$k = 0$ if cc^* is below the minimum relative income,
$k = 1$ if cc^* is equal or above the maximum relative income.

If everybody's relative income exceeds the necessity share, no one joins the first group while in the unlikely event of all households receiving less income than required to buy the subsistence basket (which presupposes cc^*

exceeding unity), even the relative income of the richest households is below y_k.

If some households save and others are not able to do so, k has a value between zero and one. The exact value of k then depends on the mean necessity share in a given period and on the distribution of income. Households in the group below k are non-saving, probably dissaving (if the propensity to dissave is positive and the inequality $y_j < cc^*$ is binding). Households with relative income exceeding cc^*, on the other hand, are saving. Hence, k denotes the share of non-saving households, while $(1 - k)$ is the share of households which save.

Hence, we can express the aggregate saving rate as a sum of two terms:

$$s = \int_0^k s_j \, y_j \, dj \; + \; \int_k^1 s_j \, y_j \, dj$$

$$= \int_0^k \alpha2 \, (y_j - cc^*) \, dj \; + \; \int_k^1 \alpha1 \, (y_j - cc^*) \, dj$$

$$= \alpha2 \int_0^k (y_j - cc^*) \, dj \; + \; \alpha1 \int_k^1 (y_j - cc^*) \, dj$$

$$= \alpha2 \int_0^k y_j \, dj \; + \; \alpha1 \int_k^1 y_j \, dj \; - \; \alpha2 \, k \, cc^* \; - \; \alpha1 \, (1 - k) cc^*$$

$$= \alpha2 \int_0^k y_j \, dj \; + \; \alpha1 \int_k^1 y_j \, dj \; - \; [\alpha1 \, (1 - k) + \alpha2 \, k] cc^*$$

$$(3.61)$$

It is obvious from equation (3.61) that changes in the income distribution within the group of savers or within the group of non-savers do not matter for aggregate saving. Only those redistributions which change either the average *relative income position* of saving and non-saving households, or their respective *population share*, or both, will have an impact on the aggregate saving rate.

The population share of non-saving households equals k, that of saving households equals $(1 - k)$. The average relative income of non-saving households equals $1/k \int_0^k y_j \, dj$, the average relative income of saving households is $1/(1-k) \int_k^1 y_j \, dj$. Since the distribution within these two groups plays no role, we can deal with these average values directly, denoting the average relative income of non-savers by $y\{ns\}$ and the average relative income of savers by $y\{s\}$. Necessarily, we have:

$$y\{ns\} \leq cc^* < y\{s\}$$

$$(3.62)$$

The income share of the entire group of non-savers equals $k\,y\{ns\}$, while all savers together are equipped with a share of $(1-k)y\{s\}$ in total income. We consistently have:

$$k\,y\{ns\} + (1-k)y\{s\} = 1$$

$$(3.63)$$

If we deal with the average income position of both groups, the aggregate saving rate becomes:

$$s = \alpha2\,k\,[y\{ns\}- cc^*] + \alpha1\,(1-k)[y\{s\}- cc^*]$$

$$= \alpha2\,k\,y\{ns\}- \alpha2\,k\,cc^* + \alpha1\,(1-k)y\{s\} - \alpha1\,(1-k)cc^*$$

$$= \alpha1\,(1-k)y\{s\} + \alpha2\,k\,y\{ns\}- [\alpha2\,k\,cc^* + \alpha1\,(1-k)cc^*\,]$$

$$(3.64)$$

To reduce variables, we can replace $(1-k)\,y\{s\}$, the income share of all savers together, by $1 - k\,y\{ns\}$. This leads to:

$$s = \alpha1(1- ky\{ns\}) + \alpha2\,k\,y\{ns\} - [\alpha2\,k\,cc^* + \alpha1(1-k)cc^*]$$

$$= \alpha1 - \alpha1k\,y\{ns\} + \alpha2\,k\,y\{ns\}- [\alpha2\,k + \alpha1\,(1-k)]cc^*$$

$$= \alpha1 + [\alpha2 - \alpha1]\,k\,y\{ns\} + [(\alpha1 - \alpha2)\,k - \alpha1)]\,cc^*$$

$$= \alpha1\,(1-cc^*) + [\alpha1 - \alpha2]k\,[cc^* - y\{ns\}]$$

$$(3.65)$$

Equation (3.65) shows rather clearly the influence of the different variables on the aggregate saving rate. Moreover, it becomes clear why in the case of either $k = 0$ or $\alpha 1 = \alpha 2$, the distribution of income is not relevant for the aggregate saving rate. In the case of $k = 0$ (i.e. when no one receives income below subsistence needs), the second term completely disappears. The same occurs if we have identical propensities to save and to dissave. In both cases the formula for the aggregate saving rate reduces to:

$$s = \alpha 1 \, (1 - cc^*)$$

Thus, all distributional parameters disappear and the aggregate saving rate is exclusively determined by the propensity to save out of free income $\alpha 1$ and the mean necessity share cc^*. The latter, in turn, moves according to the known parameters: it increases if income growth falls below its long-term trend, and it pushes up when the inflation rate of basic good prices exceeds general inflation.

However, equation (3.65) cannot be reduced to the first term on the right-hand side. The effect of the second term depends on the difference between the propensity to save and the propensity to dissave ($\alpha 1 - \alpha 2$) as well as on the share of non-savers k. The higher this share and the higher the difference between the propensity to dissave and the propensity to save, the stronger its influence. In short, with k and $y\{ns\}$ distributional parameters have an impact on saving.

The first derivative of the aggregate saving rate with respect to the mean necessity share is:

$$\frac{\partial s}{\partial cc^*} = - \alpha 1 + (\alpha 1 - \alpha 2)k < 0$$

$$(3.66)$$

In fact, if we want to scrutinise the exact effect of changes in the mean necessity share on aggregated saving, we have to take into account the dependence of k and $y\{ns\}$ on the mean necessity share. If cc^* increases and there is no redistribution of income, k will most likely increase, too. To what extent depends on the density of households in the interval of relative income between cc^*(old) and cc^*(new). If k changes, the relative income of non-savers will also change because higher relative income households will join the group of non-savers. The extent again depends on the density of households in the respective relative income groups. This might or might not change the difference between $y\{ns\}$ and cc^*. Generally, in the case of a constant income distribution, we have:

$$\frac{\partial y\{ns\}}{\partial cc^*} \geq 0$$

$$\frac{\partial k}{\partial cc^*} \geq 0$$

Despite these rather complex relationships, the first derivative of the aggregate saving rate with respect to the mean necessity share is always non-positive, as k can never exceed unity and $\alpha 1$ and $\alpha 2$ have to be non-negative.

This is also intuitively clear since an increase in cc^* diminishes the free income share of savers and boosts the negative 'free income share' of dissavers. Both effects necessarily reduce aggregate saving. Furthermore, a rising cc^* probably turns savers into dissavers, thus decreasing the aggregate saving rate even further.

What happens with the aggregate saving rate in the case of income redistribution, given the mean necessity share remains constant? As shown, to have an effect on the aggregate saving rate, a redistribution of income has to change either the division of the population between savers and non-savers, or the average relative income position of these groups, or both. Rising inequality that has such an effect corresponds either to a shrinking relative income of non-savers $y\{ns\}$ or to an increasing share of non-savers k. Hence, with increasing inequality between savers and non-savers, the term $k\,[cc^* - y\{ns\}]$ will be pushed up. Obviously, the effect of this process on the aggregate saving rate depends on the relation between the propensity to save $\alpha 1$ and the propensity to dissave $\alpha 2$. If the first exceeds the latter, increasing inequality boosts the aggregate rate of saving. If $\alpha 1$ is lower than $\alpha 2$, the opposite is true: rising inequality presses aggregate saving down. If $\alpha 1 = \alpha 2$, as shown, the income distribution has no impact on the aggregate saving rate.

Hence, the predictions of the model regarding aggregate saving are indeed similar to those at the individual level. Unless distributional parameters change, the aggregate saving rate should increase when income growth lies above its long-run growth trend or when basic price inflation is lower than general price inflation. In the opposite case, the aggregate saving rate decreases. The effect of income redistribution depends on the relationship between the parameters $\alpha 1$ and $\alpha 2$: rising inequality strengthens aggregate saving if the propensity to save exceeds the propensity to dissave, while aggregate saving will be reduced if the relationship is reversed.

3.3.4 Factors Influencing the Propensity to Save and to Dissave

It appears plausible to suppose that the respective propensities to save and to dissave differ from each other and change over time. For example, one might consider that the value of the parameter $\alpha 2$ is an increasing function of the median value of wealth among the potential dissavers since it is definitely easier to dissave out of available assets than to search for credit. Moreover, to use up wealth is usually less costly than running into debts since interest on median household's financial assets are by far smaller than interest on credit. Finally, even if one desires credit, the existence of non-liquid wealth crucially eases access to it. This correlation between median wealth and a higher $\alpha 2$ might deliver a possible explanation why rising inequality in developed countries— where median wealth, although not high, after all exists— tends to correspond to decreasing saving rates, while in poorer countries a harsh redistribution of income in favour of the rich is likely to be followed by a rise in the aggregate personal saving rate.

Additionally, an increase in the value of $\alpha 2$ is the likely outcome of financial market liberalisation. Empirical data show a swelling debt-to-income ratio to coincide everywhere with deregulations in the field of retail banking.

Furthermore, one might mull over the variance of $\alpha 1$ and $\alpha 2$ in response to the business cycle, covering the effect of uncertainty. Within the given model it becomes clear why increasing uncertainty in a business low only sometimes increases the aggregate saving rate of households while consumption tends to respond counter-cyclically. Assuming $\alpha 1$ is strengthened in a business downturn, *ceteris paribus*, the aggregated saving rate is boosted. However, since $\alpha 1$ refers not to the whole income but only to the free income share, the positive effect might be cancelled out by a shrinking free income share due to income losses caused by the business low. To further investigate this issue, we would have to compare those recessions in which saving rates have risen to those when the opposite occurred. This work has obviously not yet been done, but there are some indicators supporting such an interpretation. (In Germany, for instance, recessions with rising saving rates appeared only in the nineteen seventies, at the same time— as we show later— that the free income share reached its highest level.)

Moreover, it seems to be plausible to assume the propensity to save being shifted up in the cases of higher inflation or higher nominal interest rates. As we have seen, there is a positive relation between inflation and personal saving rates in developed countries, mainly caused by the desire to reduce capital losses. Therefore, $\alpha 1$ should somehow reflect this effect.

Of course, we could consider other factors such as real interest rates or uncertainty as possible influences on the respective propensity to save and to dissave. A great deal of further research is needed in order to determine the value of both parameters and investigate its change over time.

3.3.5 Summary: Model Predictions

According to the model provided here, the consumer saves if individual income exceeds the current value of the necessity basket, defined in reference to the general standard of living. The consumer dissaves if current income falls below basic needs.

If saving follows this simple rule, two crucial variables influencing aggregate saving can be identified: first, the rate of excess basic growth, and, second, the rate of excess basic price inflation. Excess basic growth is derived from the difference between the growth rate of the necessity basket, possibly equalling long-term growth trends of income, and current income growth. The rate of excess basic price inflation is determined by the difference between the rise of basic good prices and general inflation. The predictions are: if income growth falls below long-term growth trends, saving rates will be diminished. The same occurs if prices of basic goods rise faster than general inflation. Furthermore, aggregate saving depends on the distribution of income. Rising inequality will strengthen saving if the propensity to save exceeds the propensity to dissave. A more unequal society will be accompanied by lower saving if the relationship is reversed.

The propensity to save is considered to be (positively) influenced by the usual variables such as inflation, real or nominal interest rates and, perhaps, by the uncertainty of income expectations. The deregulation of financial markets and previously accumulated wealth are considered to increase the propensity to dissave.

The individual saving rate has been derived as a linearly decreasing function of the individual necessity share and a strictly increasing concave function of the individual relative income position. If the mean necessity share changes, individual saving responds the more lower the consumer's relative income position. Hence, in so far as determinants of the necessity share are more volatile than factors influencing the propensity to save, saving rates of low-income households should be more volatile over time than saving rates of rich consumers. At a given point in time, however, the variance of saving rates within the lower deciles should be smaller than among higher income groups since, for the former group, the trade-off between consumption and saving is much less a matter of choice.

In Chapter 5 we will check these predictions against the empirical evidence. Before we are able to do so, we have to reproduce the time path of the most decisive variable within our model governing saving at the micro and the macro level: the mean necessity share. To approximate this share requires defining of basic needs in modern societies and to find a way to measure their motion in time over several decades. This is the objective of the next chapter.

Chapter 4. The Patterns of Consumption Shares

Paragraph 4.1
How to Identify Basic Needs?

4.1.1 Two Approaches to the Historic Path of the Necessity Share

In fact, various ways exist to approximate the time path of the necessity share $cc^*(t)$. A straightforward approach would be to identify those goods and services that have to be considered basic at a given point of time. One would then measure the amount of expenditure directed into such purchases and calculate the portion of this expenditure in income. If this is done over an extended range of time, the path of the necessity share would be revealed and its link to the path of saving could be checked.

Unfortunately, this approach faces a number of difficulties. The most elementary problem arises from the degree of disaggregation in available consumption data. An exact identification of subsistence points would require very narrowly defined expenditure groups. For instance, the major group of food expenditure contains bread, potatoes, milk as well as truffles and champagne. While the first three certainly belong to basic needs, this is hardly the case for the latter two. Or a washing machine might be basic, but is this also true for a high-tech designer kitchen? Again, both goods are found in the same major category of household equipment.

But even if we had access to extended time-series of very detailed consumption data, it is difficult to determine the exact year when having a mobile phone as well as a fixed network telephone changed from being a luxury to a necessity. Or, at what precise point in time a colour-TV or a washing machine with integrated centrifuge became basic. Hardly anyone is able to answer such questions precisely.

The problem of data reliability is equally awkward. Data on very narrowly defined consumption groups—when at all available—unavoidably suffer seriously from sampling errors, statistical revisions and other distortions since their demarcation lines are harder to draw than those of wider aggregates.

Furthermore, at least in Germany, national statistics do not provide very detailed sectoral price indices, which would be required to deflate basic expenditure and to discover the real quantitative growth rate of the necessity basket. Although those indices are available for the U.S., their accuracy has to be questioned. Additionally, there is no correspondence between the detailed ordering of consumption expenses in the Consumption Expenditure Survey and the classification used in the NIPA tables to define sectoral prices. Employing broader sectoral aggregates strengthens the comparability of the data since discrepancies in detail are offset.

For all these reasons, we will refer to consumption expenditure groups at a higher degree of aggregation. For Germany, the twelve categories of the European classification of individual consumption by purpose (COICOP) will be the primary point of reference. The structure of the U.S. statistics is somewhat different, but we will deal with expenditure subgroups that, in principle, correspond to the COICOP classification.

However, employing such broadly defined sectoral consumption expenditure data means deriving a time path of $cc^*(t)$ that can, at best, approximate the move of the real necessity share. Actually, at the given degree of aggregation, not any single consumption group exists that can soundly be considered to be composed of necessities only. Rather, in almost every group very basic goods and services are found as well as luxuries. Hence, the only solution is to qualify those groups as part of the necessity share that are *dominated* by basic consumption and to exclude those groups in which, according to empirical evidence, only a small part of consumption is committed to satisfy elementary needs. To be able to draw this line, we will analyse subgroups of the wider aggregates and estimate their respective weight. We believe that given the quality of statistical data, such a procedure is the most advisable one although a sharper demarcation of the necessity basket may be desirable from a theoretical point of view.

However, this is not the only problem of the approach considered here. In fact, the purpose of calculating the necessity share is to check its relationship with the saving rate in order to confirm or refute the predictions of our model. As mentioned in Chapter 3, this is hardly possible by employing a necessity share that computes the proportion of a number of expenditure categories in *income*. In fact, *according to our model* the mean necessity share in income $cc^*(t) = C^*(t)/Y(t)$ is determined by the sum of subsistence expenditure at the respective point of time, $C^*(t) =$

$\int_0^1 p_{it} c_{it}^* \, di$. It is therefore completely independent from saving decisions. Nevertheless, it is generally true that the share of total consumption expenditure in income is smaller the higher the saving rate. Thus, even under homothetic preferences, a negative relationship between a certain share of consumption spending in income and the saving rate necessarily exists. In the homotheticity case, the necessity share in income would vary in exact proportion to the share of total consumption in income, which is higher the lower the saving effort.

Hence, the proof of a negative correlation between saving and the proportion of whatever part of consumption expenses *in income* might be considered a mere tautology. Such a negative correlation is easily explainable without reference to a hypothesis of basic needs limiting the ability to save, and will hardly be accepted as a confirmation of the latter.

Yet since the real necessity basket $C^*(t)$ can only be approximated by adding broadly defined expenditure groups, we can also consider a different point of reference. The share of basic consumption in total *consumption outlay*, $c^*(t)$ is in any respect independent from saving decisions. Although the relationship between $c^*(t)$ and the saving rate is not linear according to our model, it should be negative as well since as long as the saving rate is not extremely volatile, the time path of $c^*(t)$ moves in line with the path of $cc^*(t)$. Since the traditional models do not provide any explanation for a negative correlation between the necessity share in consumption outlay and the saving rate, this share is obviously a more appropriate variable to check our model predictions.

Hence, one way to approximate $cc^*(t)$, which we will use, is to add basic expenditure groups and to compute the change of their share in total consumption outlay over time. This is our first approach to the historic path of the necessity share.

We have to bear in mind, however, that this leads only to an approximation of $cc^*(t)$ for the following two reasons. First, expenditure groups are not sufficiently narrowly defined to exclude the appearance of luxury spending within the necessity share calculated in this way; at the same time, some basic expenses might not be covered. Second, the point of reference is consumption outlay and not income as required by a strict interpretation of our model predictions. Nevertheless, we expect the general trends of the real necessity share to be reflected in the time path of a share which is calculated in such a way.

A second approach to obtain the time path of the necessity share is to calculate the two growth rates guiding its motion over time. As defined in the previous chapter, these are the rate of excess basic price inflation and the rate of excess basic growth. Employing these rates, the time path of the necessity share can be approximated from a given initial value onwards. Of course, in this case we also have to go into the details of consumption spending since we have to characterise the particular price index measuring price inflation of basic goods. In order to define which sectoral price movements are to be included in the basic price index and at what weight, we have to distinguish necessities from luxuries. Since we have to use sectoral price indexes of broad aggregates of consumption spending similar to the case of defining the necessity share in our first approach, the derived path is again only an approximation of the real necessity share.

4.1.2 Basic Expenditure Groups versus Luxury Spending

The main task of this section is to identify those expenditure groups that can soundly be grasped as dominated by necessities in a modern society. To approach this goal, we reconsider some results of the empirical literature on consumption. One major issue of this type of research is the exploration of expenditure elasticities with respect to income and prices. Although different models find different detailed outcomes, some features are unanimously accepted. Among others, empirical evidence strongly suggests abandoning the supposition of homothetic preferences. Instead, the structure of consumption obviously depends on the levels of outlay or income respectively. (Some studies stress the distinction between these two variables, but since income and consumption expenditure are highly correlated, Engel-curves referring to income are rather similar to those using outlay as the point of reference.)

While the absolute spending for most groups of goods moves in line with total outlay, the expenditure share of some of them decreases when income (respective outlay) rises. This property is commonly used in order to distinguish necessities (income elasticity smaller than unity) from luxuries (income elasticity exceeding unity). Hence, the natural hypothesis is that income elasticity is the crucial indicator in our search for basic goods.

Things like food, drinks, clothes or shelter are usually assumed to be part of the category of necessities, while expensive durables, entertainment equipment, cars or so called personal belongings (watches, jewellery) are supposed to match the feature of luxuries. However, if we look at the empirical data, the patterns are not as clear-cut.

The link between consumption spending for particular products and real income can be analysed at the macroeconomic level by searching for changes over time, or at micro level by comparing spending patterns in cross-section at a certain point of time. Both approaches provide rather different results. Our hypothesis is that analyses of spending patterns at the micro level lead to more realistic estimates of real income elasticities, while the path at the macroeconomic level is distorted by several factors that are difficult to isolate.

For instance, scrutinising consumption expenditure shares over time requires referring not only to changes in real income, but taking note of the of relative sectoral prices movements. If sectoral inflation is higher than general inflation, upturns in the sectoral expenditure share might simply mirror a sectoral price boost. These changes must not be confused with the income effect, i.e. the change in spending due to changes in real income. Most likely, the broader the definition of consumption groups, the lower the elasticity of substitution across the borders of those groups. Hence, we have to expect a strong positive correlation between the movements of sectoral prices and of consumption shares. As far as national statistics provide sectoral prices ordered by the same system as consumption spending, the price effect can be isolated from the impact of real income changes. If sectoral prices and the classification of expenditure do not correspond, this is more complicated.

However, deviations between sectoral and general inflation are not the only causes of historic movements of consumption shares along side the income effect. The structure of consumption also changes over time due to technological innovations. For instance, as long as communication technology was limited to posting letters and using a fixed telephone network, it was difficult to spend too much on communication. The invention of mobile phones, short message service, internet and email has completely altered this situation. For a long reference period, such structural changes in consumption are very likely and it is difficult to separate their impact from the income and the price effect. If, on the other hand, the period of reference is short, real income at the macro level will hardly change sufficiently to permit conclusive estimates of income elasticities.

Therefore, income elasticities are probably more visible in cross-sectional expenditure patterns. In fact, the variance of real income across households at a point in time is much stronger than the change in mean income over time. While real income, at best, doubles over two or three decades, the difference between the lowest and the highest income quintiles often reaches a factor of three or more. Furthermore, in Engel-curves referring to the same period, the price-effect as well as the innovation effect is per se excluded.

Curves for cross-sectional expenditure shares tend to shift up and down over time. Changes in sectoral prices affect all households but the response might differ since the price elasticity of demand is not necessarily identical across income groups. Technologically induced changes in the structure of consumption are most likely to also cause a general shift of the respective Engel-curve, although they may reach some income groups earlier than others.

To summarise, the major goal of the following paragraphs consists in identifying possible candidates for subsistence points limiting the share of free income. As mentioned, the income or total expenditure elasticity is the most important indicator required to distinguish necessities from luxuries. Inelastic spending patterns suggest that an essential part of goods or services in the respective group is committed to satisfying basic needs. Another criterion, which is more difficult to examine, is the variance in spending patterns. Those parts of expenditure that are not primarily a matter of choice should display less variance across households in the same income group than spending that is financed out of the free income share.

However, to analyse such expenditure variances requires data about spending patterns of individual households *within* each income group. In fact, one would need the raw data of the surveys to evaluate this issue. A very rough approximation that could instead be used is the volatility of Engel-curves in time. Of course, we have to bear in mind here again the effect of price changes since highly volatile shares caused by highly volatile prices just prove the inelasticity of spending patterns instead of confirming the opposite. Only those frequent ups and downs in cross-sectional Engel-curves that are not caused by price movements indicate a wider range of choice in the spending decision.

Our search for subsistence points will start by reviewing the macroeconomic data about consumption shares and relative prices to get a rough intuition of the general trends. The second step is to analyse cross-sectional spending patterns and their motion, focussing on the slope of the respective Engel-curves and considering their volatility as far as possible.

Paragraph 4.2
Consumption Patterns at the Macroeconomic Level

4.2.1 Consumption Shares and Sectoral Prices in Germany

Macroeconomic time series about sectoral consumption expenditure classified by the COICOP system (and partly more detailed) are provided by the German Statistisches Bundesamt (VGR) from 1970 onwards. Moreover, the German Income and Expenditure Survey (EVS) provides sectoral consumption figures, starting from 1962/63, but is conducted only every five years. Both statistics are comparable, since they employ the same system of classification.

The general trends are in fact similar in both statistics. While the expenditure share of food and clothes, but also of furniture and household appliances has been decreasing, the share of shelter (that includes rents, imputed rents for owner occupied housing, water, electricity, and heating) has strongly shifted upwards. The same is true for the portion of expenditure spent on transportation and communication. The share of entertainment and recreation appears to be more or less identical in the national accounts, but slightly rising in the EVS. The share dedicated to eating out and hotel stays (domestic expenses only) somewhat increases in the national data but has been diminishing since 1978 in the EVS.

With respect to the level of shares and the extent of changes, some remarkable differences occur. The most striking difference emerges with respect to the share of shelter which is rising a great deal more steeply in the survey statistics than in the national average, exhibiting a difference of almost 10 percentage points. Since there are no fundamental differences in the classification system, it would be desirable to know the reason for such a significant gap. Besides sampling errors, one possible source of this deviation could be the fact that the EVS is biased towards middle-class households and excludes the very rich. Since affluent people spend a much smaller part of their budget for things like rents, heating, or electricity, this might push down the national aggregates and could thus partly explain the higher share of those consumption groups in the EVS. However, this fact is hardly sufficient to explain such a strong divergence. Lehmann (2004) investigates this issue extensively but finds no conclusive explanation either. From our point of view and due to the kind of data collection, the share of shelter provided by the EVS is likely to be more realistic than the national accounts.

Another difference concerns the share of food consumption. At almost 30 percent in the 1969 EVS, it is notably higher than the 26 percent displayed in the national statistics for 1970. However, from the mid-seventies on, both series have become similar. The share of communication and transportation is also slightly higher in the EVS.

Let us next have a look at price movements. Changes in relative prices provide an indicator on the extent to which the price level is responsible for shifting consumption shares. Relative sectoral prices are derived by dividing sectoral price indices by the general consumer price index. For Germany, sectoral prices are available from 1962 onwards. However, these German sectoral prices are not available in long-term series classified by a common classification. While prices ordered according to the modern European COICOP system are provided by the Statistisches Bundesamt from 1980 onwards, earlier sectoral prices are sorted by the old SEA 83 standard, which is not entirely comparable with the new system. In SEA 83, for instance, alcoholic drinks and tobacco have been included in the category of food and drinks, most likely pushing its sectoral inflation rate up. The traffic and the communication sector were counted together and personal belongings (covering luxury articles like jewellery, watches etc.) were merged with restaurant and hotel expenses instead of being sorted under miscellaneous. Also the categories of recreation and health expenses were defined on a broader basis in the old system. Shelter was instead defined more narrowly in SEA 83, including only rents, imputed rents and costs of energy. According to COICOP, water and heating expenses are also covered by this category.

Nevertheless, regarding the main categories, the similarities in the classification are stronger than the differences. Thus, we will generally refer to the time series as if they were ordered by a common system. As before, figures up to 1990 refer to West Germany while from 1991 the German data are employed.

Sectoral prices clearly did not move in parallel. We see an over-proportional rise in shelter costs and prices for health care and for medical products. Inflation in the traffic sector has increased over-proportionally, particularly since 1980. The same is true in prices for eating out and hotel stays. On the other hand, prices for food, drinks and clothes, but particularly for durables like household devices and furniture have been rising less than general inflation. The strongest decrease of relative prices has been reported for the communication sector.

The coefficients of correlation between the path of relative prices and the path of the compatible consumption shares are all positive and particularly high for those sectors that are considered necessities such as shelter (0.94) and food (0.93). If we refer to the time period between 1980 and 2010 only in order to exclude the effect of the change from SEA 83 to COICOP, the coefficient of correlation for food (excluding alcohol and tobacco) is as high as 0.99. For traffic and communication we obtain a correlation of 0.81 for the entire range of the series starting from 1970; it is much lower for the period between 1980 and 2010, reflecting the innovations in the communications sector which increased the communication share in spite of falling prices. For clothes, the correlation between consumption share and relative price movements is 0.80. The correlations are significantly smaller for durable goods such as furniture and household devices (0.66) as well as for the entertainment and recreation sector (0.53).

If we regress the respective consumption shares against the path of real income and relative prices, all significant own-price effects are positive, confirming our assumption of rather inelastic spending patterns across the major groups of consumption. The income effects, however, are mostly insignificant; whether they indicate real income elasticities or the influence of other factors remains an open question.

Our hypothesis of a correspondence between sectoral price movements and the historic path of consumption shares is strongly supported by the empirical evidence. However, the correlations should not be overstated since the price effect is definitely not the only cause for changes in the composition of consumption.

4.2.2 Consumption Shares and Sectoral Prices in the U.S.

Let us next have a more detailed look at the macroeconomic data from the United States. The NIPA tables provide figures on sectoral consumption outlay and sectoral prices since 1929. These figures are offered in two different systems of classification over the whole range of time. On the one hand, they are sorted by the *"major type of product"*. On the other hand, the ordering is *"by function"*. (The second categorisation is rather new. Up to 2004, NIPA tables used the categorisation *"major type of expenditure"* instead yet the difference between the two is not fundamental.) While the classification by major type of product concerns general characteristics of the items of consumption like durables, non-durable goods, and services (including several subgroups), the ordering by function or by major type of expenditure is of more interest in our context. It distinguishes the main groups of household expenditure and counts goods and services together under these categories. We focus on the classification by function. Furthermore, we limit our scope to the post-war period.

Survey data about sectoral consumption spending for the U.S. are collected by the Consumer Expenditure Survey (CEX). These data have been publicly available in a common systematic since 1984. Unfortunately, the categorisation of consumption groups in the Consumer Expenditure Survey is not identical to that used in the NIPA tables. Therefore, U.S. national and survey data are not comparable in detail.

If we evaluate the major trends of U.S. consumption shares, the following similarities to the German shares are obvious. The declining food share is one of the common patterns. The same is true with respect to the shrinking portion of outlay dedicated to purchasing clothes, household devices and furniture. In contrast to the German data, the transportation share (including car purchases, car maintenance costs and gasoline, but also expenditure for public transport) stopped increasing in the U.S. around the beginning of the nineteen fifties. This might indicate the higher level of car ownership in the U.S. at that time. More moderate increases in gasoline prices certainly also play a role.

In both U.S. data sets, the shelter share (including electricity, heating, telephone and water supply) is the largest since the beginning of the nineteen eighties. While the share in the CEX has always been rising, the NIPA figures indicate a slightly shrinking trend after 1984. However, we have to bear in mind, that both categories are not defined in the same way: mortgage payments are one major part of housing expenditure in the CEX, while the national accounts calculate rents and so called imputed rents which are frequently suspected to be subject to manipulations. As far as mortgages are indeed used to finance home ownership, which is not necessarily the case as we have seen in the Chapter 1, the CEX might more realistically reflect real housing costs.

The portion of entertainment expenses is more or less constant in the CEX data set, while the NIPA tables—displaying recreation expenditure—show a rising trend. While the share of private health expenditure is quite small (it is calculated without public or private health insurance contributions), it requires about 5 percent of an average U.S. household's budget according to the CEX. The NIPA health share has been rising even faster, currently reaching values of about 20 percent in total consumption; however, this includes all health expenses, regardless of whether they are covered by insurances or not. Thus, the real burden might be lower.

Next, we consider the path of U.S. sectoral prices, which are ordered by the major type of product and by function, i.e. in the same systematic used for classifying the NIPA consumption shares. Yet we have to bear in mind that the definition of the baskets underlying the sectoral price indices does not exactly correspond to the classification of goods and services in the CEX. Hence not every CEX consumption share has a perfectly compatible relative price.

The path of sectoral prices sorted by major type of product is rather clear. While prices for services increased over-proportionally compared to general inflation, relative prices for goods—particularly for durable goods—declined. These divergences reflect a different rate of productivity growth in these areas, although this is probably not the only explanation. The market structure, i.e. the degree of economic power, certainly plays a role. Since the production of many mass-consumption goods, but not the production of services, has shifted to low-wage countries, the location of the production process might also explain this phenomenon.

Analysing the path of sectoral prices sorted by function, we observe relative prices for education, medical care, and personal business rising tremendously. (Personal business includes things like bank service charges, expenses of handling life insurance and pension plans, brokerage charges, legal services, and funeral as well as burial expenses.) The relative price of transportation, which includes gasoline costs, is highly volatile.

As opposed to the German data, the relative price of food and drinks has been rising over-proportionally in the U.S. However, in the NIPA tables, not only tobacco and alcohol, but also prices for outdoor eating are covered by this category. This might explain the different paths. If we look at the relative price of 'food purchased for off-premise consumption' provided by the same NIPA table, it is lower, but recently increasing faster than average inflation. As is the case for Germany, prices for clothes, furniture, household devices and recreation increased under-proportionally.

As a next step, we check the correlations between the time paths of consumption shares and sectoral relative prices in the U.S. The outcome is not as clear-cut as in the German case. While most correlations are positive as expected, only some are really strong. The coefficient of correlation for the clothing share and its relative price is 0.91, for the share of medical care it is 0.98, for personal business it is 0.95, for education it is 0.93 and for furniture and household devices it is 0.97. In the housing sector (calculated by including electricity, heating, water and telephone expenses) the coefficient of correlation between the consumption share and the relative price is only 0.43. A very strong negative correlation (-0.93) is obtained for the sector of recreation, which simply mirrors the correspondence between shrinking relative prices and rising expenses. The correspondence of rising prices and a shrinking consumption share in the food sector also leads to a negative correlation that probably has little to do with real causalities.

Analysing the relationship between these macroeconomic consumption shares and log real income as well as relative sectoral prices, does not however take us far. With the exception of recreation, all significant coefficients for relative prices are positive, confirming the assumption of a low elasticity of substitution across the major consumption groups. The income coefficients, however, are for the most part not convincing and indicate that other factors have influenced the historic consumption paths. An exemption is the share of food, drinks and tobacco with a strongly negative income coefficient. This is in line with the assumption of this sector being dominated by necessities. The clothing share displays a negative income coefficient together with a completely insignificant relative price coefficient.

The relative price effect for housing is also insignificant while the income coefficient is slightly positive. For medical care, both coefficients are positive and significant. However, to interpret medical expenditure as a luxury simply because of the positive income effect is certainly misleading.

The share of furniture and household devices displays a significant positive price but a negative income coefficient that is not really conclusive. For the transportation share, both coefficients are positive and significant. This is true even for the much narrower share of new car purchases. The price elasticity for personal business is insignificant, while the income effect is positive. Recreation, as mentioned, is the only sector that appears to be price elastic, while the income coefficient is also positive. The price effect of education is insignificant.

As expected, these long-run relationships at the macro level hardly allow us to gain further clarity on subsistence points. According to the coefficients of real income, almost all goods except for food, clothing and furniture appear to be luxuries, although logic suggests that purchasing a new cupboard is much more a question of choice than paying for medical aid. Consequently, it is necessary to consider the microeconomic level. Analysing Engel-curves in cross-section will presumably provide more useful insights.

Paragraph 4.3
Consumption Patterns at the Microeconomic Level

4.3.1 Methodological Notes

Cross-sectional Engel-curves can be derived from the data of consumption expenditure surveys. We will mainly refer to the German EVS and to the CEX. A serious issue arises, however, due to the ordering of historic EVS data. While the CEX provides figures about sectoral consumption spending explicitly sorted by (before tax) income quintiles, the EVS data structured by income percentiles are not publicly available. Only in the recent surveys present consumption data referring to income groups (not percentiles). The time series of EVS data are sorted by the social status of the household head or by other criteria—such as the number of persons in a household—which are even less useful for our purpose.

So in drawing conclusions about income elasticities, we will mainly focus on the EVS surveys for 1998 and 2003, since we find information regarding income groups here, and on a set of consumption data provided by the DIW referring to 1974. We will analyse the EVS data for East and West Germany separately since—as we will see—some East German shares, particularly in 1998, are influenced by the event of German unification leading to significant deviations from consumer behaviour in the Western part of the country.

The CEX data are analysed referring to income quintiles and not to relative income since publicly available data are sorted by quintiles. We calculate all consumption shares with respect to total consumption expenditure and not to total income.

We will regress the respective consumption shares against real outlay and relative prices to gain criteria in order to distinguish necessities from luxuries. In concrete terms, we will undertake pooled cross-section and time-series OLS regressions of CEX consumption shares to log real consumption outlay and sectoral relative prices. We will use relative prices from the NIPA tables sorted by function. We have to bear in mind, however, that the variance of relative prices is not very high. Thus, spurious coefficients are possible.

We intentionally use consumption shares and not the logs of the level of the particular expenditure on the left-hand side of our regressions. The underlying assumption of the double-log equation is constant outlay elasticity across income groups, which is not very realistic from our point of view. Additionally, the usual double-log regression has other shortcomings, e.g. it fails to meet the adding-up restriction as stressed by Deaton & Muellbauer (1980). Therefore, using consumption shares as the dependent variable appears to be more appropriate. Of course within this framework, the coefficients cannot be identified with elasticities. Nonetheless, they allow for the distinction between elastic (positive coefficient) and inelastic (negative coefficient) responses to changes in total outlay.

We abstain from undertaking the same regressions employing EVS data, because of the disturbing effect of the ordering by social status. Only four recent surveys are available to search for Engel-curves over relative income, which do not provide sufficient observations to be conclusive.

However, cross-sectional Engel-curves are often not as smooth as they are considered to be in theoretical work. Hence, to look at the curves themselves provides additional information. Therefore, we will comment the curvature of the respective consumption shares over relative income or income quintiles in the text. The associated figures are freely available on the website http://bit.ly/campus39916.

4.3.2 Food

The consumption share of food (including food, drinks, alcohol and tobacco products; Figures I–III on the webseite http://bit.ly/campus39916) is a decreasing function of relative income, which suggests recognising it as a necessity. However, the CEX as well as the 1998 EVS data with respect to East Germany show a rising trend in the lower income groups. This might indicate that among the poorest households inferior foodstuff dominates, while slightly better-off people purchase better quality food, which translates into a higher expenditure share. Interestingly, the East German food share is in general significantly higher than the West German share although the difference became smaller in 2003. This could have been caused, on the one hand, by different dietary habits, since food had been very cheap in the East German past. On the other hand, the over-proportional spending on food by East Germans might also be due to the wide range of products that had not been available before 1990 and are for this very reason consumed in larger amounts. These parts of food expenditure are most unlikely to refer to basic goods. Nevertheless, the general downward slope of the food share confirms its main characteristic as a necessity.

In the CEX data, the slight increase in the food Engel-curve can additionally be traced back to the inclusion of outdoor-food (fast food as well as restaurant meals). Figure IV shows the curve exclusively for food at home. Here, the downward trend is much stronger and the upturn from the first to the second quintile almost completely vanishes.

Generally, the data suggest that purchases of "food at home" are particularly dedicated to satisfying basic needs. This is additionally confirmed by the similar shapes of all curves, which exhibit little variance. This is different for alcoholic beverages (Figure V). Tobacco, on the other hand, also displays a strong downward curve although we hesitate to define smoking as a basic requirement (Figure VI). However, for those people who smoke, the respective expense presumably is not a matter of choice. Unfortunately, in the German statistics expenses for alcoholic drinks are not calculated separately from tobacco consumption. In the early EVS, both categories are simply included in the "food and drinks" category.

Yet since alcoholic drinks together with tobacco products do not account for more than 10 to 15 percent of total food consumption (according to the detailed NIPA tables as well as the CEX), their inclusion probably does not distort the entire path by too much.

The outlay coefficient of the food consumption share is strongly negative. Surprisingly, food consumption appears to be rather price elastic (i.e. the price coefficient is negative); however, this seems to be a spurious result since the relative price variance is low. This can be seen if we regress the food share against total real outlay only, reaching almost the same outlay coefficient (-3.59) and the same fit (R-squared of 0.89 instead of 0.90). Obviously, sectoral prices do not contribute much to explaining changes in the food share over this period. The small volatility of food consumption is confirmed by the high R-squared, meaning that 90 percent of the food share's variance is explained by the variance in total outlay (Regression 27).

As expected, the expenditure inelasticity of "food at home" is even stronger and its unexplained variance is smaller (R-squared of 0.94). The price response is inelastic as expected. Yet the coefficient is insignificant which again might be a consequence of too little variance in relative prices (Regression 28).

For alcoholic beverages, the income elasticity is unclear which is probably a consequence of the highly volatile curves. The own-price response is significantly positive (Regression 29). "Food away from home" qualifies itself as a non-basic good with positive outlay elasticity, although the positive coefficient is very small. The price response is again insignificant (Regression 30). Finally, tobacco products display a significant negative outlay coefficient and a negative price coefficient. Hence, poor people spend a higher share of their income on cigarettes but price increases diminish demand (Regression 31). Hence, we will consider food consumption, particularly consumption of "food at home", to be part of the basic basket.

4.3.3 Shelter

The expenditure for shelter can clearly be identified as a necessity with a strongly decreasing Engel-curve and a rather low variance. This is true for rents as well as for electricity and heating expenses. The upward trend of the shelter share over time is obviously caused by the over-proportional increase in sectoral prices and not by the income effect (Figures VI - XII).

The East German shelter share in 1998 is significantly lower than the West German. This is mainly due to smaller apartments and lower rents in East German areas at that time. The 2003 East German shelter share is somewhat surprising because it actually rises in the two highest quintiles. However, the path might be distorted by statistical errors since a convergence to the shelter share of West Germans is in fact very likely, not only in the low and the high income range but also for middle income earners.

The CEX provides more detailed information about different types of expenditure connected with housing; all curves have the expected shape. They are upward sloping and show a higher variance for personal services, but downward sloping with almost no variance for heating and water expenses.

Mortgage payments are somewhat difficult to deal with since they are definitely necessary expenses, as far as they concern mortgages on own-home purchases, but fall into another category if they are the outcome of refinanced consumer debts. Since the NIPA data do not include mortgage payments but do include imputed rents, the problem does not arise. For the CEX, mortgage payments are part of the shelter share. In fact referring to the CEX, we also include mortgage payments in the shelter share since otherwise an essential part of necessary housing expenses would not be covered and it is not possible to distinguish both kinds of mortgages according to the data.

Regressing the CEX shelter share (rents and mortgage payments only) against total outlay and relative price, confirms shelter as a highly price inelastic necessity. The outlay coefficient is clearly negative while the price coefficient is strongly positive and significant (Regression 32). The same is true with respect to household utilities, such as fuels, water, and telephone (Regression 33). The coefficients are even stronger and the explanatory power with an adjusted R-squared of 0.87 is rather high if we regress the entire share of shelter and energy, heating, telephone and water costs to total outlay and a constructed relative price of all these kinds of expenditure (weighted by NIPA consumption data) (Regression 34).

The general CEX housing share includes some spending that should be considered luxuries. Expenditure on "Other lodges", e.g. holiday homes, belongs to this group as well as personal service. Both shares display significant positive outlay elasticities and negative responses to price changes (Regressions 35 and 36).

Generally, we should consider shelter to include rents, costs of water, electricity, heating and possibly telephone as part of the necessity share. The share of these expenses decreases with income and is much less flexible than most other parts of consumption expenditure. In fact, it is even easier to reduce spending for food and drinks in bad times than to reduce housing expenses in the short term.

4.3.4 Clothing

In contrast to food and shelter, the consumption share of clothes (in Germany including shoes, in the U.S. also including watches, jewellery and some services; see Figures XIII - XVI) does not fit the usual classification as a necessity. Rather, the consumption share strongly rises up to a relative income exceeding the mean (thus, for more than two third of the population). The share decreases slightly—if at all—only in the highest income group. This is a common feature in all German curves.

Furthermore, the East German clothing share from 1998 is significantly higher in the middle quintiles compared to the share in the West, while in 2003 the difference has largely disappeared. The CEX data, referring to apparel and services, are more ambiguous, displaying decreasing curves in some years, constant shares in others, but rising ones at most points in time.

Obviously, a good outfit is more a luxury nowadays for which an increasing share of income is spent if people can afford it. The inevitable basic expenditure is quite small due to a strong fall in prices for simple mass-wear.

The DIW (1978) data provide a separate share of so called personal belongings (watches, jewellery, etc.), which quite clearly displays the performance of luxury goods, rising across the whole range of income. In the CEX data, that category is included in "Other apparel and services", together with shoe repair and laundry; a separate picture is therefore not available.

Our assumption about the share of clothing or "apparel and services" being a luxury is confirmed by the regression. The real outlay coefficient of the clothing share is positive and significant at 0.05 confidence level (Regression 37).

Therefore, we consider the subsistence point in clothing to be very small and will not include expenditure for outfits in our necessity share. The rather strong variance in the shape of the curves additionally supports the assumption of a wide range of choice.

4.3.5 Transportation

With respect to transportation costs (Figures XVII–XXII), the classification is complicated. The curve generally increases with income, while the share is somewhat smaller in the highest income groups. There appears to be a peak among middle income households, (and a first smaller peak in the 2003 EVS data in the low income area). The East German transportation share reaches extremely high values in the upper income groups, which are primarily caused by expenditure for car purchases rather than for maintenance costs. This has to be seen as an effect of German unification. While almost every East German household bought a new car after this event, high income households were able to invest a considerable amount of money into private transportation.

This indicates that the transportation share covers rather different kinds of expenses. On the one hand, vehicle purchases are included. These exhibit the characteristics of a luxury good: the income elasticity strongly exceeds unity and the volatility is high. In contrast, expenditure for car maintenance—fuel, repair, insurance and taxes—is quite basic since a household can hardly avoid such costs except by abstaining from car ownership at all, an unfeasible decision particularly in many U.S. areas.

The CEX as well as the two recent EVS allow calculation of the transportation share without vehicle purchases. (Since East German data are unavailable, we provide the shares for the West and entire Germany.) Now, the increase is less pronounced, while the decrease in income groups beyond the median is even more significant. Additionally, in the case of the CEX, the variance in the shape of the curves is rather small. However, since car purchases are a highly discretionary form of expenditure, the data are possibly not very reliable. In the EVS, for instance, no entry is made for lower income groups and the numbers that are given for the higher percentiles are considered to be subject to a high standard error. In the early EVS surveys expenses for car purchases are not at all published separately.

In the regressions the entire transportation share has the expected positive outlay coefficient and responds inelastically to price changes (Regression 38). Car purchases are strongly income elastic (Regression 39). If we regress the transportation share without car purchases against the same set of variables, the positive income coefficient is reduced from 1.5 to 0.25 and becomes insignificant (Regression 40). If we exclude the poorest quintile from the calculation, we reach a significantly negative outlay coefficient (0.67) and a much better fit, indicated by a doubled R-squared (Regression 41).

Generally, we should assume a considerable part of transportation expenditure not to be a matter of choice in current societies. As a result, we might include transportation expenses in the necessity share (reduced by the expenditure for car purchases as far as the data are available in a reliable fashion, which seems to be the case for the U.S., but not for Germany).

4.3.6 Communication

The share of expenses dedicated to communication displays a clearly decreasing pattern in income, qualifying it as part of basic consumption (Figure XXIII). In the status sorted EVS data as well as in those sorted by relative income, the poorest households display the highest communication share. (In the status sorted data, the second lowest class exhibits an extremely low share, but here the social group is more relevant than income since it covers mainly retirees and pensioners. New communication technologies are under-proportionally used within that group.)

CEX data explicitly referring to communication are not available, thus we cannot perform any regression. Generally, a relevant part of communication expenses should be considered as satisfying basic needs in a modern society.

4.3.7 Furniture and Household Devices

Separate data are provided by the EVS with respect to the expenditure for furniture and household devices (Figure XXIV–XXV) and by the CEX (Figure XXVI) referring to household furnishings as such. All Engel-curves display a rising trend in income. Moreover, the variance of this share is considerably high. The curves shift up and down over time, whereas the sectoral price strictly decreases.

The East German curve in 1998 does not so much increase but is generally considerably higher than the furniture share in the West and both shares in 2003. This is probably still a consequence of German unification and the now wider choices of consumption goods, particularly in this category, that are available to East Germans.

Although the use of certain household devices is a basic requirement of modern life, as in the case of clothes, the quantity and quality of products purchased moves in line with income. The subsistence point, however, can obviously be reached at a small cost. Moreover, it is much easier to delay spending on durables than on food or shelter. This has been confirmed at the macroeconomic level. As shown in the first chapter, durable purchases do vary in time much more than other parts of consumption and respond strongly to the business cycle, thereby, additionally confirming their non-basic nature.

The regression of the CEX furniture shares against outlay and relative prices provides expected results. The outlay coefficient is significantly positive and the same is true for the impact of relative price (Regression 42).

Hence, expenses for furniture and household equipment are not considered to be part of the necessity share.

4.3.8 Health Care

Regarding health expenditure, there are divergent patterns in the U.S. and Germany (Figures XXVII and XXVIII). In fact, health costs displayed by the EVS are for the most part not real costs, but expenses of privately insured persons that are paid back by the insurance. Since in East Germany in 1998, and still in 2003, many fewer people were privately insured than in the West, health expenses were remarkably lower. The German health share rises with income since private insurance is the domain of higher-income earners (or the self-employed).

Due to a number of recent reforms in the health sector in Germany, the share of health costs that actually burden private households, particularly publicly insured families, has been swelling enormously. However, since these two kinds of expenses are collected together, the German health share contains a combination of real and fictive costs and, therefore, cannot be interpreted in a meaningful way.

The situation is different regarding the CEX data. Here the health share in fact covers private costs (including contributions to health insurances). The share clearly shows the pattern of a necessity, displaying income elasticity that is significantly smaller than unity. The path of the curve is dominated by a strong upward trend caused by rapidly rising prices. From the first to the second quintile, the share increases in some years which might be a consequence of the lack of health insurance within a considerable part of the lowest income group.

In the regression, the health care share behaves as expected: it is inelastic with respect to total outlay and even more so with respect to prices. About 90 percent of its variance is explained by these two factors (Regression 43).

For the U.S. we consider health expenses to be part of the basic bundle while we exclude them for Germany due to the noted data problems.

4.3.9 Entertainment and Recreation

The entertainment share (Figures XXIX and XXX), other than might have been expected, is rather flat displaying high values in low income groups and a significant variance in the second quintile.

In Germany, one reason for the high level in the lowest group might be public television contributions, which cover a relevant part of entertainment expenses in poorer households.

The shape of the CEX curves indicates that the expenditure, in part, is also necessary. However, in the regression, entertainment exhibits a significant positive outlay coefficient while the price coefficient is insignificant (Regression 44). Moreover, in the U.S. as well as in Germany the national statistics display a strictly higher entertainment and recreation share compared to surveys that are biased towards the middle-class.

For these reasons, we consider an important portion of this expenditure to be dedicated to luxury consumption. Therefore, we will not include spending for entertainment and recreation in the necessity share. However, we have to bear in mind that a certain part of these expenses cannot be adequately understood as a luxury.

4.3.10 Education

The expenditure share for education (Figure XXXI and XXXII) is quite interesting since it displays unexpectedly high values in the lowest income groups in Germany as well as in the U.S. The share has shifted upwards significantly between 1998 and 2003 in Germany reflecting higher private payments for school equipment and rising university fees.

The high education share in low income groups may be strengthened by the fact that most students belong to these groups. However, this is by far not a full explanation as can be seen in the status sorted EVS curves. They show that unemployed people in particular face high costs for education relative to their income. Thus, despite the high values in the upper income group, a considerable share of education expenses is certainly not a matter of choice.

The regression provides a significant negative outlay coefficient confirming education as a necessity. The relative price coefficient is strongly positive, i.e. demand is rather price inelastic (Regression 45). Hence, we include education expenses in the necessity share.

4.3.11 Restaurants and Hotels

The share of expenses dedicated to attending restaurants and hotels exhibits the expected rising pattern (Figures XXXIII and XXXIV). The CEX provides data for eating out as a subcategory of food spending which we have already considered. It too is smoothly rising.

Consequently, spending in restaurants and hotels are qualified as a luxury and not included in the necessity share. (This qualification is questionable for that part of eating out concerned with fast food chains or take away shops. The very flat curve for the U.S. indicates that the expenditure share for eating out does not vary a lot across the various income groups.)

Paragraph 4.4 Summary:
The Historic Path of the Necessity Share

4.4.1 What Belongs in the Necessity Basket?

After analysing the details of consumption patterns, we have a better understanding which expenditure categories can be adequately grasped as dominated by basic consumption and which should be understood as luxury spending.

The outcome of our analysis can be summarised as follows: the expenditure categories of food (excluding eating out, particularly in restaurants), shelter (including all costs of housing, namely rents, imputed rents or mortgage payments, costs of heating, electricity and water supply), communication and education share the feature of being necessities. They all display outlay elasticities smaller than unity and, for the most part, low volatility of spending patterns over time. Although these expenditure categories undeniably include also luxury spending, we consider their subsistence points to be relatively high. Therefore, these categories are understood to be dominated by basic needs and, hence, to be part of the necessity basket.

Due to the considered data problems in Germany, only health expenditure in the U.S. belongs to the basic basket. The transportation share –excluding vehicle purchases as far as possible—will also be understood as part of basic expenditure. (As we are referring to surveys, we have to treat the transportation share excluding new cars very carefully since car purchases are highly discretionary and data for narrowly defined household groups might not be reliable. This seems to be particularly true for the German data.)

In contrast, spending for clothes, furniture, household devices, entertainment, recreation, restaurants and hotels (and possibly car purchases) is qualified as luxury consumption despite some basic expenses that are also covered by these categories. Since these kinds of expenditure rise over-proportionally with income, their subsistence points are considered to be low. Furthermore, the time of purchase of most of these goods is widely a matter of choice.

As already considered in the first section of this chapter, the categorisation used here is approximate. Neither the whole amount spent on items considered as necessities satisfy basic needs nor does every expense for items considered luxuries appropriately match the features of luxury consumption. People certainly need clothes as well as certain household devices. Furthermore, we have referred to the public television contributions appearing in the entertainment share in Germany.

On the other hand, a considerable proportion of expenditure by wealthier people on food and drinks is certainly not dedicated to satisfying basic needs. Undoubtedly, one could improve the categorisation by using more disaggregated figures if they were available in both a reliable fashion and common systematic. However, for the time being we will deal with this general classification in order to investigate whether this approach is able to contribute to an explanation of saving rate differentials in cross-section and over time. If we are successful, one might think about further refinements.

4.4.2 First Approach to the Necessity Share

In the first section of this chapter we considered two possibilities to approach the time path of the necessity share $cc^*(t)$. The first was simply to add expenditure categories that can be qualified as dominated by basic consumption and to calculate the share of such purchases in total consumption outlay. (We rejected using income as the point of reference to obtain a variable that is in any respect independent from saving.) The second approach was to calculate the rate of excess basic growth and of excess basic inflation and to compute the motion of the necessity share in line with these rates from a given initial value onwards.

Thus, based on our first definition we will calculate the time path of the necessity share from the addition of the shares of the following expenditure categories in total consumption outlay:

Germany:

- VGR necessity share $(c1^*_{VGR})$: food and drinks; shelter (rents, imputed rents, water supply, electricity, heating); communication; transportation; and education. Additionally we include insurance costs, which are listed under "other expenses" and are also certainly necessary.
- EVS necessity share $(c1^*_{EVS})$ same categories without insurance costs.
  (Source: VGR, EVS)

United States:

- NIPA necessity share $(c1^*_{NIPA})$: food and beverages purchased for off-premises consumption; tobacco; housing (incl. rents, imputed rents, water supply, electricity, heating); communication; transportation (excluding new car purchases); health care; education; and insurance costs.
- CEX necessity share $(c1^*_{CEX})$: food at home; tobacco products; shelter (including rents and mortgage payments, without other lodging); utilities, fuels and public services; transportation (without vehicle purchases); health care; and education.
  (Source: NIPA, CEX)

Generally, the necessity share calculated by adding consumption shares is denoted by the symbol $c1^*$. As mentioned above, from the U.S. NIPA tables, data on the details of consumption expenditure are available for the entire period starting from 1929. However, to exclude the extreme volatility of macroeconomic data during Great Depression and World War II, we do not perform any calculation for the period before 1950. U.S. survey data from the Consumer Expenditure Survey (CEX) are available from 1984. For Germany, the required figures from the National Accounts have been publicly available since 1970. The Income and Consumption Survey (EVS) provides data from 1962/63 at five-year intervals. As before, data up to 1990 concern West Germany only.

To check the robustness of the relationship between saving and necessity spending we additionally calculate a luxury share from the same sources. The luxury share includes:

Germany:

- VGR luxury share: clothes and shoes; household furnishing and equipment; entertainment and recreation; hotels and restaurants; personal belongings (jewellery, watches, luxury articles, etc.).
- EVS luxury share: same categories without personal belongings.
  (Source: VGR, EVS)

United States:

- NIPA luxury share: clothing, footwear, and related services; furnishings, household equipment; recreation; food services and accommodation; and personal items (jewellery, watches, etc.).
- CEX luxury share: other lodging; household furnishings and equipment; apparel and services; vehicle purchases, and entertainment.
  (Source: NIPA, CEX)

The constructed luxury share and the necessity share do not add to unity since ambiguous spending categories are excluded by both. Therefore, a separate check of the correlation between saving rate and luxury share might provide additional information. According to our model predictions, the saving rate should be negatively correlated to the necessity share but positively correlated to the luxury share. The prediction of the standard models, in contrast, is more the opposite since saving and luxury consumption are considered to be substitutes.

4.4.3 Second Approach to the Necessity Share

The necessity share calculated according to our second definition is symbolised by $c2^*$. To reveal its time path, we have to operationalize the rate of excess basic growth and the rate of excess basic inflation. In order to define the first rate, we stick to our assumption that the necessity basket, in quantitative terms, follows long-term trends of income growth. Let us suppose the growth rate of the necessity basket equals a 10-year moving average of (previous) real income growth per head. Hence, the rate of excess basic growth corresponds to the difference between this trend and current income growth. If current income growth is lower than its previous

10-year average, excess basic growth will be positive, and negative if current income growth exceeds its trend.

To define the rate of excess basic inflation, we have to determine which sectoral price indexes should be included in the basic price index. Since sectoral price data are even more difficult to collect than sectoral consumption expenditure data, and are noisier than the latter, we will include only the major basic expenditure categories. For Germany we will include the sectoral price index for food, shelter (including rents, imputed rents, energy, water and heating costs), traffic and communication. As weights we use the VGR consumption shares since the EVS shares are not available annually. The rate of basic price inflation is the weighted sum of these specific inflation rates. The rate of excess basic inflation is obtained by subtracting general consumer price inflation from the rate of basic price inflation.

For the U.S., the basic price index is similarly defined: we include food, housing (including rents, imputed rents, electricity, water, heating, telephone), transportation, health and education. The exclusion of health expenditure for Germany has already been justified above. Educational expenses are included for the U.S. since they presently require more than 2 percent of an average U.S. household's budget. For Germany the respective proportion has always been below 1 percent so it does not have a significant influence on the index anyhow. The respective NIPA consumption shares are employed as weights since CEX data do not start before 1984.

For Germany, reliable data for income, growth and saving are not available before 1950. The time-series for excess basic growth could consistently start 10 years later. Yet the German consumption shares that we need as weights for the rate of excess basic inflation are not available before 1970. Therefore, all calculations of the German $c2^*$ refer to the period between 1970 and 2010. Computations of the U.S. necessity share $c2^*$ concern the period between 1955 and 2009.

To simulate the time path of the necessity share we finally have to assume an initial value. We use 50 percent in both cases. In cross-section, this is often the relative income position below which households do not save. In Kuznets' (1953) data set for 1950, the group with a relative income of 0.5 dissaved, while the next group with a relative income of 0.75 saved.

Of course, one might argue that the choice of 50 percent as the initial value is rather arbitrary. However, the initial value of the necessity share is not decisive for the result of the tests of our model predictions. The initial value determines the absolute level of $c2^*$ exclusively; however, the level neither plays a role for the general results of the regressions, nor does it control the fit of the simulations carried out in the previous chapter. In all cases, it is only the curvature of $c2^*$ that matters.

To get an intuition of similarities and divergences of the paths, we plot the three necessity shares derived for each country: first, $c1^*_{VGR}$ calculated by adding the respective expenditure shares from the National Accounts, second, $c1^*_{EVS}$ using survey data, and, third, $c2^*$ moving in line with the rate of excess basic growth and excess basic inflation. Comparing these paths is not a test of the actual relevance of the two excess basic variables. In fact, it remains an open question whether the necessity share measured by adding expenditure categories or the share that grows in line with the rates of excess basic inflation and excess basic growth, is a better approximation of the real necessity share.

Since the levels of all shares are necessarily different, we do not use the same scale for the various curves. (That's why three numbers in parallel are plotted on the x-axis of the graph. Each number refers to one of the curves. The ordering of the curves is the same as below the figure.) The main point we intend to evaluate by the graph is whether shares that are calculated in different ways display common trends and where major differences lie.

Figure 16 provides the results for Germany. Scrutinising these paths, it is obvious that the German necessity share $c1^*$ from the EVS ($c1^*_{EVS}$) starts at a similar level as the necessity share from the VGR ($c1^*_{VGR}$). The former, however, increases much stronger, starting from the beginning of the nineteen nineties. Recalling the previous paragraph, we actually discovered a significant divergence in the path of the shelter share and—less significantly—the food share between survey and VGR data in Germany. Since both types of expenditure belong in the necessity basket, these divergences are reflected in the path of the necessity share.

The path of the necessity share $c2^*$, in fact, corresponds much more closely to $c1^*_{EVS}$ than to $c1^*_{VGR}$. $c2^*$ rises somewhat steeper than $c1^*_{EVS}$, indicating that the assumption of the necessity basket to growth according to a 10-year average of income growth might be slightly strong.

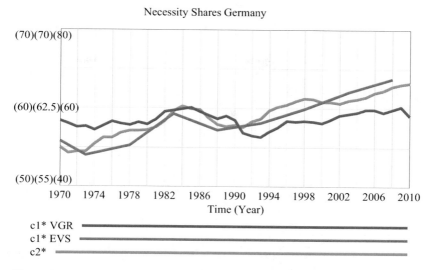

Figure 16. German Necessity Share, Source: destatis, EVS

Irrespective of this difference, the general curvature of $c1^*_{EVS}$ and $c2^*$ is very similar. This can be confirmed by checking their respective correlations. While the coefficient of correlation between $c1^*_{VGR}$ and the simulated share $c2^*$ is as low as 0.56, and the correlation between $c1^*_{VGR}$ and $c1^*_{EVS}$ (computed for those years, in which EVS data are available) is 0.63, $c1^*_{EVS}$ and $c2^*$ are linked by a coefficient of correlation of 0.96.

Among the common trends of all shares is a rising trend in the second half of the seventies up to a first peak in the mid-eighties, followed by a falling trend until the beginning of the nineties and an upturn since 1995. One obvious difference between $c1^*_{VGR}$ and the other two shares is the sudden drop of the former in 1991. In this year, figures for all of Germany are applied for the first time and $c1^*_{VGR}$ jumps downwards due to extremely low basic prices (rents, energy, water, etc.) in the Eastern part of the country. $c2^*$ is influenced also by a negative rate of excess basic inflation but the lower income per head due to the inclusion of the East made the rate of excess basic growth strongly positive and balanced the influence of the inflation variable. Since $c2^*$ covers the income difference, it reflects the path of the real necessity share in this year probably better than $c1^*_{VGR}$. (The EVS is only conducted for 1988 and 1993; hence, the transition from West German to German figures is smoothed.)

Next, let us take a look at the necessity share in the respective approximations for the United States. Figure 17 provides the result of our calculations.

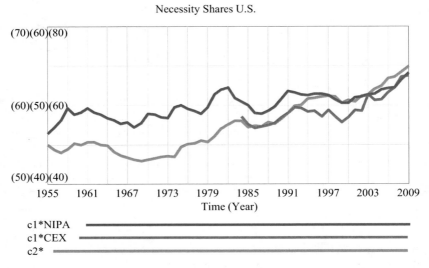

Figure 17. U.S. Necessity Share, Source: NIPA, CEX

Again, $c2^*$ is more compatible with the CEX necessity share $c1^*$ $(c1^*_{CEX})$ than with the $c1^*$ from the National Accounts $(c1^*_{NIPA})$. The curve of $c2^*$ appears to be somewhat too steep also in the case of the U.S. The general trends, however, are similar. All three shares indicate a temporary low in the eighties and a rising trend since the second half of the nineties.

The coefficient of correlation is quite high for all relationships. While $c1^*_{NIPA}$ and $c2^*$ are correlated by a coefficient of 0.86, the correlation between $c1^*_{CEX}$ and $c2^*$ is 0.90. $c1^*_{NIPA}$ and $c1^*_{CEX}$ are correlated by a coefficient of 0.96.

This suggests that consumption data from the National Accounts are generally a less reliable source to approach the necessity share compared to either survey data or the calculation of $c2^*$ using detailed price and growth figures.

4.4.4 The Individual Necessity Share

Some final remarks are necessary concerning the individual necessity share that we use to check our model predictions at the microeconomic level. The individual necessity share was defined in Chapter 3 in reference to the mean necessity share assuming that it depends on the general standard of living in a country at a given point in time. The formula provided there was:

$$cc_j^*(t) = \frac{C^*(t)}{Y_j(t)} = \frac{cc^*(t)}{y_j(t)}$$

Since we only deal with approximations for $cc^*(t)$, $cc_j^*(t)$ has to be also approximated. We use one of the two approximations of the mean necessity share, $c1^*$ or $c2^*$ and divide it by the household's relative income.

One might consider another way to approximate the individual necessity share. Similar to the computation of $c1^*$, one could add *income-group specific* consumption expenditure for those groups of goods and services that we have considered to be necessities and calculate the share of this basic expenditure in *income-group specific* consumption outlay.

The share of basic expenditure in total outlay calculated in such a way shrinks with a rising relative income position. Changes of this share over time might, indeed, indicate changes in the individual necessity share. Nevertheless, such a share does not only reproduce the shortcomings of the macro necessity share $c1^*$; even more serious distortions have to be expected.

The reason is as follows: the categorisation distinguishing necessities from luxuries for deriving $c1^*$ was approximate. The criterion was to qualify such expenditure categories as part of the necessity share, categories which are *dominated* by basic needs, and to exclude those in which luxury spending constitutes the major part. We acknowledged that such a definition of the necessity share also contains luxury spending; vice versa, the luxury expenditure groups contain elementary expenses. Yet insofar as the qualification as necessity or luxury reflects the major part of spending in the respective expenditure category, the characterisation appears to be justified.

However, it is more than questionable whether this approach is applicable to the micro level of income-group specific expenditure shares. The composition of the respective shares out of necessary or luxury consumption goods certainly differs according to income groups. For instance, those expenditure categories that we consider to be dominated by luxuries for the average household most likely contain mainly basic goods for low-income families. (We have already considered the dominance of public television contributions as a major part of the recreation share of poorer families in Germany. Similarly, low-income earners need from time to time new clothes or a new washing machine if the old one is broken. Such expenditure can hardly be understood as luxury spending.) Therefore, the share of basic expenditure categories in individual consumption outlay definitely underestimates the real necessity share for low-income households.

In fact, the share of basic expenditure groups in total outlay can never exceed unity and will hardly ever approach unity for the simple reason that some spending is indispensable for other expenditure groups, even by the poorest households. At the same time, the share of basic expenditure groups surely overestimates the individual necessity share of the rich as their spending for apparent necessities (food, drinks, etc.) includes a remarkable, perhaps a dominant, proportion of luxury consumption.

If we compare the two shares per income group, the individual necessity share (approximated by dividing the mean necessity share by individual relative income) is indeed a great deal higher in the bottom range of the income scale compared to the share of basic expenditure groups in their total consumption outlay. In contrast, the former is lower than the latter in the upper income groups.

From our point of view, the individual necessity share derived from the mean necessity share ($c1^*$ or $c2^*$) is a better approximation of real individual subsistence needs and, hence, the more appropriate variable to understand saving decisions. Therefore, when we talk about the individual necessity share in the next chapter, it will be from this understanding.

A rule to predict individual saving rates that refers to the mean necessity share and relative income has, in addition, a number of practical advantages compared to a formula that requires calculating income-group specific basic expenditure shares. Since reliable disaggregated consumption expenditure data for each relative income group are often simply not available, a formula that exclusively refers to the mean necessity share has a much wider range of application. Finally, this approach is more satisfying from a theoretical point of view. If we define the individual necessity share in reference to the mean, the distinction between saving and non-saving households follows naturally from the assumption that all those households at a relative income position below the mean necessity share dissave, while all others save. We will see in the next chapter that this almost perfectly matches the actual distinction between savers and non-savers. In contrast, nobody can ever reach a share of basic expenditure in total consumption outlay that exceeds unity. Predicting saving rates by this share therefore requires defining a limit, and to assume that households save if their share is below this limit and dissave in the opposite case. To set such a limit, however, is rather arbitrary. Also for these reasons, we will continue to define the individual necessity share in reference to the mean necessity share.

On some occasions, however, the share of basic expenditure categories in individual outlay will also be analysed. Although this share underestimates real basic spending, it might provide additional information. Under very special circumstances, the mean necessity share might not be the adequate reference point, for instance, when different parts of a country are simply not linked sufficiently to refer to the same mean. Remarkably, different individual shares of some basic expenditure categories are an indicator for such a situation. One example is Germany during the years immediately after unification.

The concept of an individual necessity share c_j^* derived from the mean necessity share is based on the assumption of a common necessity basket that is not significantly influenced by the respective household's income position. It has already been mentioned that such an approach only roughly approximates reality. Required expenditure is certainly not completely independent from income. Therefore, the real necessity share curve over relative income is possibly somewhat less concave than our formula suggests.

Nonetheless, we maintain our hypothesis, that the crucial determinant of individual saving behaviour is the individual necessity share derived from the mean necessity basket c_j^*.

Chapter 5. Does Our Model Match the Facts?

Paragraph 5.1
Model Predictions and the Stylised Facts
of Saving

The predictions of a model built on the hypothesis that basic needs, dependent on the general standard of living in the respective country, limit the ability of an individual consumer to save are the following. First, in cross-section, saving rates should be a strictly rising function of relative income since the free income share rises with a household's current income position as does the possibility to save. For the same reason, saving rates should increase with the level of permanent income. Since the free income share of low-income consumers will be enduringly low or absent, they will save almost nothing over their life span.

Second, in the long run and across countries, we should miss a significant correlation between real income and saving. However, since the subsistence point most likely covers average income almost completely in very poor countries, such countries should display particularly low saving rates. Only if countries overcome this destitute status, a free income share arises and saving will occur at significant rates. Beyond a certain level income should stop boosting saving since the necessity basket also starts to grow with a rising standard of living.

Third, saving rates at the macro level should be positively correlated to growth since periods of high income growth are most likely those in which current income growth exceeds its long run trend and the rate of excess basic growth is negative.

Fourth, if basic price inflation exceeds general inflation the saving rate should, *ceteris paribus*, shrink; saving by lower-income households should be particularly diminished. As far as determinants of the necessity share are more volatile than factors influencing the propensity to save (which is very likely), saving rates of low-income households should be more volatile over time than saving rates of rich consumers. At a given point in time, however, the variance of saving rates within a certain income group should be smaller in the lower deciles than in the higher deciles since for the first the trade-off between consumption and saving is much less a matter of choice.

These predictions almost perfectly correspond to the stylised facts of saving as considered in the first chapter. We found a strong positive link between saving rates and relative income, and the saving rate-relative income curve had mainly a concave shape. We reviewed the literature confirming a positive influence of income growth on saving. The relationship between saving rates and real income was corroborated to be very weak, more significant in low- and middle-income countries than in the OECD-sample. It was explicitly confirmed that between a low- and a middle income country, higher income is linked to higher saving rates while beyond a certain level this relationship disappears. Finally, considering the German, U.S. and the Mexican example we have shown that saving rates of lower income percentiles are indeed more volatile over time compared to saving rates of the affluent. At a given point in time, there was evidence of a lower variance of saving rates across households in the low-income deciles.

But there is even more empirical evidence that can be explained by our model. As mentioned, one should suppose a variance of $\alpha 1$ and $\alpha 2$ in relation to the business cycle. According to our model, rising uncertainty during a business low only increases the saving rate if its positive effect on the propensity to save is not cancelled out by a decrease of the free income share. Hence, recessions with rising saving rates should occur particularly when the mean necessity share is relatively low. In fact, such recessions happened in Germany during the mid-seventies and early eighties when the necessity share was at its lowest level.

Finally, our model provides an explanation for the negative relationship between the saving rate and inequality in developed countries. As we have seen, its prediction is that rising inequality diminishes the personal saving rate if the propensity to dissave exceeds the propensity to save. It is very likely that the first is higher in developed than in developing countries for several reasons. Higher levels of existing wealth certainly make it easier to dissave or to access to credit. It was the extreme peak in property prices in the U.S.—together with a deregulated credit market and low interest rates—that opened the possibility of refinancing and enlarging consumer credit by new mortgages on the existing homes of millions of U.S. citizens. A poor citizen of, say, Mexico City has probably fewer possibilities of getting into extended debt. Furthermore, we have to bear in mind that financial markets in the developed world were deregulated only during the previous decades. This is an additional factor that should be considered to facilitate credit access and increase the propensity to dissave.

Hence, our approach is able to explain a number of stylised facts that presented the traditional models with serious difficulties in providing a consistent justification. Varying basic needs are surely not the only possible explanation. But they are indeed a comprehensive one.

All these considerations suggest that the time path of the necessity share contributes to an explanation of saving rate differentials. To test the strength of the relationship we have to go into the details of empirical data at the micro and macro level: this is the purpose of the remainder of this chapter. We start by analysing cross-sectional saving rates as provided by the recent German EVS surveys and check whether our approach contributes to a better understanding of saving behaviour. Then we do the same with the U.S. cross-sectional saving rates collected by Kuznets (1953) over a number of years in the first half of the 20th century.

Afterwards, we switch to the macro level. Here, we test the correlations between the time path of the necessity share in its various definitions and changes in the personal saving rate. Finally, we reproduce the historic path of the personal saving rate for the U.S. and for Germany by our saving rule and compare this simulation to the real path.

Paragraph 5.2
Model Predictions and Empirical Evidence at the Microeconomic Level

5.2.1 The Necessity Share and German Saving Rates

A general match between the empirical facts and the predictions of our model is necessary but not sufficient to confirm our approach. Therefore, we will scrutinise in detail to what degree individual saving behaviour can be reproduced by our rule of thumb.

To obtain German saving data in cross-section, we employ the recent Income and Consumption Surveys (EVS of 1993, 1998, 2003 and 2008). Unfortunately, these are the only EVS's providing information about relative income groups, while data from the earlier surveys are available only under other types of ordering (social status, household type, etc.). The EVS consumption as well as the income and saving figures are generally considered to be reliable.

In Chapter 3, we suggested following a simple rule of thumb guiding individual saving decisions:

$$s_j(t) = \begin{cases} \alpha 1(t)\left(1 - cc_j^*(t)\right), & \quad if \quad cc_j^*(t) \leq 1 \\ \alpha 2(t)\left(1 - cc_j^*(t)\right), & \quad if \quad cc_j^*(t) > 1 \end{cases}$$

$$(5.1)$$

In this formula, $cc_j^*(t)$ denotes the individual necessity share in income. In the previous chapter, we argued that this share can be best approximated by the ratio of the mean necessity share to individual relative income. Thus, individual saving is considered to be positive if individual income is higher than that required to purchase a common basket of necessary goods and services defined for a certain country at a given point in time. If individual income is lower than the current value of this basket, the consumer is assumed to dissave.

We apply this formula to reproduce individual saving rates. We start with the mean necessity share $c1^*$ computed from EVS consumption data as defined above ($c1^*_{EVS}$). We refer to the EVS necessity share since we deal with EVS cross-sectional saving rates. The calculated values for $c1^*_{EVS}$ in consumption outlay were 61.15 percent in 1993, 62.40 percent in 1998, 63.90 percent in 2003 and 65.26 percent in 2008. For comparison, $c1^*_{VGR}$ was 56.32 percent in 1993, 58.34 percent in 1998, 59.28 percent in 2003 and 59.74 percent in 2008. So $c1^*_{VGR}$ was clearly lower than $c1^*_{EVS}$, but displayed the same positive trend. The share $c2^*$ was 57.3 percent in 1993. This level is similar to $c1^*_{VGR}$, but it rose much more strongly, reaching the level of $c1^*_{EVS}$ of 65.4 percent in 2008.

To obtain the mean necessity share in income we calculate:

$$cc1^*(t) = \big(1 - s(t)\big)c1^*_{EVS}(t)$$

$$(5.2)$$

The reference to the mean necessity share in income is unproblematic in this case since we use this share exclusively for a prediction of cross-sectional saving rates and not for an explanation of aggregated saving rates and their change in time.

$\alpha 1$ is set to 0.25 and $\alpha 2$ to half of it. Calculating the saving rates for 1993, 1998, 2003 and 2008 by our model, and comparing them to the real rates, gives the paths provided by Figures 18–21 (*real sr* denotes the saving rate that is provided by statistical data, while *model sr* stands for the saving rate predicted by our model) .

Obviously, the mean necessity share $cc1^*$ derived from adding the respective EVS expenditure categories and calculating their share in mean income is quite close to the relative income position separating saving from non-saving households. This indicates, that $c1^*\_EVS$ is probably not too bad an approximation of the real necessity share. Moreover, the upturn of the necessity share corresponds to a general downward trend in saving rates, notably for households at the lower end of the earnings scale.

This particular negative trend of the saving rate of poorer households is even more visible in Figure 22, which provides a comparison of the real cross-sectional saving rates in the respective years.

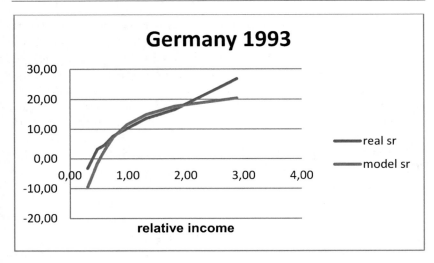

Figure 18. Model Saving Rates 1993, Source: EVS

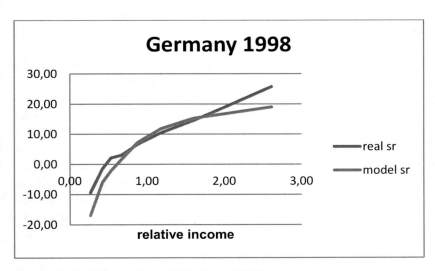

Figure 19. Model Saving Rates 1998, Source: EVS

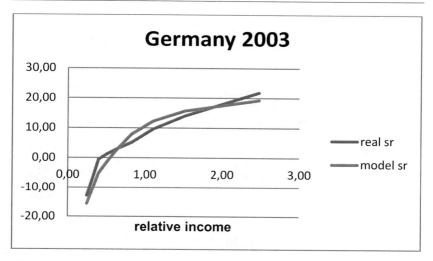

Figure 20. Model Saving Rates 2003, Source: EVS

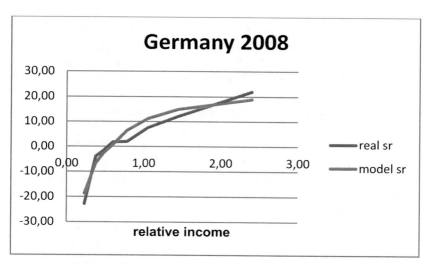

Figure 21. Model Saving Rates 2008, Source: EVS

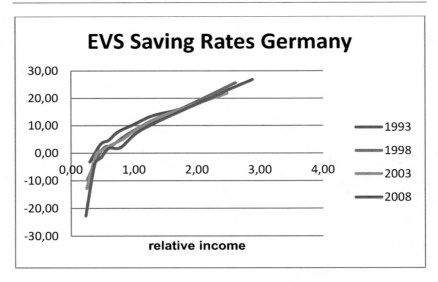

Figure 22. EVS Saving Rates 1993–2008, Source: EVS

Clearly, the rising necessity share diminishes saving in lower income groups much more strongly than at the top of the income scale.

Of course, it is obvious from Figures 18–21 that the simulated saving curve is a little too concave. Saving rates in the middle income range are somewhat overestimated while the highest income group saves more eagerly than our model predicts. This suggests that the assumption of a linear relationship between the free income share and saving is perhaps an over simplification. Saving might not correspond to a fix proportion of free income, but the share possibly increases in the upper income range. However, considering the very simple rule we used, the general match between model and real saving in cross-section and in trend between 1993 and 2008 is noteworthy.

Our approach is able to provide an explanation for a number of additional empirical facts. These concern the separate results of the surveys for East and West German households. If we calculate separately the East and West German saving rates for 1993, 1998, 2003 and 2008, again employing the necessity share $c1^*_{EVS}$, the outcome is highly interesting. In fact, we calculate these saving rates by a simplified formula that is directly derived from the formula used to predict the saving rates of different income groups:

$$s_{West}(t) \approx \alpha 1 \left(1 - \frac{c1^*_{EVS}(t)}{y_{West}(t)} \right)$$

resp.

$$s_{East}(t) \approx \alpha 1 \left(1 - \frac{c1^*_{EVS}(t)}{y_{East}(t)} \right)$$

Hence, we refer to East and West Germans as if they correspond to two distinct income groups defined by their relative income with respect to the German mean. Of course, this formula is a simplification since in both parts of Germany there are better-off households as well as low-income families and the latter are possibly dissaving. But if we assume the propensity to dissave equals the propensity to save, we can deal with this simplified rule.

Since we refer to a number of years, we do not use $cc1^*$ in this case but $c1^*$. We assume a propensity to save of 0.3 (since $c1^*$ is smaller than $cc1^*$). Predicting the average East and West German saving rate by this formula, we obtain the results provided in Table 3.

It is obvious that the match for West Germany is quite close. The difference to the real value of the saving rate is much less than 1 percentage point in all years and the negative trend of saving is perfectly covered. However, if we use the same rule for East Germany, the match is remarkably worse with a deviation of more than 7 percentage points in 1993 and about 5 percentage points in 1998.

Year	Model saving rate (West)	Real saving rate (West)	Diff.	Model saving rate (East)	Real saving rate (East)	Diff.
1993	12.79	13.29	-0.5	4.72	12,35	-7,63
1998	12.10	12.07	0,03	5.91	10,99	-5,08
2003	11.66	11.77	-0,11	5.87	9,45	-3,58
2008	11.35	10.96	0,39	4.98	9,29	-4,31

Table 3. Model Predictions East/West, Source: EVS

Even after the turn of the millennium, the fit does not become any more convincing. Thus, East German saving rates are strikingly underestimated by our model, particularly in the nineteen nineties. Moreover, the model predicts increased saving efforts between 1993 and 2008, while the real saving rate of East Germans declined. Hence, to simply assume a higher propensity to save for the Eastern part of Germany does not solve the puzzle. Does our model suggest a reason for the serious failure to reproduce East German saving rates?

We believe it does. In line with our general saving rule, we used the mean German necessity share as point of reference. However, we already considered in Chapter 4 that particular cases may exist for which the reference to the mean standard of living is not the adequate approach. In fact, German unification brought together people from completely different social environments and with diverging social experiences. This event took place just three years before 1993 and eight years before 1998. Even after the turn of the millennium, the living conditions in the Eastern and the Western part of Germany were still very distinct. Some of the discrepancies had become smaller, but had not disappeared. Moreover, East Germans situated in the higher income range after 1990 had experienced incomparably stronger income growth than the typical West German at the same income position.

For these reasons it is more than questionable to presume East and West German households have the same necessity basket in 1998, not to mention 1993. Instead, significant East-West-differences in the volume and value of the necessity basket still have to be considered for 2003 and 2008. Consequently, the reference to a common German necessity share is simply not justified. Since the German mean is dominated by expenditure patterns of the West, this was not a problem for predicting saving rates in that part of the country. But for the East, the approach had to fail.

If we calculate the East and the West necessity shares $c1^*$ for the year 1993 separately, they are almost identical with 61.15 percent and 61.38 percent respectively. When assuming a common necessity basket, however, the necessity share of a typical East German household should by far exceed the share of an average household in the West since the average relative income position of East Germans (in relation to the German mean) was as low as 0.73 compared to 1.07 for West Germans in 1993. In 1998 this value was 0.79 in the East compared to 1.05 in the West. These exact values continued to exist in 2003 and 2008. Hence, our model, calculating the East German necessity share by the German mean necessity share and the relative income position of East Germans, widely overestimates real East German necessity spending and slightly underestimates the income share required for basic needs in the West.

To become clearer about necessity spending in East and West Germany, let us take a look at the shelter share, the main part of the necessity share. The shelter share includes outlay for rents, heating, water and electricity, spending categories that are undoubtedly basic and mainly fixed. Here, the difference between East and West in 1993 is striking. While the shelter share occupied 27.2 percent of consumption outlay in the West, it was only 22.1 percent in the East.

The shelter share later increased tremendously in East and West. In this process the difference became smaller, but was still noticeable in 1998 with a shelter share of 32.2 percent in the West and 29.9 percent in the East. Actually, eight years after unification typical East Germans still lived in smaller apartments or houses compared to West Germans. Furthermore, rents were on average somewhat lower in the East. In 2003, the shelter share became almost identical in both parts of the country at about 32 percent. Yet we have to take into account that it was 32 percent of a still much lower average consumption level in the East. Hence, in absolute terms average shelter spending was still significantly lower in the East part of the country. Figures 23–25 show the shelter share over relative income for both parts of the country in 1993, 1998 and 2003.

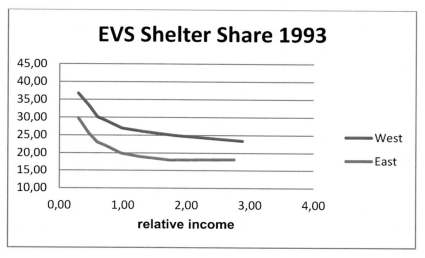

Figure 23. EVS Shelter Share 1993, Source: EVS

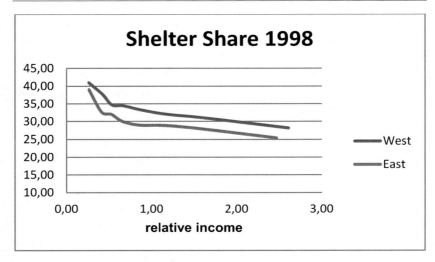

Figure 24. EVS Shelter Share 1998, Source EVS

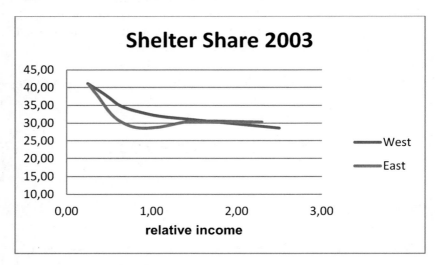

Figure 25. EVS Shelter Share 2003, Source: EVS

Obviously, the proportion of shelter expenditure in the total outlay of East German households is still noticeably lower in 1998 at each relative income position. This corresponds perfectly to the fact that in each relative income group in the East saving is significantly higher compared to the West.

Some convergence of the shelter share in the higher income range is visible only in 2003.

Based on these considerations, the solution to the German savings puzzle is easily found. Due to serious differences between the average standard of living in the East and in the West of Germany, a presupposed common German necessity basket is simply the wrong reference point. If we amend our formula, eliminating all references to the German mean, the East German saving rate in 1993 and 1998 can be predicted almost perfectly. We just have to employ the East German necessity share $c1^*_{EVS\_East}$ defined by the share of basic expenditure categories in total East German consumption outlay. This means, we have to apply the following rule:

$$s_{East}(t) \approx \alpha1 \left(1 - c1^*_{EVS_{East}}(t)\right)$$

$$(5.3.)$$

Supposing a propensity to save of 0.30 as before, this rule almost perfectly predicts East German saving for 1993 and 1998 and generally much better than the formula that includes the German reference point. Moreover, the direction of the change in East German saving between 1993 and 1998—a clear fall—is now matched.

Table 4 provides the exact values for comparison.

Year	Real saving rate (East)	Model saving rate (East) German c1*	Diff.	Model saving rate (East) East c1*	Diff.
1993	12.35	4.72	-7.63	11.59	-0.76
1998	10.99	5.91	-5.08	11.24	0.25
2003	9.45	5.87	-3.58	10.62	1.17
2008	9.29	4.98	-4.31	10.32	1.07

Table 4. Model Predictions East/West, Source: EVS

Interestingly, from 2003 on this approach starts to overestimate East German saving. If we continue to treat East Germany as if it was an autonomous region, the calculated saving rate is more than 1 percentage point higher than the real saving rate of East Germans, confirming a process of convergence between East and West. Nevertheless, this approach is still closer to the real value than our original formula employing the German necessity share divided by the East German relative income position (relative to the German mean).

In Chapter 1, we already considered the salient difference between the East and West German saving curves over relative income in 1993 and 1998, which suggested the East Germans to be particularly eager savers. However, we have also shown that the gap almost completely disappeared if the East and the West specific mean income levels were taken as the reference to calculate the relative income position of the respective income group instead of using the German mean. We now better understand the reason. In 1993 and 1998, and even after the turn of millennium, expenditure for shelter as the main part of the necessity basket was still significantly lower in the East than in the West. This was on the one hand due to East-West differences in prices. On the other, it followed from the fact that the point of reference for the standard of living in the East was obviously not yet close to the German average, which was dominated by the data for the West.

Five years later and more than a decade after German unification, the differences between East and West Germany became somewhat smaller. This convergence was indicated by the closer match of the East German saving rate as predicted by a model that uses the German mean necessity share $c1^*$ as point of reference. Checking the shelter share in the different income groups for 2003, the Eastern shares have indeed somewhat approached those of the West. Therefore, the formula for predicting saving rates referring to a common mean necessity share now works slightly better but remains worse than the East average income as reference point.

Hence, the East German individual necessity share is better approached, if we calculate East German relative income positions in reference to East German mean income. As a consequence, the free income share of an East German was higher than that of a West German at the same income position. For this reason, the mean saving rate in the East, although lower than in the West, was much closer to the latter than a comparison of income levels in East and West suggested. Our previous formula defining the necessity basket and relative income in relationship to the German mean, had to consistently underestimate saving in the East. Taking note of these relationships, the different saving behaviour in Eastern and Western Germany can be well explained.

As a next step, let us carry out some regressions. The purpose is to evaluate the explanatory power of the individual necessity share cc_j^*. We will use EVS data for 1993, 1998, 2003 and 2008. The EVS provides consumption shares and saving rates for 8 relative income groups.

First, we carry out a pooled cross-sectional and time-series regression of saving rates per income group against the income group specific necessity shares in consumption spending for Germany as a whole. (Again we use the necessity share in consumption spending, instead of income, to avoid any influence of the saving rate on the result since we deal not only with cross-sectional values here). The outcome, as provided in the Annex (Regression 46), is quite convincing with a negative coefficient, a p-value close to zero and an adjusted R-squared of 0.87.

In fact, the negative coefficient as such is not surprising since the necessity share is built in such a way that it consists of goods and services with low income elasticity. Since the income elasticity of saving is higher than unity, both variables have to be negatively correlated. Nevertheless, the very strong correspondence indicated by the high R-squared suggests that the relationship is not coincidental.

If we carry out the same pooled cross-sectional/time series regression referring to relative income instead of the necessity share, the fit is clearly worse with an R-squared of only 0.81 (Regression 47). This confirms that the necessity share provides additional information.

If we use the individual necessity share in income instead of that in consumption outlay as the point of reference, the outcome is in fact identical to the first regression. The R-squared is hardly improved, now reaching 0.88 instead of 0.87. All other values are mainly identical. Hence, the influence of the saving rate on the result, if we use income instead of consumption shares, is almost negligible.

Summarising the outcome of this section, we find that our hypothesis on the individual necessity share contributing to an explanation of saving rate differentials in cross-section, to be strongly supported by the German EVS data for 1993, 1998, 2003 and 2008.

5.2.2 Reproducing U.S. Saving Rates of the Mid-20th Century

We next take a look at U.S. saving rates in cross-section. Kuznets (1953) provides us with saving data ordered by relative income for a number of years around World War II. On aggregate, these were years of deflation, economic crisis and extreme uncertainty, but also of a war-induced economic upswing. As mentioned in Chapter 1, aggregate saving has been extremely volatile during that time.

Thus, it might be questionable to what degree saving rate differentials can actually be explained by the motion of the necessity share during such a restless period. However, if we simulate cross-sectional saving rates according to our rule and compare them to the real saving data provided by Kuznets, we discover a very close match indeed.

In this case we will calculate the mean necessity share $c1^*$ by using the NIPA tables, adding expenditure for food and drinks, shelter (including rents, water, electricity, heating and telephone), health care and local transportation. (Private transportation is considered to still be a luxury at that time.) Again, we calculate the mean necessity share in income $cc^*(t)$.

This necessity share will be used as the point of reference for the individual necessity share. For the pre-war and wartime periods, we use a common propensity to save and to dissave of 0.25, for the post-war period we use 0.2. This difference is justified by the different degree of uncertainty. In fact, one had to assume much stronger varying propensities in the ever changing environment of this particular era. But since we are mainly interested in proving the impact of the individual necessity share here, we do not want to complicate the analysis by varying propensities.

Figures 26–32 provide the curves that are derived from this rule and compare them with the real saving rates in cross-section. We observe an almost perfect match in 1929 and 1942 and a rather good fit for 1948 and 1950. The deviation is higher in 1935 and particularly so in 1945.

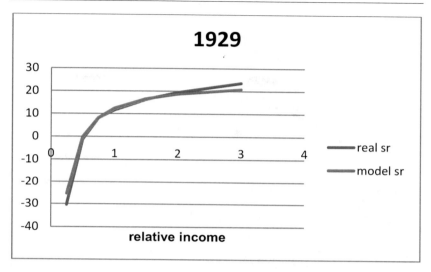

Figure 26. Model Saving Rates 1929, Source: Kuznets (1953), NIPA

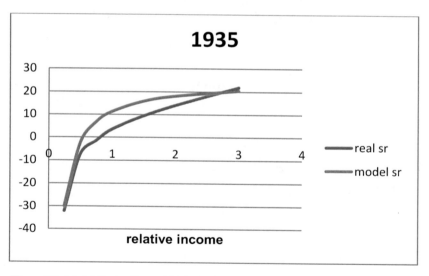

Figure 27. Model Saving Rates 1935, Source: Kuznets (1953), NIPA

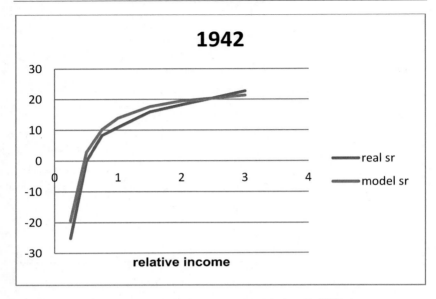

Figure 28. Model Saving Rates 1942, Source: Kuznets (1953), NIPA

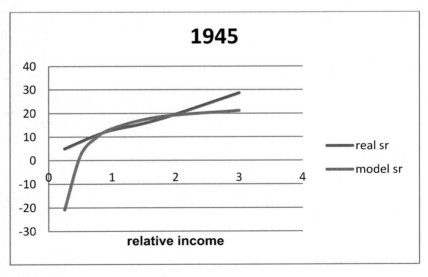

Figure 29. Model Saving Rates 1945, Source: Kuznets (1953), NIPA

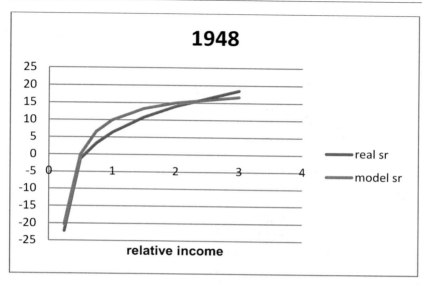

Figure 30. Model Saving Rates 1948, Source: Kuznets (1953), NIPA

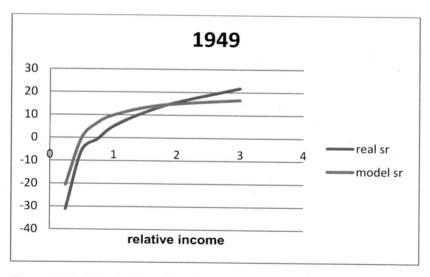

Figure 31. Model Saving Rates 1949, Source: Kuznets (1953), NIPA

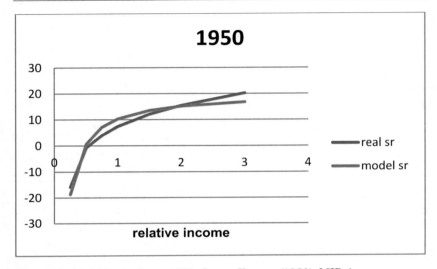

Figure 32. Model Saving Rates 1950, Source: Kuznets (1953), NIPA

In the latter case this is not surprising, since the aggregated saving rate reached extreme highs during the late war-years; in cross-section according to Kuznets, even the poorest saved, which had obviously little to do with a sudden decrease in the necessity basket. However, considering the circumstances of this particular period, far from being business as usual, the degree by which real saving rates in cross-section can be reproduced by our rule is remarkable.

This is confirmed if we undertake a pooled cross-section and time-series regression of Kuznets' saving data for the various years and income groups against the respective individual necessity shares cc_j^* (Regression 48). The fit is very strong with an adjusted R-squared of 0.85. To see that this fit is not derived from a strong relationship between individual saving rate and relative income alone, we again carry out an additional regression, scrutinising the latter (Regression 49).

We actually obtain a strong and significant coefficient of relative income, but the R-squared of 0.65 is clearly a worse fit than the regression of cross-sectional saving rates against the necessity share.

Even more surprising, the formula provided by the regression as the best linear estimation of saving rates, corresponds exactly to the saving rule derived from our model. The intercept is 21 while the coefficient of the necessity share is 0.21. Therefore, the suggested best linear estimator of cross-sectional saving rates is:

$$s_j = 0.21 \left(100 - cc_j^* \right)$$

$$(5.4)$$

which corresponds to our model. The only difference is that we assumed $\alpha 1$ to be varying and somewhat higher in pre-war and war times than in the more certain period after World War II. The regression can of course only provide one coefficient. (The 100 instead of unity is caused by the fact that we used saving rates and necessity shares as percentage from 100 instead of a ratio of one).

It is a pity that no reliable cross-sectional saving data from later periods of U.S. history are available to check our model. Nevertheless, the empirical evidence provided by Kuznets' data set strongly supports our hypothesis that the necessity share has explanatory power.

We conclude that our approach is able to very well explain the saving rate differentials at the micro level for the U.S.

Paragraph 5.3
Model Predictions and Empirical Evidence at the Macroeconomic Level

5.3.1 Preliminary Notes

In Chapter 3, the following formula determining the aggregated saving rate was derived from our model:

$$s_{agg}(t) = \alpha 1(t)[1 - cc^*(t)] + [\alpha 1(t) - \alpha 2(t)]k(t)[cc^*(t) - y\{ns\}(t)]$$

$$(5.5)$$

Hence, the necessity share was considered to be the main variable also influencing saving behaviour at aggregated level. If the propensity to save $\alpha 1(t)$ equals the propensity to dissave $\alpha 2(t)$, the aggregated saving rate rises with this propensity and depends negatively on the necessity share $cc^*(t)$. In this case, aggregated saving is not affected by the distribution of income. If the propensity to save significantly deviates from the propensity to dissave, redistributions of income (changing the share of non-savers k and/or the average relative income position of non-savers $y\{ns\}$) matter for the aggregated saving rate. If $\alpha 1(t)$ exceeds $\alpha 2(t)$, rising inequality boosts saving, while in the opposite case a rising gap between rich and poor diminishes the aggregated saving rate. The objective of the following paragraphs is to check whether such a rule matches the empirical data at the macro level.

The first step to test our main hypothesis that subsistence points contribute to an explanation of saving behaviour, is to scrutinise whether a negative correlation between necessity share and saving rate can indeed be found at the aggregate level. This will be tested for the mean necessity share in either approximation, $c1^*$ and $c2^*$.

As already argued in Chapter 4, the construction of $c1^*$ is very rough and its path only approximates the movement of the real necessity share.

The categories in the necessity basket $C^*(t)$ contain a number of goods and services that belong to luxury consumption. Perhaps, a boost in $c1^*$ might just be caused by the expansion of such goods and services that are not basic. Since the basic price index uses the same systematic, the rate of excess basic inflation might overestimate the increase of real basic prices for the same reason. Hence, a negative correlation between $c1^*$, respectively $c2^*$, and the saving rate might not be accepted as a sufficient proof of a negative link between saving and basic spending. Therefore, we will additionally check the reverse relationship, i.e. the correlation between luxury spending and saving.

As the final step, we will examine to what degree our formula is indeed able to reproduce the main trends of the path of the personal saving rate in the U.S. and in Germany given reasonable parameter values.

5.3.2 Saving Rate and Basic Needs in Germany

Let us start with Germany. The necessity share $c1^*$ from the National Accounts ($c1^*_{VGR}$) and from the Income and Consumption Survey ($c1^*_{EVS}$) is defined exactly as in Chapter 4. The same applies to the luxury share.

Necessity share and luxury share do not add to unity, since such kinds of consumption that cannot clearly be identified as either basic or luxurious are excluded. We exclude all parts of "Other expenditure" except for insurance costs (necessity) and personal belongings (luxury). Health expenses are not taken into account due to the already mentioned data problem: relevant private spending for medical care is a relatively recent phenomenon in Germany but the statistics merge this real spending with health expenses of privately insured persons who get their expenses reimbursed through their insurance policies.

To derive the necessity share $c2^*$, the rate of excess basic growth and the rate of excess basic inflation are calculated as defined in Chapter 4. As the initial level, we use 50 percent. The calculation starts in 1970.

If we observe the paths of the EVS necessity share and the EVS saving rate, it is quite obvious, that they are negatively correlated (Figure 33).

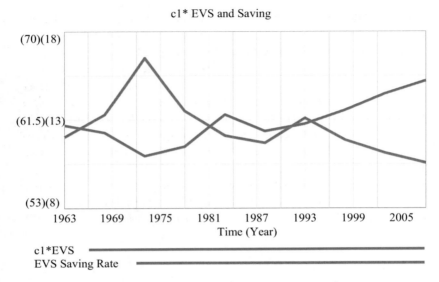

c1*EVS ——————————
EVS Saving Rate ——————————

Figure 33. Necessity Share and Saving in Germany, Source: EVS

The EVS saving rate peaks only in the mid-seventies when the EVS necessity share reaches its lowest value. Afterwards, the necessity share increases while the saving rate decreases. There is another short downturn of the necessity share between 1983 and 1988 where the saving rate continues to decrease while over the next 5 years both increase. These are the only two exceptions from the contradictory trend, and in each the change is not very strong.

The relationship between saving rate and EVS luxury share also corresponds perfectly to our model predictions (Figure 34). The movement of the latter is always in line with the saving rate, except again for the time between 1983 and 1993. If we compare the path of the luxury share from the national accounts (VGR) to the path of the German National Accounts saving rate, the correlation is similarly striking (Figure 35).

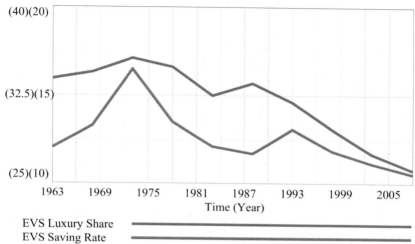

Figure 34. Luxury Share and Saving in Germany, Source: EVS

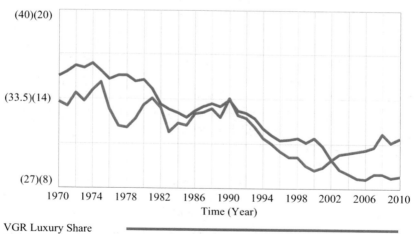

Figure 35. Luxury Share and Saving Germany, Source: VGR

If we regress the EVS saving rate against the EVS necessity share $c1^*_{EVS}$, we obtain a significant negative coefficient. Taking into account, that we are using only 10 observations, this is quite a strong result. The fit with an adjusted R-squared of about 0.70 is also fairly good (Regression 50). Employing the EVS luxury share as regressor for the EVS saving rate provides the predicted positive coefficient that is significant, and an adjusted R-squared of 0.5 (Regression 51). If we use the disaggregated EVS data for the different household groups sorted by social status (which strongly increases the number of observations) regressing their saving rate against their relative income position and the three components of the necessity share, all coefficients of the shares have the predicted negative signs, and most of them are significant. The coefficient of relative income, in contrast, is positive as expected (Regression 52).

Regressing the VGR saving rate against the necessity share $c1^*_{VGR}$, leads to a negative but not sufficiently significant coefficient (Regression 53). The fit, however, is very poor. More convincing is the regression of the saving rate against the luxury share that provides the expected positive sign and a significant coefficient, while the adjusted R-squared is as high as 0.64 (Regression 54).

The fit is similarly strong if we regress the German saving rate against the necessity share $c2^*$. Here the negative coefficient is significant and the adjusted R-squared of 0.64 is quite convincing.

There are several reasons for the poor fit of $c1^*_{VGR}$. Beside possibly distorted data (we mentioned several differences to the $c1^*_{EVS}$), one single event has an important effect: the sharp fall in the mean necessity share in 1991 due to German unification, which is accompanied by an equally sharp fall of the aggregated saving rate. (The event did not immediately influence the EVS data, since the survey was conducted in 1988 and 1993 only.) This single observation has a significant influence on the regression result since the absolute change of both variables in this particular year is one of the strongest over the entire range of time. The true reason of diminished saving in 1991 is of course falling income per head because 1991 was the first year in which the figures include East Germany. Since the income variable is completely excluded in this regression, the outcome is biased. (This is different for $c2^*$ since the rate of excess basic growth became strongly positive in 1991 due to falling income, diminishing the effect of negative excess basic inflation due to very low basic prices in the East. In fact, $c2^*$ also declined in 1991, but the fall was not as pronounced.)

Indeed, if we carry out the same regression of the saving rate against the necessity share $c1^*_{VGR}$ reducing the period to the years from 1970 to 1990 (West Germany), we now obtain a significant negative coefficient and the match, with an adjusted R-squared of 0.31, is also fairly good (Regression 56). Moreover, if we regress the German National Accounts saving rate against the major component of the necessity share, the shelter share (including rents, imputed rents, electricity, heating and water fees), we obtain a significant negative coefficient and a stronger fit indicated by an adjusted R-squared of 0.54.

Thus, empirical data about consumption shares in Germany are, by and large, in line with our approach. All regressions provide coefficients that correspond to the predictions of our model and most of them are significant. Moreover, the fit is rather good, indicated by adjusted R-squares that mostly exceed 0.5.

We emphasise again that all shares are calculated as *expenditure shares* and not income shares in order to avoid any hidden influence of saving on the regressor. Within the framework of the usual consumption models, no link between the saving rate and such shares should exist. If anything, a negative relationship to the luxury share is consistent with the usual assumption that luxury spending is a substitute to saving.

One might nevertheless argue that all these correlations are simply caused by the correspondence of time trends. The share of expenditure categories covered by the necessity share has been rising since the mid-seventies, while the share of those groups defined as luxuries generally decreased. Because the saving rate has been falling since the mid-seventies, this correspondence might have led to the signs of the coefficients that have been found.

Certainly, regressions never provide any proof of causalities. In fact, some of the regressions carried out so far display a low Durbin-Watson statistic revealing a high degree of autocorrelation. This should caution us to interpret the results with care. On the other hand, particularly the regressions against the EVS necessity and luxury share provide a Durbin-Watson-Statistic between 1.89 and 2.27. Here, autocorrelation is obviously not a relevant problem. Moreover, it is simply not true that the respective series had only one trend that is just shared (or opposed) by the saving rate. Rather, there are ups and downs in the paths of the respective consumption shares and the strong parallelism with the peaks and lows of the saving rate is striking. This is particularly true for the EVS necessity share and the National Accounts luxury share.

To avoid autocorrelation, it is usually suggested that annual changes instead of levels are referred to. However, to calculate changes of a rate results in a time series that is particularly noisy. Yearly changes in the saving rate are mainly in the range of plus/minus one percentage point while the standard error might easily reach half of it. We have seen in the U.S. data that the NIPA and the FoF saving rate are mainly compatible in their levels, but show almost no correlation in their changes. Therefore, we abstain from carrying out regressions using changes in the saving rate as the dependent variable.

To sum up, a significant negative relationship between the EVS saving rate and the EVS necessity share $c1^*_{EVS}$, as well as between the VGR saving rate and the necessity share $c2^*$ has been confirmed in this section. The same is true for the positive relationship between saving rate and luxury share from the EVS as well as from the VGR. In fact, the results of all regressions strongly confirm our hypothesis of an empirical link between basic needs and saving.

5.3.3 Saving Rate and Basic Needs in the U.S.

We next check the relationships between consumption shares and saving rates for the U.S. As mentioned, the NIPA tables provide sufficient data to derive the necessity share as well as the luxury share for the entire post-war time. We start calculations from 1950. Definitions of all shares are the same as in Chapter 4.

As in the case of Germany, the respective necessity and luxury shares do not add to unity. While the necessity share again might include some luxuries, the luxury share is clearly dominated by goods and services which are highly income elastic and flexible over time. According to common understanding, these kinds of expenses should behave contrary to saving. Particularly in the debate about the decline in the U.S. personal saving rate, it has often been argued that vanishing thrift has been caused by a higher desire for luxury items. In this context, exactly those goods and services which we included in the luxury share are often referred to: new cars, electronic devices, all kinds of expensive durables, recreation expenses, holiday homes, costly clothes and accessories.

Also calculated for the U.S. is the necessity share $c2^*$ moving in line with the rate of excess basic growth and excess basic inflation. We use the statistical data from 1946 onwards, hence $c2^*$ starts in 1955.

Because of the unreliable CEX income figures, we do not compute a separate saving rate from the survey. As already pointed out in Chapter 1, the path of CEX saving (calculated from the residual between income and consumption) is very implausible. It starts with negative values in the middle of the eighties, rising permanently afterwards. The falling trend of the personal saving rate in this period, however, was confirmed by NIPA as well as by FoF data and has never been seriously questioned. Therefore we abstain from employing a special CEX saving rate. Instead, all consumption shares will be compared to the NIPA or the FOF saving rate. (With respect to these rates, the result is generally similar since they are highly correlated.)

A decline of $c2^*$ is observable up to the mid-seventies corresponding to a slightly rising trend in NIPA saving. The necessity share then starts to rise strongly while the saving rate shows no clear trend until the mid-eighties. During the nineties, both paths are again clearly contradictory: a further boost to the necessity share is accompanied by a steep fall in saving.

For the NIPA luxury share we see some parallels to the peaks and lows of the path of saving in the sixties and seventies while in the first half of the eighties the trends are more opposed. The CEX luxury share is somewhat higher than the share computed using NIPA figures. One reason might be the inclusion of "Other lodging", a category that is not explicitly available in the NIPA tables. But in principle, the paths of these luxury shares are very similar.

We observe a general downward trend in luxury spending in the second half of the eighties, a slight upswing in the nineties and another decline after the turn of the millennium. During the nineties, when saving faced an unprecedented decline, the luxury shares displayed a slight uptrend, although not recovering by far to the values of the eighties. Rather, the increase was in the range of less than 2 percentage points and is hardly a plausible cause for the slump in saving.

But as mentioned, not only the luxury share but also the necessity share $c2^*$ went up during the nineties and the increase was much more significant in the latter case. In fact, one trend has to be spurious, since the real basic and the real luxurious proportion in consumption spending can hardly grow in parallel.

If we scrutinise the development of the two shares within each income group according to the CEX data, we observe a notable rise in the necessity share in the two highest income groups. (We have to bear in mind that the upper quintile of the CEX does not correspond to the very rich, but to better-off middle-class families.) Interestingly, the slight upturn of the luxury share during the nineties that we observed in the aggregate share, is not present in the CEX data for the two upper quintiles, but rather for the two lowest. Since the first two are mainly those who contribute to personal saving, there is probably no contradiction between their saving path and the path of their luxury share.

Movements in the luxury shares should of course not be interpreted as implying that the poor enjoyed extended luxury spending in the nineties while the rich did not. In fact, the personal income of these quintiles developed rather differently: while poorer households experienced almost no increase—often even losing purchasing power during this period—wealthier families received a remarkable income plus. Hence, the rising luxury share of the poor might simply indicate that they tried to maintain the accustomed standard of living, while the shrinking share of better-off households indeed points towards the rising costs of those basics essential for a middle-class standard of living (but not so much for the poor). Certainly, one has to analyse this in more detail to become clear about the issue. It is really a pity that reliable CEX quintile saving rates are not available to compare them to the movement of these consumption shares.

We conclude that the disaggregated CEX consumption shares are in line with our model predictions that saving increases and decreases with the free income share (which is positively correlated to the luxury and negatively to the necessity share). Hence, rising basic costs for those households who are usually savers, but have turned partially into dissavers (and accumulators of rising debt), is surely a serious reason for the tumbling U.S. saving rate in the decade before the turn of the millennium.

We next carry out a number of regressions to check whether the general intuition about correlations was true or misleading. In fact, if we regress the FOF Saving rate against the NIPA necessity share $c1^*_{NIPA}$, we obtain the expected negative coefficient and it is significant (Regression 58). The adjusted R-squared is 0.21. The coefficient of the NIPA luxury share is significantly positive and the fit, with an adjusted R-squared of 0.35, is even better. (Regressions 59) Regressing the FOF saving rate against the CEX necessity share $c1^*_{CEX}$ and the CEX luxury share, also provides the predicted coefficients; in both cases significant at 0.05 confidence level (Regression 60 and 61).

The lack of significance might be caused by the shorter time period (CEX data are available only from 1984 onwards) and the extreme variance of the FoF saving rate, particularly during this time period. In fact, if we instead use the NIPA saving rate as the dependent variable, the sign of all coefficients is the same, but they are significant (Regressions 62 and 63).

A very strong fit is found if we regress the NIPA saving rate against the CEX basic housing expenditure share (housing expenditures without other lodging, furniture and household devices). Here, a significant negative coefficient occurs and the adjusted R-squared is 0.46 (Regression 64).

This result supports the assumption that the NIPA saving rate (different from the FoF saving rate) is dominated by middle-class saving. The strong positive correlation to the wage share discovered in Chapter 1 was already an indicator for this. Since the CEX over-proportionally also reflects consumption behaviour of middle-class people, this might explain the stronger correspondence. Moreover one can certainly suppose that upper class saving is little influenced by the necessity share. As already expressed, our model is intended to primarily explain the saving behaviour of the median household and not so much that of the wealthiest. The saving behaviour of the latter is most likely guided by other motives.

If we finally regress the NIPA saving rate against the necessity share $c2^*$ we again obtain a significant negative coefficient. The adjusted R-squared of this regression is 0.65 (Regression 65).

To sum up, the coefficients of all consumption shares exactly correspond to the predictions of our model and most of them are significant. The fit in most cases is also quite remarkable. This supports our assumption of an empirical link between the saving rate and the composition of consumption spending. Moreover, the generally positive correlation between luxury share and saving rate rejects the assumption that extended luxury spending was responsible for declining saving in the U.S. during the nineties and after the millennium. We saw luxury spending just slightly increasing from a very low level during that decade, while the necessity share moved upwards.

However, the outcome of these regressions is somewhat less convincing than in the case of Germany since in the U.S. just one major time trend dominates the paths of the shares. The necessity share went up (only $c2^*$ dropped until the mid-seventies) and the luxury share shrunk. The saving rate rose only moderately until the mid-eighties while it broke down afterwards. Considering these general trends, the signs of the coefficients are not surprising. Hence, the Durbin-Watson tests for the respective residuals provide values close to zero in all cases, implying a high degree of autocorrelation.

Simply observing similarities in the paths of consumption shares and saving rates again does not prove much. Both time series might be driven by completely divergent forces and the correlation might occur only by chance due to the same time trend. However, the common findings for two countries, which are usually considered to be rather distinct in their saving behaviour, are after all remarkable. Thus, the most modest conclusion summarising the U.S. data analysed so far is that we have not found evidence rejecting our model while many facts can be interpreted as supporting our hypothesis.

5.3.4 Is Our Model Able to Reproduce the Historic Path?

a) Operationalizing the required variables

The next step is to check whether major trends of the real saving path can be reproduced by the saving rule derived from our model. Therefore, we again repeat the formula for the aggregated saving rate from Chapter 3:

$$s(t) = \alpha1(t)\big(1 - cc^*(t)\big) + \big(\alpha1(t) - \alpha2(t)\big)k(t)\big(cc^*(t) - y\{ns\}(t)\big)$$
$$(5.6)$$

Hence, we need empirical values for the following variables to be able to simulate the saving path according to this rule: $cc^*(t)$, the mean necessity share, $k(t)$, the number of non-savers and $y\{ns\}(t)$, the average relative income of nonsavers.

As already stressed, measuring the share of whatever part of consumption expenditure *in income* inevitably leads to a variable that is influenced not only by the structure of consumption, but by the saving rate. Such an approach should be avoided since it is highly questionable to employ a variable that depends on saving in a rule that explains and reproduces the path of saving,. Hence, we have to deal with one of the two approximations of $cc^*(t)$ defined in Chapter 4: either the measured share of basic expenditure in total consumption outlay, $c1^*$, or the simulated necessity share $c2^*$ growing in line with the rate of excess basic growth and excess basic inflation. We will model the saving rate using each of the respective shares to determine which one works better.

But $cc^*(t)$ is not the only variable that has to be operationalised. As soon as we abandon the assumption of equal propensities to save and to dissave, the second term in the savings formula becomes relevant. Thus, we have to specify values for the share of non-savers $k(t)$ and the average relative income of non-savers $y\{ns\}(t)$. Unfortunately, it is almost impossible to derive exact annual values for these variables from available statistics. For this reason we also have to approximate these values.

We assume that the density distribution of relative income can be approached by a Gamma-distribution. Referring to this kind of density distribution appears to be sensible whenever issues of income distribution are to be addressed since a Gamma-distribution is perfectly capable of modelling a right-skewed distribution at various levels of inequality.

The expected value of a Gamma (r, λ)-distribution is r/λ, while the variance is r/λ^2. One has to consistently assume $r = \lambda$, when the density of relative income is to be modelled since mean relative income is always unity. The higher the chosen values for r and λ, the more equal the respective distribution.

In the following, we assume the density distribution of relative income to correspond to a Gamma $(2,2)$-distribution. If relative income follows such a distribution, 26 percent of the population have a relative income position of less than 0.5, i.e. this group earns less than half of the average income. Approximately 60 percent of the population have earnings below the mean income. Only very few families earn more than 4 times the average.

If we compare the values of relative income of certain deciles derived from a Gamma $(2,2)$ density distribution with known values for some years in Germany and in the U.S., it is obvious that this kind of distribution can indeed be taken as a realistic approximation to the real spreading of income.

For our purposes, small differences between the assumed and the real income distribution are not in any case so important since the aggregate saving rate does not depend on the entire income distribution but only on the two parameters k and y{ns}. If a Gamma (2,2) distribution of relative income density is assumed and the necessity share reaches just 50 percent, the share of non-savers in the population is 26 percent and the average relative income position of non-savers is 0.3. Any percentage point increase (or decrease) of the necessity share in the range between 45 and 70 percent (which are the values we are dealing with), increases (or diminishes) the share of non-savers in the population by approximately 0.7 percentage points and their average relative income by approximately 0.5 percentage points. These are the values we will incorporate into our model for both countries and for the whole range of time. Hence, for the moment we will exclude changes in the income distribution. Their particular effect will be considered later on.

b) The optimal path under constant propensities to save and to dissave

First we check the model assuming constant propensities to save and to dissave over the entire range of time. The quality of a simulation will be evaluated by the payoff and by the coefficient of correlation between the historic and the simulated path. The payoff measures the (negative) sum of squared differences between the model's path and the historic path. A simulation is better the closer the payoff comes to zero. The payoff naturally rises with the number of data points. Therefore, a comparable match will necessarily provide a worse payoff for the U.S. than for Germany.

We start with the data from the German EVS. In this case data are available from 1963 to 2008 in steps of five years. The statistics of the optimal match in this case is provided by Table 5. A comparison of the model path and the historic path of the EVS saving rate gives Figure 36.

Despite the highly simplifying assumption of constant propensities to save and to dissave over a time range of almost 50 years, and the use of exactly one explanatory variable, the ups and downs of the historic path are almost perfectly matched. The coefficient of correlation between the real and the model path of the German EVS saving rate is as high as 0.85.

Germany ($c1^*_{EVS}$)
Maximum payoff found at:
unadjusted propensity to save = 0.44
unadjusted propensity to dissave = 0.96
Payoff = -6.96624
Coefficient of Correlation: 0.85

Table 5. Model Parameters, Source: EVS

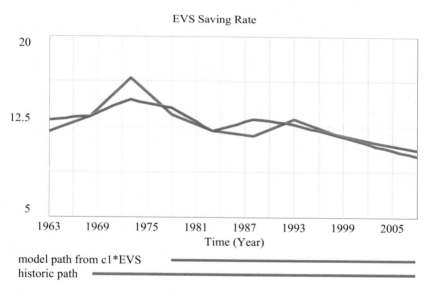

EVS Saving Rate

model path from c1*EVS

historic path

*Figure 36. Model Path from c1*_EVS, Source: EVS*

Table 6 provides the optimal values of the two propensities, the payoff and the coefficient of correlation of those calibrations that refer to the VGR necessity share $c1^*_{VGR}$ and the necessity share $c2^*$. The available range of time is 1970 until 2010.

Germany ($c1^*_{VGR}$)	Germany ($c2^*$)
Maximum payoff found at:	Maximum payoff found at:
unadjusted propensity to save = 0.40	unadjusted propensity to save = 0.28
unadjusted propensity to dissave = 0.99	unadjusted propensity to dissave = 0.22
Payoff = -89.6513	Payoff = -36.5936
Coefficient of Correlation 0.34	Coefficient of correlation: 0.80

Table 6. Model Parameters, Source: VGR

Figure 37 and 38 show the respective paths comparing them to the historic path of the German VGR saving rate.

The fit of the model that uses $c1^*_{VGR}$ is clearly worse compared to the one employing $c1^*_{EVS}$ as well as to the one referring to $c2^*$. The coefficient of correlation of the model path that uses $c1^*_{VGR}$ is as low as 0.34 compared to a correlation of more than 80 percent in both other cases. The payoff of the first is also quite poor. It has been already considered in Chapter 4 that the German VGR necessity share $c1^*_{VGR}$ is probably quite distorted and generally less reliable than $c1^*_{EVS}$. If this is true, it explains the poor fit of the respective path.

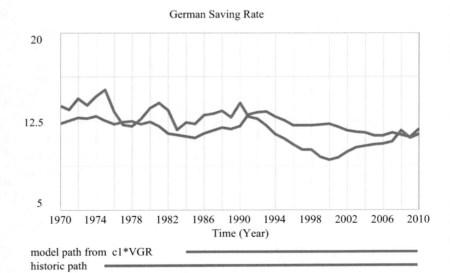

*Figure 37. Model Path from c1*_VGR, Source: VGR*

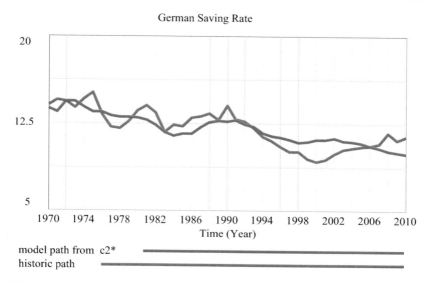

Figure 38. Model Path from c2*, Source: VGR

In contrast, the match is quite convincing when employing $c2^*$. The coefficient of correlation to the historic path of saving is, at 0.80, only somewhat lower than in the case of using $c1^*_{EVS}$. For the 30 years up to 2000, the peaks and lows of the real saving rate are mainly covered although the extent of the variation is not in all cases matched. Only the upswing of the VGR saving rate in the previous decade is not matched. Yet, this upturn of saving does not exist in the EVS data since from 2002 onwards, VGR saving and EVS saving do not follow common trends. While the VGR saving rate increases, the EVS saving rate continues to shrink. A possible explanation for this might be that the EVS data more adequately reflect the saving decisions of the vast majority of people, while the VGR saving rate is pushed up by an extremely high saving effort by a very rich minority.

If this assumption is true, the recent saving boost in Germany was primarily caused by saving decisions of wealthy households instead of the median saver. This provides an explanation for the failure of our model in this particular period since the development of the mean necessity share is certainly not highly relevant for the budgeting and saving decisions of the rich.

Reliable saving data for the U.S. from surveys do not exist. This is why we abstain from employing the CEX necessity share and start by using

$c1^*_{NIPA}$ in our calculation. Here, we refer to the time period between 1950 and 2009. Secondly, we use the U.S. $c2^*$ calculated by NIPA data as a point of reference. Since data for excess basic growth are required, we cannot start before 1955. The optimal parameter values for both models are provided by Table 7.

U.S. ($c1^*_{NIPA}$)	U.S. ($c2^*$)
Maximum payoff found at:	Maximum payoff found at:
unadjusted propensity to save = 0.36	unadjusted propensity to save = 0.20
*unadjusted propensity to dissave = 1.35	*unadjusted propensity to dissave = 0.52
Payoff = -225.149	Payoff = -116.126
Coefficient of correlation: 0.60	Coefficient of correlation: 0.82

Table 7. Model Parameters, Source: NIPA

Similar to the case of Germany, the model that employs $c2^*$ works much better than the model using $c1^*_{NIPA}$, although the payoff is not entirely comparable since the model employing $c1^*_{NIPA}$ covers 60 years while the time span of the simulation that refers to $c2^*$ is 5 years shorter. However, the difference in the coefficient of correlation amounts to 20 percentage points, which clearly indicates a better fit for the second approach. The reason is most likely the same as in the case of Germany. Consumption shares provided by the National Accounts are obviously much more prone to statistical error than data of surveys. If National Accounts are used, calculating the necessity share by growth rates and the rate of basic inflation seems to approximate to true necessity spending more adequately than simply adding consumption shares. In fact, this necessity share $c2^*$ in both countries strongly corresponds to the necessity share $c1^*$ from the EVS and the CEX respectively

The obtained model paths for both approaches are plotted in Figures 39 and 40.

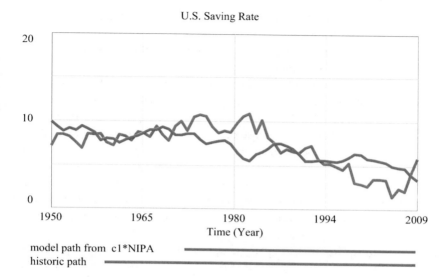

*Figure 39. Model Path from c1*_NIPA, Source: NIPA*

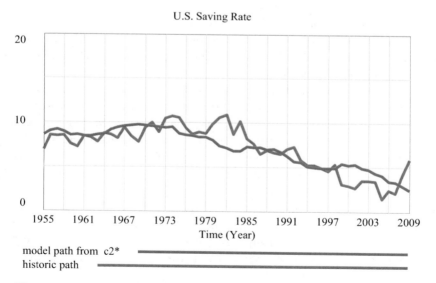

Figure 40. Model Path from c2, Source: NIPA*

The figures confirm that the correspondence between the model path and the historic path is more convincing in the case of the model that uses $c2^*$. Here, the general trends of the saving path are reflected reasonably well, while smaller variances are not reproduced.

This is particularly true for the two saving peaks in the first half of the nineteen eighties which had obviously other reasons than a sudden down-turn of the necessity share. The fall of the U.S. saving rate during the nineteen nineties is mainly covered, while the sudden upswing after the outbreak of the financial crisis 2007 is not matched by the model path. However, the failure in the latter case is not surprising since the boost to saving after 2007 was surely not caused by increased saving efforts by private households, but by dried-out financial markets and an abrupt stop in the flow of new credit. Taking into account the very simple formula that has been applied, a correlation of more than 80 percent is a good result.

To sum up, by including the necessity share as the only explanatory variable, we obtain a simulation that covers 0.85 percent of the variance of the EVS saving rate (using $c1^*_{EVS}$) and 80 percent of the variance of the German VGR saving rate (using $c2^*$) in Germany, and 82 percent of the variance of the U.S. NIPA saving rate (again using $c2^*$) for a range of time of 40 up to 55 years.

This strongly supports our hypothesis that the necessity share or the rates of excess basic growth and excess basic inflation (according to which the necessity share $c2^*$ had been calculated) are indeed crucial variables in explaining saving behaviour.

However, the assumption of a constant propensity to save and to dissave over half a century, which underlies the previous simulations, is certainly not realistic. Since our rule of thumb is derived from optimal behaviour, we should expect the propensity to save to be influenced by the usual suspects such as the interest rate, the inflation rate, et cetera. The assumption of a constant propensity to dissave is also questionable. Nei-ther have U.S. households been carrying the current load of debts for the past 40 years, nor has the level of household indebtedness been constant in Germany. Rather, consumer credit (other than mortgages) is a relatively new phenomenon in Germany and had been almost absent before the mid-eighties. Thus, in both cases a growing trend of private debts has to be taken into account.

c) Sensitivity of the simulated path of saving to the impact of various variables

By analysing the stylised facts of saving, we have already considered a positive correlation between saving and the CPI inflation rate. In fact, this correspondence is not surprising. To save the same amount is certainly a different issue whether the inflation rate is zero or reaches 10 percent thereby devaluating accumulated wealth. Hence, we could assume the propensity to save to be influenced by inflation. Higher nominal rates help to shield financial wealth against inflationary losses while higher real rates reward saving with a richer return. Consequently, all these variables might be considered to have an impact on the propensity to save.

In this sub-section, each effect will be introduced and tested separately by a very simple formula. We assume the propensity to save to be the sum of a constant (the unadjusted propensity to save) and a linear effect of the respective variable. Each effect enters the calibration with a lower limit of zero and an upper limit of 1. The respective rates are measured as percentages of unity. Hence, if inflation had an effect of, say, 1, this would imply an inflation rate of 5 percent pushing up the propensity to save by 5 percentage points, say, from 0.25 to 0.3. This is certainly not identical with a boost to the saving rate by 5 percentage points. In fact, since the propensity to save refers to the free income share exclusively, the final effect on saving depends on the extent of the latter.

The propensity to save should certainly not exceed unity since the main hypothesis of our model is that no one can ever save more than his free income share. Hence, the unadjusted propensity to save is assumed to reach values between zero and unity, while the effects mentioned additionally appear without pushing the value of the resulting propensity to save to values beyond 1. An upper limit of 1 does not per definition exist for the propensity to dissave; thus, values exceeding unity are not excluded in advance.

People's saving behaviour might actually be less guided by the current value of a variable than by its expected value, particularly since the exact value of, say, current inflation or current real rates in the respective year, is simply not known before its end. In order to take into account the role of expectations, it is common to introduce highly complicated formulas to include the (certainly unknown!) probability distribution of the respective variable in the far-off future. We will instead employ a very simplified approach. Since neither the inflation rate nor the real interest rate has a general growth trend, the ordinary principle of expecting this year's value to be the same as the previous year's value is not implausible. Hence, it is possible that lagged values of the respective variables influence saving behaviour more significantly than current values. Therefore, for each variable, a current and a lagged effect will be tested. For the latter, the variable enters with a time lag of one year.

One has to bear in mind that within the employed saving rule, a delay not only shifts a certain effect by one year, but the influence on saving also changes. The reason again is that the saving rate does not directly respond to the propensity to save. If the free income share varies, a lagged effect might influence saving in a different way than an immediate effect.

In the calibrations, we search for the optimal value of the two propensities and of the effect of the respective variable. To become clear about *how* the various effects indeed influence the simulated path, we will additionally carry out a sensitivity test for each variable. Such a test displays the variance of the simulated saving path in dependence on a varying (current or lagged) effect. In all tests, the unadjusted propensity to save is assumed to equal the value derived as optimal for the respective effect. The same is true for the propensity to dissave. In all calculations we refer to the necessity share $c2^*$. The curves are commented in the text, while the graphics themselves are freely available on the website http://bit.ly/campus39916.

Before we introduce the first effect, we observe the general sensitivity of the path regarding changes in the propensity to save and to dissave itself. We vary $\alpha1$ by plus/minus 0.01 around its optimal value and $\alpha2$ from zero to 1.5. (Table I on the website http://bit.ly/campus39916) The effect of a changing propensity to save is mainly a shift of the entire path up or down, while the curvature is little affected. Only if the propensity to save becomes very low, does the path get flatter. However, for the range of variation analysed here there is almost no divergence in the profile. This is different for the propensity to dissave. Varying values of $\alpha2$ not only shift the simulated path up or down, but have a clear impact on the profile. The lower the propensity to dissave, the less curved the path. The reason is easily understandable: an upturn of the necessity share pushes down aggregated saving more heavily if it turns savers into dissavers, while the effect is much smaller if the respective households only stop saving.

Particularly for Germany, assuming a higher propensity to dissave more adequately provides a path that matches the peak in the second half of the nineteen eighties and the subsequent fall. However, it implies a strong downward trend of saving before this period that does not correspond to the real path. Therefore, the optimal value of the propensity to dissave in Germany for the entire range of time is as low as 0.22.

Next, we analyse the impact of inflation and of nominal and real interest rates on the propensity to save. We start with inflation. Let $\alpha 1_{unadj}$ denote the propensity to save that is not adjusted for the impact of inflation and ε_{infl} the effect of inflation. Hence, we carry out a simulation of the saving path, in which the propensity to save $\alpha 1(t)$ varies according to following rule:

$$\alpha 1(t) = \alpha 1_{unadj} + \varepsilon_{infl} * \text{inflation rate}(t)$$

$$(5.7)$$

resp.

$$\alpha 1(t) = \alpha 1_{unadj} + \varepsilon_{infl_{lag}} * \text{inflation rate}(t-1)$$

$$(5.8)$$

Table 8 displays the sensitivity of the modelled saving rate for the current and the lagged inflation effect. Table II on the website additionally provides the respective graphics. Obviously, the effect of lagged inflation is stronger than that of current inflation in both countries. Including a lagged inflation effect improves the payoff significantly.

Hence, lagged inflation, particularly in the U.S., probably has an effect on the propensity to save. The less significant effect for Germany might follow from the fact that inflation rates did not climb at similarly high values as in the United States. Hence, U.S. households had more reasons to take them into account when adjusting their saving behaviour.

The relevance of the lagged inflation effect is underlined by the sensitivity analysis. For Germany, peaks of inflation in the seventies and in the first half of the eighties clearly correspond to peaks of the saving rate. This applies also to the U.S.. Of course, due to the construction of our model, lagged effects do not only result in a shift by one year, but in a somewhat different shape.

Germany	U.S.
Maximum payoff found at:	Maximum payoff found at:
unadjusted propensity to save = 0.25	unadjusted propensity to save = 0.17
unadjusted propensity to dissave = 0.11	unadjusted propensity to dissave = 0.45
*effect inflation rate = 0.32	***effect inflation rate = 0.56**
Payoff = -34.7266	Payoff = -89.4241
Maximum payoff found at:	Maximum payoff found at:
unadjusted propensity to save = 0.25	unadjusted propensity to save = 0.17
unadjusted propensity to dissave = 0.12	unadjusted propensity to dissave = 0.47
*lagged inflation effect = 0.34	***lagged inflation effect = 0.75**
Payoff = -33.7931	Payoff = -66.6817

Table 8. Model Parameters, Source: VGR, NIPA

Next, we check the influence of nominal interest rates. As mentioned, inflation will certainly cause the desire to balance losses in wealth by stronger saving effort. Yet the ability to do so is much greater if nominal rates are high. Although the time series of inflation and nominal rates are highly correlated, they are not identical by far, so nominal rates might contain additional information explaining differentials in saving.

For the German interest rate, we employ the average annual yield of German public bonds. For the U.S., we use the Federal Reserve's effective rate. Both rates are available for the whole range of time. The formula follows the same scheme as before.

Hence, we now check:

$$\alpha 1(t) = \alpha 1_{unadj} + \varepsilon_{i.nom} * \text{nominal interest rate}(t)$$

(5.9)

resp.

$$\alpha 1(t) = \alpha 1_{unadj} + \varepsilon_{i.nom_{lag}} * \text{nominal interest rate}(t-1)$$

(5.10)

The results of the respective calibrations are provided by Table 9. The sensitivity analysis is added by Table III on the website.

Germany	U.S.
Maximum payoff found at:	Maximum payoff found at:
unadjusted propensity to save = 0.20	unadjusted propensity to save = 0.17
unadjusted propensity to dissave = 0	unadjusted propensity to dissave = 0.47
*effect nominal interest rate = 0.62	***effect nominal interest rate = 0.44**
Payoff = -28.8274	Payoff = -86.7907
Maximum payoff found at:	Maximum payoff found at:
*unadjusted propensity to save = 0.20	unadjusted propensity to save = 0.17
*unadjusted propensity to dissave = 0	unadjusted propensity to dissave = 0.49
*lagged nominal interest effect = 0.62	***lagged nominal interest effect = 0.54**
Payoff = -30.4105	Payoff = -71.3892

Table 9. Model Parameters, Source: VGR, NIPA

In Germany, the effect of the nominal rate is obviously stronger than the effect of the inflation; particularly the effect of current nominal rates clearly improves the simulation. For the U.S. the lagged effect provides a better fit, while it is worse compared to the inflation effect. A plausible explanation for this divergence is the different structure of the capital markets and the higher relevance of interest-bearing saving accounts in Germany. In the U.S., saving in stocks and other kinds of assets has a stronger role. This could explain why in the U.S. nominal rates are less important as a factor guiding saving behaviour.

Next, we check the effect of the real interest rate. To obtain real rates, we refer to the same interest rates as above, but subtract the respective inflation rates. Our simulation is guided by following formula:

$$\alpha1(t) = \alpha1_{unadj} + \varepsilon_i * \text{real interest rate}(t)$$

$$(5.11)$$

resp.

$$\alpha 1(t) = \alpha 1_{unadj} + \varepsilon_{i\_lag} * \text{real interest rate}(t-1)$$

$$(5.12)$$

The outcome of the respective calibrations is provided by Table 10 and the graphics with the outcome of the sensitivity analysis by Table IV on the website.

Germany	U.S.
Maximum payoff found at:	Maximum payoff found at:
unadjusted propensity to save = 0.26	*unadjusted propensity to save = 0.20
unadjusted propensity to dissave = 0.20	*unadjusted propensity to dissave = 0.53
*effect real interest rates = 0.27	***effect real interest rates = 0.32**
Payoff = -35.2875	Payoff = -109.881
Maximum payoff found at:	Maximum payoff found at:
unadjusted propensity to save = 0.27	unadjusted propensity to save = 0.20
unadjusted propensity to dissave = 0.21	unadjusted propensity to dissave = 0.53
*lagged real interest effect = 0.12	***lagged real interest effect = 0.28**
Payoff = -36.3753	Payoff = -111.409

Table 10. Model Parameters, Source: VGR, NIPA

The real interest rate effect is extremely weak in both countries. In fact, the payoff is almost not improved at all by assuming an influence of current or lagged real rates on the propensity to save. The difference between current and lagged effects is not crucial in this case. Hence, any hypothesis of a strong effect of real rates on saving is, again, rejected.

However, the nineteen eighties in the U.S., particularly the first half, have been the years of Reaganomics with extremely high nominal and—due to falling inflation—real interest rates. In this period, there is indeed a very strong correspondence between the double peaks in the saving rate and the path of the real interest rate. In fact, in this particular period the parallelism is stronger than it was in the cases of inflation or nominal rates.

However, the other peaks of real interest rates do not correspond to particularly high values of the saving rate. The situation in Germany is similar. It was the uptrend in saving in the years before unification that was accompanied by particularly high real rates. However, supposing a strong real rate effect would in general rather increase the difference between the simulated and the real path.

It is striking that the correspondence between the peaks of saving and real interest rates in both countries only occurred in periods, in which real rates reached exceptionally high values. This was the case in the mid-eighties in the U.S. and in the late eighties in Germany. During more regular periods, when real rates are only slightly above the average, an effect on saving is not present.

This leads us to another approach. Perhaps real interest rates only (measurably) encourage saving when they reach extremely high values, while saving is neutral regarding smaller changes in real rates. Hence, we test the following specification:

$$\alpha 1 = \alpha 1_{unadj} + \{\varepsilon_{i.extr} * \text{real interest rate, if } i_{real} > 4; \ 0 \text{ otherwise}\}$$

$$(5.13)$$

If we check for optimal parameter values, including the effect of an extremely high real rate (excluding any effect of current or lagged real rates in general), we obtain the results printed in Table 11. The sensitivity analysis is available in Table V on the website.

Germany	U.S.
Maximum payoff found at:	Maximum payoff found at:
unadjusted propensity to save = 0.27	unadjusted propensity to save = 0.20
unadjusted propensity to dissave = 0.21	unadjusted propensity to dissave = 0.54
*effect of extremely high real interest rate = 0.26	***effect of extremely high real interest rate = 0.80**
Payoff = -32.5303	Payoff = -81.2047

Table 11. Model Parameters, Source: VGR, NIPA

In fact, in both countries the effect of extremely high interest rates improves the fit of the simulation much more than the inclusion of a real rate effect (be it current or lagged). This suggests that the hypothesis is not too far from reality: the propensity to save responds to the real interest rate, but only if the latter reaches very high values. Otherwise, the response is negligible.

In truth, there is an additional factor which we have not yet introduced into our model despite its undoubtedly relevant influence on *measured* saving. We have talked about capital gains being particularly relevant for saving in stocks and other securities. In Chapter 1 we already considered a crucial measurement problem influencing the displayed path of the saving rate. The core of this problem is that the measured saving rate regards dividends used for further stock purchases as saving, while realised capital gains that are again accumulated are not considered as saving. For the individual saver, however, the difference between these two types of revenues is not crucial. If the saver does not own stocks directly but shares in investment funds that redistribute parts of their profit, from his point of view it is indistinguishable to what degree such revenues correspond to dividends and to what extent they result from realised capital gains. In fact, particularly since the mid-nineties, companies have increasingly used profits to repurchase own stocks instead of redistributing dividends. These stock-repurchases led to a large flow of cash from the business to the household sector that was not accounted for as income. If households used only a small fraction of these flows for consumption purposes, the measured saving rate had to decrease, even if households reaccumulated a higher share of their total revenues than before. Maki & Palumbo (2001) actually show that in the nineteen nineties measured saving dropped the most for families in the uppermost quintile who experienced—and realised—the largest capital gains.

In fact, the curve of the aggregate saving rate during the recent decade partly mirrors the ups and downs of the stock market. In the late nineteen nineties, when stock markets prospered, saving out of realised capital gains certainly played an important role, while after the temporary stock market crash in 2000, traditional investments in bank accounts or at the money market regained ground. After 2004, the stock market again started to boom, breaking down in 2008. Such shifts in assets influence the measured saving rate although it actually neither causes nor reflects any change in the individual propensity to save. It is beyond the scope of this book to analyse in more detail the influence of stock market movements on the saving rate; nevertheless, we test the possible outcome of the introduction of a stock market effect into our model.

To do so, we employ time-series, provided by the World Bank, measuring the share of stock market capitalisation in GDP. These data are available from 1976 to 2010. In fact, no significant influence is discernible before the late nineteen eighties since the value of listed shares in GDP had been widely constant beforehand. A strong upward trend of stock market wealth started in the nineteen nineties.

Our hypothesis is: the higher the value of listed stocks compared to GDP, the more capital gains will be realised in the respective year. Since reaccumulating such gains pushes measured saving down, the effect of booming stock markets on saving is assumed to be negative. To test whether the inclusion of such an effect improves the fit, we test the following formula to model the propensity to save:

$$\alpha 1(t) = \alpha 1_{unadj} - \varepsilon_{stocks} * \text{stock market capitalisation to GDP}(t)$$

$$(5.14)$$

It has to be stressed that, in contrast to the other effects, the stock market effect is supposed to be an effect that mainly concerns *measured* saving and not so much the individual propensity to save itself.

In fact, it has been argued in a number of studies that prospering stock markets let people feel wealthier thereby suppressing their saving effort. However, we consider the measurement problem to be the more crucial one compared to the other effect.

To test the sensitivity of the model path with respect to the stock effect, we vary the latter between 0 and 0.1. The result of the simulation is provided by Table 12. The outcome of the sensitivity analysis is available in Table VI on the website. The influence of the stock market on saving since the beginning of the nineteen nineties is actually clearly visible for both countries. In each case the payoff is closer to zero here than in the case of any other single effect. In Germany, the improvement of the match following from the inclusion of the stock market effect is somewhat weaker than in the U.S., but still remarkable. This difference reflects the less vital (but increasingly relevant) role of the stock market in Germany.

Germany	U.S.
Maximum payoff found at:	Maximum payoff found at:
unadjusted propensity to save = 0.26	unadjusted propensity to save = 0.20
unadjusted propensity to dissave = 0	unadjusted propensity to dissave = 0.01
*stockeffect = 0.08	*stockeffect = 0.09
Payoff = -23.3331	Payoff = -64.1223

Table 12. Model Parameters, Source: VGR, NIPA, World Bank

Whether this effect is due to the measurement problem being considered, or whether stock market wealth discourages saving, is of course not answered by this simulation. However, since data about wealth holdings and saving rates in cross-section do not provide any evidence for the hypothesis that higher wealth discourages saving, we tend to the first interpretation.

While we departed from the assumption of a constant propensity to save, the propensity to dissave was, thus far, assumed to be fixed. This might be equally inadequate for a time period of about 40 to 60 years. Conditions to get access to private credit have certainly changed during this time. Interestingly, the calibrations always provided higher values for the propensity to dissave in the U.S. compared to Germany. This is clearly in line with reality. U.S. households are, on average, worryingly indebted today, which suggests a strong propensity to search for credit.

However, this has not been the case for the previous five decades. We mentioned in Chapter 1 the extreme rise in mortgage debt during the second half of the nineteen nineties and even more so between the beginning of the millennium and 2007, a rise that was not covered by real estate investment at all. Rather, mortgages were a cheap way to refinance consumer credit in times of soaring property prices and low interest rates. We argued in Chapter 1 that the fall in the FOF saving rate in the late nineties was to a remarkable degree caused by rising indebtedness. The acquisitions of financial assets did not shrink by far, being instead rather volatile. Yet household indebtedness is not a negligible phenomenon in today's Germany either, even if the extent is not comparable to the United States.

In fact, the deregulation and liberalisation of financial markets made it much easier to access credit. In contrast, credit was hardly available after the financial market crash in 2007/2008. Thus, the conditions changed for the propensity to dissave. It is certainly realistic to include this effect into our model, deviating from the assumption of a constant propensity to dissave for almost half a century. Although the deregulation of financial markets was certainly not a one-year event, for simplicity we will assume just two single changes in the propensity to dissave. Hence, we test the following approach:

$$\alpha 2(t) = \begin{cases} \alpha 2_{unadj} + \varepsilon_{lib} & \text{if liberalisation year} \le t < 2008 \\ a2_{unadj} & \text{otherwise} \end{cases}$$

$$(5.15)$$

The first steps in the U.S. towards deregulation were already happening during the nineteen eighties. The immediate effect was rising household indebtedness. We include 1985 as the year for liberalisation in the U.S. In Germany, essential measures of financial deregulation did not take place before the unification. We use 1991 as the year for liberalisation in this case.

To separate the liberalisation effect, we return to a constant propensity to save in the following calibrations. The liberalisation effect is assumed to be situated between zero and one. The result of the calibrations is provided by Table 13.

Germany	U.S.
Maximum payoff found at:	Maximum payoff found at:
unadjusted propensity to save = 0.25	unadjusted propensity to save = 0.18
unadjusted propensity to dissave = 0	unadjusted propensity to dissave = 0.18
*effectlib = 0.18	***effectlib = 0.27**
Payoff = -18.9046	Payoff = -83.8459

Table 13. Model Parameters, Source: VGR, NIPA

The payoff is significantly improved by the inclusion of a liberalisation effect in both countries. For Germany, this effect is even more relevant than the stock market effect. Hence, to assume a change in the propensity to dissave is obviously realistic.

But there is still another parameter that has been assumed to be constant over the entire range of time, although in reality it certainly changed. We have talked about the distribution of income. In fact, an increase in the propensity to dissave due to the deregulation of financial markets definitely plays a stronger role in reducing aggregate saving if the share of non-savers increases and/or their income is reduced due to redistribution. As noted before, the effect of rising inequality on saving depends on the relationship between the propensity to save and to dissave. If the first exceeds the latter, a redistribution of income from the bottom to the top boosts saving, while in the opposite case it shifts the saving rate down.

Finally, we test the effect of income redistributions separately. It is almost unanimously accepted that in OECD countries inequality has risen since the beginning of the nineteen eighties. We observed the curve of the Gini coefficient for developed countries in Chapter 1, analysing the relationship between inequality and saving. In the OECD sample, rising inequality was found to move in line with shrinking saving rates.

We will model the effect of income redistributions by assuming a yearly decrease of the standard relative income of nonsavers (that is the relative income of non-savers in the case of a Gamma (2,2) distribution and a necessity share of 50 percent) of maximal 0.005 percentage points from 1980 on. Hence, we vary $y\{ns\}$ according to following rule:

$$
y\{ns\} = \begin{cases} y\{ns_{Gamma(2,2)}\} & \text{if } t \leq 1980 \\ y\{ns_{Gamma(2,2)-\varepsilon_{redistr}}\} * (t-1980) & \text{if } t > 1980 \end{cases}
$$

$$(5.16)$$

In the simulations provided so far, about 27 percent of the population in the U.S. were non-savers in 1980 since the necessity share was at a level of about 52 percent; in Germany, the proportion of non-savers was a little higher due to a slightly higher necessity share (54 percent).

The average relative income of the U.S. non-savers was consistently about 0.31 in 1980, and slightly higher in Germany. If the redistribution effect reaches its maximum, the standard relative income of the non-savers shrinks to 0.155. Due to the increased necessity share, the share of non-savers now reaches about 40 percent in both countries (in Germany somewhat less than in the U.S.) and the relative income of non-savers amounts to approximately 0.25. This is very low, indeed. The real redistribution of income was probably not so strong. On the other hand, the real redistribution—particularly in the U.S.—did not only concern the poorer households, but former middle-class people as well, turning savers into dissavers. This effect is excluded here to keep the model as simple as possible. The share of non-savers k increases in our model during the nineties, but only due to a rising necessity share.

If we carry out the respective calibration for Germany, we obtain zero as the optimal effect of redistribution. This is not surprising bearing in mind that the propensity to save always exceeds the propensity to dissave in the German calibrations (0.28 to 0.21). Under this condition, the effect of increasing inequality on saving would be positive. Whereas saving in the late nineteen nineties was always overestimated by our simulations, a significant redistribution effect would amplify this deviation. However, if we include a liberalisation effect on the propensity to dissave (supposing 1991 as the year of liberalisation and ending in 2008) both effects become positive.

The calibration for the U.S. provides a positive redistribution effect at the upper limit of 0.005, even without introducing a liberalisation effect. Here, the propensity to dissave exceeds the propensity to save in all simulations. Therefore, the redistribution effect contributes to an explanation of the falling trend of saving in the nineties. If we include the liberalisation effect, we obtain the results provided in Table 14. Redistributions of income from the bottom to the top, obviously, contributed to the fall of the U.S. saving rate in the previous 20 years.

Germany	U.S.
Maximum payoff found at:	Maximum payoff found at:
*unadjusted propensity to save = 0.26	unadjusted propensity to save = 0.18
*unadjusted propensity to dissave = 0.06	unadjusted propensity to dissave = 0.17
*redistribution effect = 0.002	**redistribution effect = 0.005**
*effectlib = 0.16	***effectlib = 0.21**
Payoff = -18.7269	Payoff = -76.7652

Table 14. Model Parameters, Source: VGR, NIPA

Let us summarise our results so far. Beside the necessity share, inflation as well as nominal rates appear to contribute to an explanation of saving behaviour. Real interest rates were found to have a significant effect only if they reach extremely high values. The stock market effect appeared to be quite strong, particularly in the United States. The modelling of the liberalisation effect was somewhat artificial due to the assumption of just one jump and one drop in the propensity to dissave. The inclusion of this effect, nevertheless, significantly improved the match. Redistributions of income seem to also contribute to an explanation for the fall of the saving rate in both countries.

d) Simulating the savings path including relevant effects

In the simulations provided so far, many effects actually referred to time series that are correlated to each other such as inflation and nominal rates. Moreover, all these effects cannot be assumed to influence saving independently from each other. We explicitly considered the interdependence between the redistribution effect and the liberalisation effect. This is certainly not the only connection playing a role. However, our main purpose in this chapter is to confirm the influence of the necessity share on saving. Therefore, we will only include the most relevant additional effects in our final simulation to get a more realistic model deviating from the assumption of constant propensities to save and to dissave over half a century. One effect that will be included influences the propensity to save, and the second modifies the propensity to dissave. Moreover, redistributions of income from the bottom to the top are considered to be relevant. As the variable influencing the propensity to save, we actually employ current nominal interest rates for Germany, and lagged nominal interest rates for the U.S. For the propensity to dissave, we include the liberalisation effect. Table 15 provides the optimal parameter values under these circumstances. Figures 41 and 42 provide a visual representation of the fit of the simulated path in both countries.

Germany	U.S.
Maximum payoff found at:	Maximum payoff found at:
unadjusted propensity to save = 0.21	*unadjusted propensity to save = 0.15
unadjusted propensity to dissave = 0	*unadjusted propensity to dissave = 0.17
effectlib = 0.13	***effectlib = 0.19**
redistribution effect = 0.005	***redistribution effect = 0.005**
***effect nominal interest rate = 0.54**	***lagged nominal interest effect = 0.49**
Payoff = -13.7144	Payoff = -39.9221
Coefficient of correlation: 0.93	Coefficient of correlation: 0.94

Table 15. Model Parameters, Source: VGR, NIPA

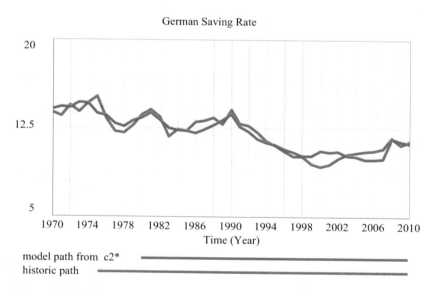

Figure 41. Model Path German Saving Rate I, Source: VGR

Figure 42. Model Path U.S. Saving Rate I, Source NIPA

The difference to the graph based on constant propensities to save and to dissave is particularly obvious in the case of the United States. While the former simulation failed to match the savings peak in the mid-eighties, this is well covered now. For Germany, the difference is not crucial, but the match is clearly improved by the inclusion of the two effects.

If, as a second approach, we employ the stock market effect instead of the liberalisation effect, the fit is slightly worse in Germany and slightly better for the United States. Table 16 provides the results. In Figure 43 and 44 the paths are plotted.

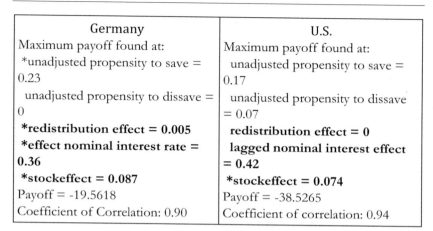

Germany	U.S.
Maximum payoff found at:	Maximum payoff found at:
*unadjusted propensity to save = 0.23	unadjusted propensity to save = 0.17
unadjusted propensity to dissave = 0	unadjusted propensity to dissave = 0.07
*redistribution effect = 0.005	**redistribution effect = 0**
*effect nominal interest rate = 0.36	**lagged nominal interest effect = 0.42**
*stockeffect = 0.087	***stockeffect = 0.074**
Payoff = -19.5618	Payoff = -38.5265
Coefficient of Correlation: 0.90	Coefficient of correlation: 0.94

Table 16. Model Parameters, Source: VGR, NIPA

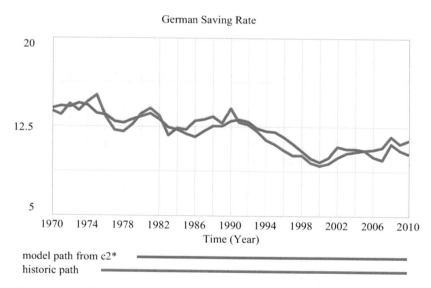

Figure 43. Model Path German Saving Rate II, Source: VGR, World Bank

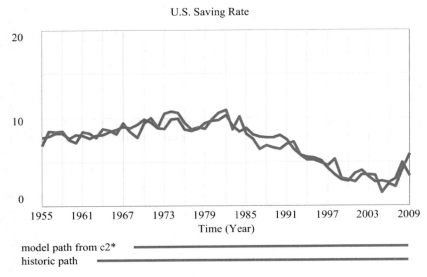

Figure 44. Model Path U.S. Saving Rate II, Source: NIPA, World Bank

Interestingly, the stock market effect is much stronger and more relevant if we use the FoF saving rate as the point of reference. Table 17 provides the results and Figure 45 plots the path.

Generally, the inclusion of a stock market effect provides a match that is similar to the liberalisation effect in the case of the United States. In Germany, the fit is slightly worse if we refer to the stock market, but it reaches a coefficient of correlation of 90 percent

U.S. FoF Saving rate
Maximum payoff found at:
unadjusted propensity to save = 0.23
*unadjusted propensity to dissave = 0
redistribution effect = 0.0037
stock effect = 0.1477
lagged nominal interest effect = 0.46
Payoff = -107.704
Coefficient of correlation: 0.93

Table 17. Model Parameters, Source: NIPA, FoF, World Bank

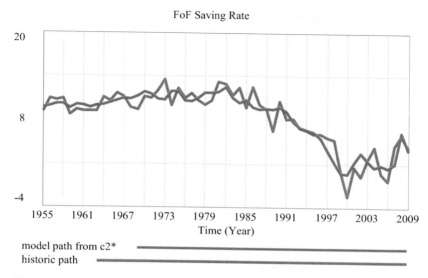

Figure 45. Model Path FoF Saving Rate, Source: NIPA, FoF, World Bank

To conclude, by including one monetary variable and either the liberalisation or the stock market effect, the path of saving is reproduced very well by the simulations. Only small peaks and lows, especially in the sixties and eighties, are not covered perfectly. This is not surprising since we completely ignored changes in tax incentives and other institutional changes that certainly encouraged or discouraged saving.

Thus, taking into account that our approach includes either only two variables (the necessity share and the current or lagged inflation rate and a dummy for the liberalisation effect) or three variables (if we refer to the stock market instead of the liberalisation effect), while the time period covers 41 or 55 years, the match is remarkable. In fact, more than 90 percent of the variation of the saving rate in both countries, over approximately half a century, is explained by our model.

e) Checking the null hypothesis

To check the real contribution of the necessity share to an explanation of saving rate differentials, we will finally evaluate the possible fit of the null hypothesis. The latter corresponds to a model including all tested monetary variables (the inflation rate, the real and the nominal interest rate, each at current and lagged values), but excluding any reference to the necessity share. Hence, under the null hypothesis, consumers save the same share of their respective personal disposable income at a certain point in time. For the aggregate saving rate we therefore have:

$$s(t) = \alpha 1(t)$$

$$(5.17)$$

The propensity to save is determined by a constant and the monetary variables that were considered to influence saving behaviour:

$$\alpha 1(t) = \alpha 1_{unadj}$$

$$+ \ \varepsilon_{infl} \ * \ \text{inflation rate}(t)$$

$$+ \ \varepsilon_{infl\_lag} \ * \ \text{inflation rate}(t-1)$$

$$+ \ \varepsilon_{i.nom} \ * \ \text{nominal interest rate}(t)$$

$$+ \ \varepsilon_{i.nom\_lag} \ * \ \text{nominal interest rate}(t-1)$$

$$+ \ \varepsilon_i \ * \ \text{real interest rate}(t)$$

$$+ \ \varepsilon_{i_{lag}} \ * \ \text{real interest rate}(t-1)$$

$$(5.18)$$

Table 18 provides the optimal values of the different parameters under the null hypothesis.

The match of the null hypothesis is remarkably worse compared to the match of our model in both countries. For the U.S. saving rate, the best payoff found by the null hypothesis is just -240 compared to -38 reached by our saving rule. The coefficient of correlation of our best model simulation to the real path of the NIPA saving rate is 0.94, while the null hypothesis at best reaches a match of 0.55. The deviation is somewhat lower for Germany but still remarkable. While our simulation displays a payoff of -13, the null hypothesis reaches -33. Moreover, the coefficient of correlation has deteriorated from 0.93 in the case of our saving rule, to 0.81.

Null Hypothesis Germany (6 variables)	Null Hypothesis U.S. (6 variables)
Maximum payoff found at:	Maximum payoff found at:
unadjusted propensity to save = 0.08	*unadjusted propensity to save = 0.05
lagged nominal interest effect = 0	*lagged nominal interest effect = 0
lagged inflation effect = 0.12	* lagged inflation effect = 0.30
lagged real interest effect = 0.13	* lagged real interest effect = 0.05
effect inflation rate = 0.42	*effect inflation rate = 0.28
effect nominal interest rate = 0.13	*effect nominal interest rate = 0.01
*effect real interest rates = 0.28	*effect real interest rates = 0.05
Payoff = -33.9686	Payoff = -240.575
Coefficient of correlation: 0.81	Coefficient of correlation: 0.55

Table 18. Null Hypothesis, Source: VGR, NIPA

In the case of the U.S., the fit achieved by the null hypothesis including such a wide range of variables is worse compared to our first model that referred alone to the necessity share, assuming constant propensities to save and to dissave. This model actually reached a payoff of -116 compared to -240 of the hull hypothesis and the coefficient of correlation was also stronger.

For Germany, the match of the null hypothesis is similar to the simplified first approach, but worse compared to the simulation employing EVS data and referring alone to the necessity share. To evaluate this result, we have to bear in mind that the null hypothesis included six variables instead of one.

If we additionally include the stock effect as an additional variable, the payoff and the coefficient of correlation of the null hypothesis is improved, but still worse compared to our model. In fact, we reach a payoff of -23 for Germany and of -52 for the United States. The coefficient of correlation is 0.88 for Germany and 0.92 for the U.S. However, this is only somewhat better than our first approach that referred to the necessity share alone, and clearly worse compared to our model that included two additional variables.

Therefore, the test of the null hypothesis suggests rejecting the assumption of no effect of the necessity share on saving. Rather, for the U.S. as well as for Germany, a model including subsistence points turns out to be able to explain the real path of saving much better than models reduced to the traditional variables.

To evaluate the contribution of the necessity share to explaining saving behaviour, Table 19 provides a final comparison of the three main approaches for reproducing the historic path of the personal saving rate, and the results for the null hypothesis.

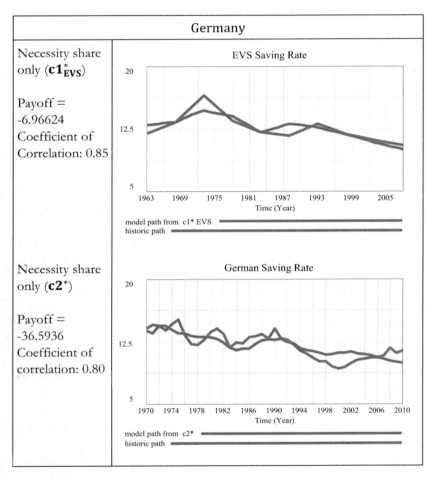

Germany	
Necessity share (**c2***), nominal interest rate and liberalisation effect (incl. income redistributions) Payoff = -13.7144 Coefficient of correlation: 0.93	**German Saving Rate**
Necessity share (**c2***), nominal interest rate and stock market effect (incl. income redistributions) Payoff = -19.5618 Coefficient of Correlation: 0.90	**German Saving Rate**

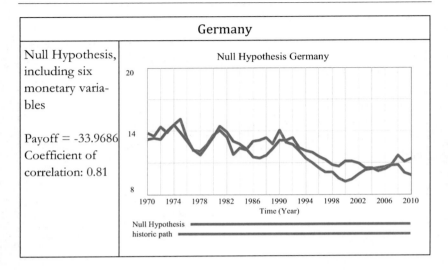

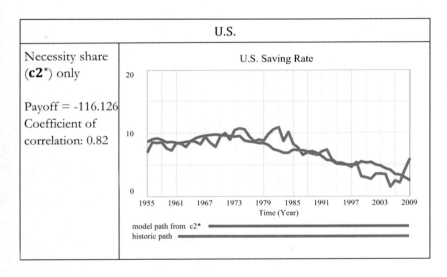

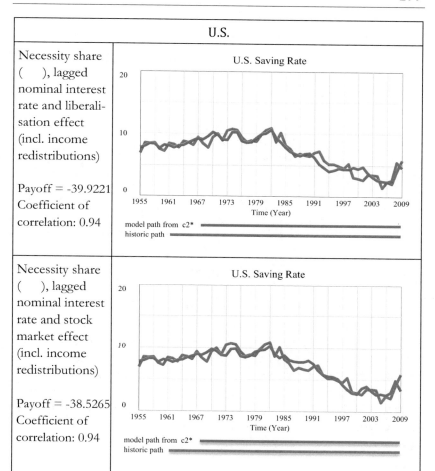

U.S.	
Necessity share ( ), lagged nominal interest rate and liberalisation effect (incl. income redistributions) Payoff = -39.9221 Coefficient of correlation: 0.94	U.S. Saving Rate model path from c2* historic path
Necessity share ( ), lagged nominal interest rate and stock market effect (incl. income redistributions) Payoff = -38.5265 Coefficient of correlation: 0.94	U.S. Saving Rate model path from c2* historic path

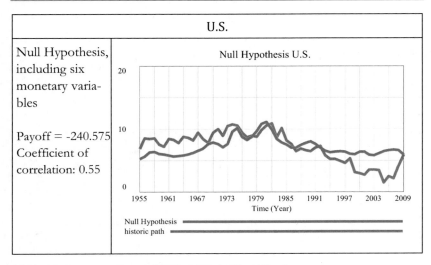

Table 19. Summary, Source: VGR, NIPA, World Bank

The first row for each country provides the result if we use the necessity share as the only explanatory variable. The second row shows the fit of the path that includes the additional factors: current or lagged nominal interest rates, one dummy variable for the effect of financial market liberalisation and the effect of more income inequality. The third row provides the model path when a stock market effect instead of an effect of liberalisation is included. The fourth row shows the fit of the null hypothesis employing 6 monetary variables (more than any of the other models), but excluding any reference to the necessity share.

f) Conclusions

We conclude that the necessity share, growing according to the rate of excess basic growth and excess basic inflation, contributes significantly to an explanation of saving behaviour. By including this share as a single explanatory variable, we obtain a simulation that covers 82 percent of the variance of the NIPA saving rate between 1955 and 2009 and 82 percent of the variance of the German VGR saving rate. The model that uses the survey necessity share $c1^*$ obtained from the German EVS reaches a match of 85 percent of the variance of the German EVS saving rate between 1963 and 2008. Hence, necessity spending turns out to be a crucial variable explaining saving behaviour.

Additionally, current or lagged nominal rates appear to contribute to a better match of the path of the real saving rate. In contrast, real interest rates only have weak effects, while extremely high real interest rates (exceeding 4 percent) seem to push saving. Moreover, the assumptions of a liberalisation effect and of an effect of income redistributions improve the fit. Finally, a stock market effect has been shown to guarantee a better match of the real savings path for recent decades for the U.S.

The discovered effects are easily explicable. High nominal rates facilitate stronger saving, supplying the saver with additional resources. It is also not incomprehensible that real rates have a measurable effect only at extreme values. A stock market effect on measured saving, due to the different treatment of dividends versus realised capital gains, has already been considered in Chapter 1.

In the end, we provided a simulation that reproduced more than ninety percent of the variation of the real path of saving in both countries. This is a strong result considering that the simulation refers to a period of 41 years in Germany and 55 years in the U.S. Of course, our model does not cover every small variation of the U.S. and the German saving rate since we excluded the influence of the institutional environment such as varying taxes, introduced or abolished saving incentives as well as the partial privatisation of the pension system in Germany connected to the Riester reforms. Changes in those conditions undeniably play a role in encouraging or discouraging saving. However, the strong fit reached by our simulations shows that the crucial factors explaining the path of saving over time are found in another area.

Summary

The focal point of our research throughout this book is the hypothesis that basic needs, which move in line with the general standard of living, have a crucial influence on saving. We argue that the choice to spend or to save does not concern the entire amount of disposable income of a consumer but only the free income share. This share represents the part of income that is left once all basic needs have been satisfied. To solve the saving puzzle, we attempt to uncover the motion of the free income share.

Since we are convinced that people follow simplified rules rather than attempt to solve a stochastic intertemporal optimisation problem (particularly since the required information is unavailable) we provide a rule of thumb that might plausibly guide saving behaviour. This rule states that consumers save if current income exceeds the amount required to purchase the current necessity basket, while they dissave, or demand credit, if income falls below basic needs. The propensity to save out of free income or the propensity to dissave are assumed to vary over time and to be influenced by monetary variables and the institutional environment.

If individual saving follows such a rule, the aggregate saving rate is crucially influenced by the mean necessity share. Moreover, if the propensity to save is not identical to the propensity to dissave, distributional parameters—or more precisely, the share of non-savers in the population and their share of total income—play a relevant role.

Defining subsistence points for modern societies is not without problems. Since subsistence points should not only include the indispensable necessities of a human being's biological survival, but also represent the basic requirements for *social* survival, we define this category according to the common standard of living in an industrialised country.

Following a detailed analysis of cross-sectional consumption shares, we identify a number of consumption expenditure categories that are dominated by basic needs. On this basis, the path of the mean necessity share in

Germany and in the United States is reproduced in two approximations. First, we compute the share of these expenditure categories in total consumption outlay $(c1^*)$. Second, we calculate the rates of excess basic expenditure and of excess basic growth; the time path of the necessity share is assumed to grow according to these two rates $(c2^*)$. While the rate of excess basic inflation measures the extent by which price increases of basic goods exceed the general rate of inflation, the rate of excess basic growth is derived from the hypothesis that necessity growth follows a 10-year moving average of income growth.

For the United States, the three approximations to the real necessity share, $c1^*_{NIPA}$, $c1^*_{CEX}$ and $c2^*$, are found to be well correlated, although the relationship between $c2^*$ and $c1^*_{CEX}$ is stronger. For Germany, the correlation of $c2^*$ and $c1^*_{EVS}$ is particularly strong, while $c1^*_{VGR}$ deviates from both shares. The national accounts expenditure shares are found to be somewhat spurious, particularly in Germany,

The predictions of our model for saving behaviour are as follows. First, cross-sectional saving rates should be a strictly rising function of relative income since the free income share rises with a household's current income position. For the same reason, saving rates should rise with permanent income. Permanently low-income consumers are most likely unable to save over their entire life span since they are never equipped with a relevant free income share.

Second, over the long run and across different countries, we should not find a significant correlation between real income and saving. But since subsistence needs are likely to almost entirely equal average income in very poor countries, these countries should display particularly low saving rates. Only if such countries overcome their destitute status can a free income share emerge and saving occur at significant rates. Beyond a certain level, however, income should stop boosts to saving since the necessity basket also starts to grow with a rising standard of living.

Third, at the macroeconomic level, saving rates should be positively correlated to income growth since periods of high income growth are most likely those in which current income growth exceeds its long-term trend and, hence, the supposed growth rate of the necessity basket.

Fourth, if basic price inflation exceeds general inflation, the saving rate should, *ceteris paribus*, decrease. Saving by lower-income households should be particularly diminished. As far as determinants of the necessity share are more volatile than factors influencing the propensity to save, saving rates of low-income households should be more volatile over time than saving rates of richer consumers. At a given point in time, however, the variance of saving rates within the lower deciles should be smaller than among higher income groups since for the lower deciles, the trade-off between consumption and saving is much less a matter of choice.

All these predictions match perfectly the empirical data. In Chapter 1 we identify the stylised facts of saving. The most striking features of saving behaviour in cross-section are, first, the steeply rising curve of individual saving rates over relative income and, second, the high share of households at the lower end of the earnings scale, who save nothing and possess no accumulated wealth.

Observing the time path of saving rates of different quintiles, saving rates of lower-income households are found to be more volatile than saving rates of better-off families. Furthermore, empirical evidence from the German Income and Expenditure survey suggests that saving rates in the bottom deciles display significantly less variance across households at a given point in time.

The most robust stylised fact at the macroeconomic level is a positive link between the saving rate and income growth. The vague correspondence between the aggregate saving rate and per capita income in cross-country comparisons as well as over time is confirmed. This link is only significant when comparing very poor countries to middle-income countries; above a certain level, however, income has no significant impact on the saving rate.

Our saving rule is able to explain additional empirical evidence. Even if the propensity to save and to dissave varies depending on the business cycle, increasing uncertainty during a downturn increases the saving rate only in certain instances since the propensity to save refers to the free income share only. This positive effect might be cancelled by a decrease of this share due to income losses. Strikingly, recessions with rising saving rates happened in Germany in the mid-seventies and early eighties, just when the necessity share was at its lowest level.

Most studies reject a significant link between real interest rates and saving. Indeed, even if higher real rates strengthen the propensity to save, this will not be observable if the necessity share rises simultaneously. This effect can again easily offset a higher propensity to save, especially if the effect of the real interest is not strong.

Our model provides an explanation for a negative relationship between the saving rate and inequality in developed countries. We predict that rising inequality reduces the personal saving rate if the propensity to dissave exceeds the propensity to save. Such a situation is more likely in developed countries since a higher level of available wealth makes it easier to dissave or to get access to credit. As is well-known, it was the extreme peak in U.S. property prices that—together with low interest rates—opened the possibility to millions of U.S. citizens of refinancing and enlarging consumer credit by new mortgages on existing homes. For limited periods of time, increasing inequality might decrease the saving rate instead of pushing it up.

We conclude that our approach is able to explain a number of stylised facts which cannot be adequately accounted for by traditional models of saving. We investigate the relationship between the necessity share and the saving rate for the U.S. and Germany and find a significant negative relation for both countries. Moreover, we reproduce cross-sectional saving rates and compare the results with Kuznets' data set on U.S. saving between 1929 and 1950 and with the four recent Income and Expenditure Surveys (1993–2008) in Germany. The match of real saving rates is quite good in both cases. Moreover, we show that the reference to the necessity share is able to provide a consistent explanation for diverging saving behaviour in East and West Germany during the nineteen nineties.

Finally, using our saving model we reproduce the time path of the personal saving rate for the U.S. from 1955 to 2009 and for Germany from 1970 to 2010. The outcome is quite convincing. The reference to the necessity share as the only determinant—assuming the propensity to save and to dissave to be constant—actually provides a simulation that is able to account for 82 percent of the variance of the NIPA saving rate, 85 percent of the variance of the EVS saving rate and 80 percent of the variance of the German VGR saving rate for the period under consideration.

In a next step, we depart from the assumption of a constant propensity to save and to dissave and check the relevance of a number of variables which are usually considered to influence saving behaviour. Among the tested variables, current and lagged nominal interest rates are found to have a significant effect on the propensity to save. Real rates are shown to have an impact on saving only if they reach extremely high values, exceeding 4 percent. The effects of financial market deregulation and of income redistributions are also found to be significant. Finally, booming stock markets appear to have a negative impact on measured aggregate saving.

The additional inclusion of an effect of current or lagged nominal rates on the propensity to save, and of an effect of financial market deregulation on the propensity to dissave, significantly improves the fit of our estimation for both countries. A similar result is obtained by introducing a stock market effect influencing *measured* saving rather than real saving behaviour. For both cases, income redistributions from the bottom to the top are considered and turn out to improve the match significantly.

The null hypothesis employing six monetary variables but excluding any reference to the necessity share, is found to match the real variances by 81 percent in Germany and 55 percent for the United States. Estimating the null hypothesis also provides a much worse payoff. A difference in the fit of almost 40 percentage points for the U.S. and of about 10 percentage points for Germany is considered to be sufficient to reject the null hypothesis.

The ability of our model to reproduce more than 90 percent of the variation of the U.S. and the German saving rate over more than four and five decades respectively, strongly supports the hypothesis that the necessity share is relevant in explaining the actual saving behaviour of households. We obtain such a strong fit even though we ignore changes in tax incentives or other institutional parameters that encouraged or discouraged private saving.

To conclude, a model in which households only start saving after all basic needs are satisfied is able to explain the major stylised facts and to reproduce cross-sectional saving rates as well as the historic path of personal saving in time, covering its variation to a remarkable degree. Our hypothesis, that necessity spending limits the choice between consumption and saving, is strongly supported by the empirical evidence and our saving rule can soundly be considered to provide an adequate representation of the decision process of real consumers.

References

Abel, A. B. (1990), Asset Prices under Habit Formation and Catching up with the Joneses, The American Economic Review, vol. 80, no. 2, May, 38–42.

– (1999), Risk Premia and Term Premia in General Equilibrium, Journal of Monetary Economics, vol. 43, no. 1, 3–33.

Aghevli, B.B., Boughton, J.M., Montiel, P., Villanueva, D., Woglom, G., (1990), The Role of National Saving in the World Economy, International Monetary Fund Occasional Paper 67.

Alessie, R., Lusardi, A. (1997), Consumption, Saving and Habit Formation, Economics Letters, vol. 55, no. 1, 103–8.

Alessie, R., Lusardi A., Kapteyn A. (1995), Saving and Wealth Holdings of the Elderly, Ricerche Economiche, vol. 49, 293–315.

Allen, T.W., Carroll, C.D. (2001), Individual Learning About Consumption, in: Macroeconomic Dynamics, vol. 5, no. 2 (April), 255–71.

Ando, A., Guiso, L., Visco I. (eds.) (1994), Saving and the Accumulation of Wealth. Essays on Italian Household and Government Saving Behaviour, Cambridge: Cambridge University Press.

Antoniewicz, R.L. (1996), A Comparison of the Household Sector from the Flow of Funds Accounts and the Survey of Consumer Finances, Board of Governors of the Federal Reserve System (U.S.), Finance and Economics Discussion Series, no. 96-26.

Atkinson, A. (1971), The Distribution of Wealth and the Individual Life-Cycle, Oxford Economic Papers, New Series, vol. 23, no. 2, July, 239–54.

Atkinson, A., Brandolini, A. (2001), Promise and Pitfalls in the Use of Secondary Data-Sets: Income Inequality in OECD Countries as a Case Study, Journal of Economic Literature, vol. 39, no. 3, 771–99.

Atkeson, A., Ogaki, M. (1996), Wealth-Varying Intertemporal Elasticities of Substitution: Evidence from Panel and Aggregate Data, Journal of Monetary Economics, vol. 38, no. 3, 507–34.

Attanasio, O. P. (1998), A Cohort Analysis of US Household Saving Behavior, National Bureau of Economic Research, Journal of Human Resources, vol. 33, no. 3, 575–609.

– (1994), The Intertemporal Allocation of Consumption: Theory and Evidence, NBER Working Paper no. 4811.

–   (1997), Consumption and Saving Behaviour: Modelling Recent Trends, Fiscal Studies, vol. 18, no. 1, 23–47.
–   (1998). A Cohort Analysis of Saving Behaviour by U.S. Households, Journal of Human Resources, vol. 33, no. 3, 575–609.
Attanasio, O. P., Banks, J. (1998). Trends in Household Saving: A Tale of two Countries, Working Paper no. 98/15, The Institute of Fiscal Studies, London.
–   (2001), The Assessment: Household Saving – Issues in Theory and Policy, Oxford Review of Economic Policy, vol. 17, no. 1, 1–19.
Attanasio, O. P., Banks, J., Meghir, C., Weber, G. (1999), Humps and Bumps in Lifetime Consumption, Journal of Business and Economic Statistic, vol. 17, no. 1, Jan., 22–35.
Attanasio, O. P., Browning, M. (1995), Consumption over the Business Cycle and over the Life Cycle, American Economic Review, vol. 85, no. 5, 1118–37.
Attanasio, O. P., Davis, S. (1996), Relative Wage Movements and the Distribution of Consumption, Journal of Political Economy, vol. 104, no. 6, 1227–62.
Attanasio, O. P., Hoynes, H. W. (2000), Differential Mortality and Wealth Accumulation, Journal of Human Resources, vol. 35, no. 1, 1–29.
Attanasio, O. P., Székely, M. (1998), Household Savings and Income Distribution in Mexico, IDB Working Paper no. 322.
–   (2000), Household Saving in Developing Countries: Inequality, Demographics and all that. How different are Latin America and South East Asia?, Working Paper no. 427, Inter-American Development Bank.
Attanasio, O. P., Weber, G. (1989), Intertemporal Substitution, Risk Aversion and the Euler Equation for Consumption, Economic Journal, vol. 99, no. 395, Supplement, 59–73.
–   (1993), Consumption Growth, the Interest Rate and Aggregation, Review of Economic Studies, vol. 60, no.3, 631–49.
–   (1994), The UK Consumption Boom of the Late 1980s. Aggregate Implications of Microeconomic Evidence, Economic Journal, vol. 104, no. 427, 1269–302.
–   (1995), Is Consumption Growth Consistent with Intertemporal Optimisation? Evidence form the Consumer Expenditure Survey, Journal of Political Economy, vol. 103, no. 6, 1121–57.

Bacchetta, P., Gerlach, S. (1997), Consumption and Credit Constraints: International Evidence, Journal of Monetary Economics, vol. 40, no. 2, 207–38.
Bailliu, J. N., Reisen, H. (1998), Do Funded Pensions Contribute to Higher Aggregate Savings? A Cross-Country Analysis, Weltwirtschaftliches Archiv, Bd. 134, H. 4, 692-711.
Baltagi, B.H. (1995), Econometric Analysis of Panel Data, New York: Wiley.
Banks, J., Blundell, R. (1994), Household Saving Behaviour in the UK, in: Poterba, J. (ed.), International Comparisons of Household Saving, Chicago: The University of Chicago Press, 169–206.

Banks, J., Blundell, R., Preston, I. (1994), Life-Cycle Expenditure Allocations and the Consumption Costs of Children, European Economic Review, vol. 38, 1391–1410.

Banks, J., Blundell, R., Tanner, S. (1998), Is There a Retirement-Savings Puzzle?, The American Economic Review, vol. 88, no. 4 (Sep.), 769–88.

Barro, R.J. (1991), Economic Growth in a Cross-Section of Countries, Quarterly Journal of Economics, vol. 106, no. 2, 407–43.

Barro, R.J., Sala-i-Martin, X. (1995), Economic Growth, International Edition 1995, New York: McGraw-Hill.

Becker, G.S. (1962), Irrational Behavior and Economic Theory, Journal of Political Economy, vol. 70, no. 1, 1–13.

Behrends, S., Krebs, T. (2002), Einkommens- und Verbrauchsstichprobe 2003 – Den finanziellen Überblick wahren, Wirtschaft und Statistik, Nr. 11, 952–8.

Bernheim, D., Scholz, J.K. (1993), Private Saving and Public Policy, in: Poterba, J.M. (ed.), Tax Policy and the Economy, vol. 7, 73–110, Cambridge, Mass./ London: MIT Press.

Bernheim, D., Shoven, J.B. (eds.) (1991), National Saving and Economic Performance, Chicago and London: The University of Chicago Press.

Bernheim, D., Skinner, J., Weinberg, S. (2001), What Accounts for the Variation in Retirement Wealth among U.S. Households?, The American Economic Review, vol. 91, no. 4 (Sep.), 832–57.

Bertaut, C. (2002), Equity Prices, Household Wealth, and Consumption Growth in Foreign Industrial Countries: Wealth Effects in the 1990s, IFDP Working Paper no. 724, Federal Reserve Board.

Bertaut, C., Haliassos, M. (1997), Precautionary Portfolio Behavior from a Life-Cycle Perspective, Journal of Economic Dynamics and Control, vol. 21, no. 8–9, 1511–42.

Bertola, G., Foellmi, R., Zweimüller, J. (2006), Income Distribution in Macroeconomic Models, Princeton: Princeton University Press.

Biewen, M. (2000), Income Inequality in Germany during the 1980s and 1990s, Review of Income and Wealth, vol. 46, no. 1, 1–19.

Blinder, A.S. (1975), Distribution Effects and the Aggregate Consumption Function, Journal of Political Economy, vol. 83, no. 3, 447–75.

Blundell, R., Browning, M., Meghir, C. (1994), Consumer Demand and the Life-Cycle Allocation of Household Expenditures, Review of Economic Studies, vol. 61, no. 1, 57–80.

Bodkin, R.G. (1959), Windfall Income and Consumption, American Economic Review, vol. 49, no. 4, 602–14.

Borensztein, E., Montiel, P. J. (1991), On Savings, Investment and Growth in Eastern Europe, International Monetary Fund, Working Paper no. 91/61.

Börsch-Supan, A., Essig, L. (2005), Household Saving in Germany. Results of the First SAVE Study, in: Wise, D. A. (ed.), Analyses in the Economics of Aging, Chicago: The University of Chicago Press.

Börsch-Supan, A., Reil-Held, A., Rodepeter, R., Schnabel, R., Winter, J. (2001), The German Savings Puzzle, Research in Economics, vol. 55, no. 1, 15–38.

Börsch-Supan, A., Schmidt, P. (2001), Early Retirement in East and West Germany, in: Riphahn, R. T., Snower, D. J., Zimmermann, K. F. (eds.), Employment Policy in Transition. The Lessons of German Integration for the Labor Market, Berlin: Springer, 83–102.

Bosworth, B. (1990a), International Differences in Saving, American Economic Review, vol. 80, no. 2, May, 377–81.

– (1990b), The Global Decline in Saving: Some International Comparisons, Brookings Discussion Papers in International Economics, 83.

– (1993), Saving and Investment in a Global Economy, Brookings Institution.

Bosworth, B., Burtless, G., Sabelhaus, J. (1991), The Decline in Saving: Some Microeconomic Evidence. Brookings Papers on Economic Activity, vol. 22, no. 1, 183–256.

Bound, J., Krueger, A.B. (1991), The Extent of Measurement Error in Longitudinal Earnings Data: Do Two Wrongs Make a Right?, Journal of Labor Economics, vol. 9, no. 1, 1–24.

Bound, J., Brown, Ch., Duncan, G.J., Rodgers, W.L. (1994), Evidence on the Validity of Cross-sectional and Longitudinal Labor Market Data, Journal of Labor Economics, vol. 12, no. 3, 345–68.

Bradford, D. (1990), What is National Saving? Alternative Measures in Historical and International Context, in: Walker, C., Bloomfield, M., Thorning, M. (eds.), The U.S. Savings Challenge: Policy Options for Productivity and Growth, Boulder: Westview Press, 31–75.

Branch, E.R. (1994), The Consumer Expenditure Survey: A Comparative Analysis, Monthly Labor Review, vol. 117, no. 12, 47–55.

Browning, M., Collado, M.D. (2001), The Response of Expenditures to Anticipated Income Changes: Panel Data Estimates, American Economic Review, vol. 91, no. 3, 681–92.

Browning, M., Crossley, T.F. (2001). The Life-Cycle Model of Consumption and Saving, Journal of Economic Perspectives, vol. 15, no. 3, 3–22.

Browning, M., Lusardi, A. (1996), Household Saving: Micro Theory and Micro Facts, Journal of Economic Literature, vol. 34, no. 4, 1797–1855.

Byrne, J.P., Davis, E. P. (2003), Disaggregate Wealth and Aggregate Consumption: An Investigation of Empirical Relationships for the G7, Oxford Bulletin of Economics and Statistics, vol. 65, no. 2, 197–220.

Caballero, R.J. (1990), Consumption Puzzles and Precautionary Savings, Journal of Monetary Economics, vol. 25, no. 1, 113–36.

– (1991), Earnings Uncertainty and Aggregate Wealth Accumulation, American Economic Review, vol. 81, no. 4, 859–71.

Cagetti, M. (2003), Wealth Accumulation Over the Life Cycle and Precautionary Savings, Journal of Business and Economic Statistics, vol. 21, no. 3 (July), 339–53.

Callen, T., Thimann, C., (1997), Empirical Determinants of Household Saving, Evidence from OECD Countries, International Monetary Fund, Working Paper no. 97/181.

Campbell, J. Y. (1987), Does Saving Anticipate Declining Labour Income? An Alternative Test of the Permanent Income Hypothesis, Econometrica, vol. 55, no. 6, 1249–73.

Campbell, J. Y., Cocco, J. F. (2007), How Do House Prices Affect Consumption? Evidence from Micro Data, Journal of Monetary Economics, vol. 54, no. 3, 591–621.

Campbell, J. Y., Cochrane, J. (1999), By Force of Habit: A Consumption-Based Explanation of Aggregate Stock Market Behavior, Journal of Political Economy, vol. 107 (April), 205–51.

Campbell, J., Deaton, A. (1989), Why Is Consumption So Smooth?, Review of Economic Studies, vol. 56, no. 3, 357–73.

Campbell, J., Mankiw, R. (1989), Consumption, Income and Interest Rates: Reinterpreting the Time Series Evidence, in: Blanchard, O. J., Fischer, S. (eds.), NBER Macroeconomics Annual, vol. 4, Cambridge/Mass.: MIT Press, 185–216.

– (1991), The Response of Consumption to Income: A Cross-Country Investigation, European Economic Review, vol. 35, no. 4, 723–56.

Carroll, Ch.D. (1992), The Buffer-Stock Theory of Saving: Some Macroeconomic Evidence, Brookings Papers on Economic Activity, vol. 23, no. 2, 61–156.

– (1994), How Does Future Income Affect Current Consumption?, The Quarterly Journal of Economics, vol. 109, no. 1, 111–47.

– (1997), Buffer-Stock Saving and the Life Cycle/Permanent Income Hypothesis, Quarterly Journal of Economics, vol. 112, no. 1, 1–55.

– (2000a), Lecture Notes on Solving Microeconomic Dynamic Stochastic Optimization Problems, Manuscript, Department of Economics, Johns Hopkins University.

– (2000b), Requiem for the Representative Consumer? Aggregate Implications of Microeconomic Consumption Behavior, American Economic Review, vol. 90, no.2, Papers and Proceedings of the One Hundred Twelfth Annual Meeting of the American Economic Association, 110–15.

– (2000c), Why Do the Rich Save So Much?, in: Slemrod, J.B. (ed.), Does Atlas Shrug? The Economic Consequences of Taxing the Rich, Cambridge/Mass.: Harvard University Press, 463–84.

– (2001a), Death to the Log-Linearized Consumption Euler Equation! (And Very Poor Health to the Second-Order Approximation), Advances in Macroeconomics (B.E. Journal of Macroeconomics), Nov., vol. 1, no. 1, Article 6.

–   (2001b), A Theory of the Consumption Function, with and without Liquidity
    Constraints, Journal of Economic Perspectives: vol. 15, no. 3, 23–45.
–   (2004a), Theoretical Foundations of Buffer Stock Saving, Manuscript, Johns
    Hopkins University, June, NBER Working Paper no. 10867.
–   (2004b), Housing Wealth and Consumption Expenditure, Paper Prepared for
    Academic Consultants Meeting of Federal Reserve Board (January), available at
    http://econ.jhu.edu/people/ccarroll/papers/FedHouseWealthv2.pdf.
Carroll, Ch.D., Kimball, M. (1996), On the Concavity of the Consumption Func-
    tion, Econometrica, vol. 64, no. 4, 981–92.
–   (2001), Liquidity Constraints and Precautionary Saving, NBER Working Paper
    no. 8496.
Carroll, Ch.D., Overland, J., Weil, D. N. (2000), Saving and Growth with Habit
    Formation, American Economic Review, vol. 90, no. 3, 341–55.
Carroll, Ch.D., Slacalek, J. (2006), Sticky Expectations and Consumption Dynam-
    ics, Johns Hopkins University, Mimeo.
Carroll, Ch.D., Summers, L.H. (1991), Consumption Growth Parallels Income
    Growth: Some New Evidence, in: Bernheim, B.D., Shoven, J.B. (eds.), Na-
    tional Saving and Economic Performance. Chicago and London: The Univer-
    sity of Chicago Press, 305–43.
Carroll, Ch.D., Samwick, A.A. (1997), The Nature of Precautionary Wealth, Jour-
    nal of Monetary Economics, vol. 40, no. 1, 41–72.
–   (1998), How Important is Precautionary Saving?, Review of Economics and
    Statistics, vol. 80, no. 3, 410–19.
Carroll, Ch.D., Weil, D.N. (1994), Saving and Growth: A Reinterpretation, Carne-
    gie-Rochester Conference Series on Public Policy, vol. 40, 133–92.
Case, K.E., Quigley, J.M., Shiller, R.J. (2005), Comparing Wealth Effects: The
    Stock Market versus the Housing Market, Advances in Macroeconomics, vol.
    5, no. 1, 1–34.
Catte, P., Girouard, N., Price, R., Andre, Ch. (2004), Housing Market, Wealth and
    the Business Cycle, OECD Economics Department Working Papers no. 394.
Cocco, J., Gomes, F.J., Maenhout, P.J. (2005), Consumption and Portfolio Choice
    Over the Life Cycle, Review of Financial Studies, 18 (2), 491–533.
Coleman, A. (1998), Household Savings: A Survey of Recent Microeconomic
    Theory and Evidence, New Zealand Treasury Working Paper no. 98/8.
Constantinides, G. (1990), Habit Formation: A Resolution of the Equity Premium
    Puzzle, Journal of Political Economy, vol. 98, no. 3, 519–43.
Coronado, J. (1998), The Effects of Social Security Privatization on Household
    Saving: Evidence from the Chilean Experience, Federal Reserve System (U.S.),
    Finance and Economics Discussion Series no. 1998-12.
Danziger, S., Van Der Gaag, J., Smolensky, E., Taussig, M. K. (1983), The Life-
    Cycle Hypothesis and the Consumption Behavior of the Elderly, Journal of
    Post Keynesian Economics, vol. 5, no. 2, 208–27.

Darby, M.R. (1977), Effects of Social Security on Income and the Capital Stock, UCLA Economics Working Papers no. 095A.

Dean, A., Durand, M., Fallon, J., Hoeller, P. (1989), Saving Trends and Behaviour in O.E.C.D. Countries, OECD Economics Department Working Papers no. 67.

Deaton, A. (1987), Panel Data from Time Series of Cross Sections, Journal of Econometrics, vol. 30, no. 1, 109–26.

– (1991), Saving and Liquidity Constraints, Econometrica, vol. 59, no. 5, 1221–48.

– (1992), Understanding Consumption, Oxford/New York: Oxford University Press.

– (1997a), Saving and Growth, Working Paper no. 180, Research Program in Development Studies, Princeton University.

– (1997b), The Analysis of Household Surveys: A Microeconometric Approach to Development Policy, Baltimore: The Johns Hopkins University Press.

Deaton, A., Case, A. (1987), Analysis of Household Expenditures, LSMS Working Paper, no. 28, Washington.

Deaton, A., Muellbauer, J. (1980), Economics and Consumer Behaviour, Cambridge: Cambridge University Press.

Deaton, A., Paxson, C. (2000), Growth and Saving among Individuals and Households, Review of Economics and Statistics, vol. 82, no. 2, 212–25.

Deininger, K., Squire, L. (1996), A New Data Set Measuring Income Inequality, World Bank Economic Review, vol. 10, no. 3, 565–91.

– (1998), New Ways of Looking at Old Issues: Inequality and Growth, Journal of Development Economics, vol. 57, no. 2, 259–87.

Demirguc-Kunt, A., Levine, R. (1999), Bank-Based and Market-Based Financial Systems. Cross-Country Comparisons, World Bank, Development Research Group, (June).

Denizer, C., Wolf, H.C. (1998), Aggregate Savings in the Transition, The World Bank Saving Across the World Project, Dec., Working Paper.

– (2000), The Saving Collapse during the Transition in Eastern Europe, The World Bank, Policy Research Working Paper Series no. 2419.

DIW (1978), Göseke, G., Bedau, K.-D., Klatt, H., Einkommens- und Verbrauchs-schichtung für die größeren Verwendungsbereiche des privaten Verbrauchs und die privaten Ersparnisse in der Bundesrepublik Deutschland 1955–1974, DIW Beiträge zur Strukturforschung, Heft 49.

Dixit, A.K., Stiglitz, J.E. (1977), Monopolistic Competition and Optimum Product Diversity, American Economic Review, vol. 67, no. 3, S. 297–308.

Döhrn, R. (1988), Zur strukturellen Entwicklung des privaten Verbrauchs seit 1960, RWI Mitteilungen, Jg. 39, S. 55–87.

Dreger, Ch., Kosfeld, R. (2003), Consumption and Income. Panel Economic Evidence for West Germany, Applied Economics Quarterly, vol. 49, 75–88.

Duesenberry, J. (1949), Income, Saving, and the Theory of Consumer Behavior, Cambridge/Mass.: Harvard University Press.

Dvornak, N., Kohler, M. (2007), Housing Wealth, Stock Market Wealth and Consumption: A Panel Analysis for Australia, Economic Record, vol. 83, issue 261, 117–30.

Dynan, K.E. (1994), Relative Wage Changes and Estimates of the Rate of Time Preference, Federal Reserve Board (September), Mimeo.

– (2000), Habit Formation in Consumer Preferences: Evidence from Panel Data. American Economic Review, vol. 90, no. 3 (June), 391–406.

Dynan, K.E., Maki, D. (2001), Does Stock Market Wealth Matter for Consumption?, Federal Reserve System (U.S.) Finance and Economics Discussion Series no. 2001-23.

Dynan, K.E., Skinner, J., Zeldes, S.P. (2004), Do the Rich Save More?, Journal of Political Economy, vol. 112, no. 21, 397–444.

Edwards, S. (1995), Why are Saving Rates so different Across Countries? An international Comparative Analysis, NBER Working Paper no.5097.

– (1996), Why are Latin America's Savings Rates So Low? An International Comparative Analysis, Journal of Development Economics, vol. 51, no. 1, 5–44.

Elmendorf, D. (1996), The Effect of Interest-Rate Changes on Household Saving and Consumption: A Survey, Federal Reserve Board Finance and Economics Discussion Series Working Paper no. 1996–27.

Engelhardt, G.V. (1996), House Prices and Home Owner Saving Behavior, Regional Science and Urban Economics, vol. 26, no. 3-4, 313–36.

Engen, E., Gale, W., Uccello, C. (1999), The Adequacy of Retirement Saving, Brookings Papers on Economic Activity, vol. 30, no. 2, 65–188.

Fachinger, U. (2001), Einkommensverwendungsentscheidungen von Haushalten, Sozialpolitische Schriften, 83, Berlin: Duncker und Humblot.

Feldstein, M. (1980), International Differences in Social Security and Saving, Journal of Public Economics, vol. 14. no. 2, 225–44.

Feldstein, M., Horioka, C. (1980), Domestic Savings and International Capital Flows, The Economic Journal, vol. 90, no. 6, 314–29.

Feldstein, M., Samwick, A. (1992), Social Security Rules and Marginal Tax Rates, National Tax Journal, vol. 45, no. 1, 1–22.

Fernandez-Corugedo, E., Price, S., Blake, A. (2003), The Dynamics of Consumers' Expenditure. The UK Consumption ECM Redux, Working Paper 204, Bank of England.

Fischer, S., Sahay, R., Vegh, C. (1996), Stabilization and Growth in Transition Economies. The Early Experience, Journal of Economic Perspectives, vol. 10, no. 2, 45–66.

Flavin, M. (1981), The Adjustment of Consumption to Changing Expectations about Future Income, Journal of Political Economy, vol. 89, no. 5, 974–1009.

Friedman, M. (1953a), Essays in Positive Economics, Chicago: The University of Chicago Press.

– (1953b) Choice, Chance, and the Personal Distribution of Income, Journal of Political Economy, vol. 61, no. 4 (August), 277–90.

– (1957), A Theory of the Consumption Function. Princeton: Princeton University Press.

– (1963), Windfalls, the 'Horizon', and Related Concepts in the Permanent-Income Hypothesis, in: Christ, C.F, Friedman, M., Goodman, L.A., Griliches, Z., Harberger, A.C., Liviatan, N., Mincer, J., Mundlak, Y., Nerlove, M., Patinkin, D., Telser, L.G., Theil, H., Measurement in Economics. Studies in Mathematical Economics and Econometrics in Memory of Yehuda Grunfeld, Stanford: Stanford University Press, 3–28.

Friend, I., Kravis, I. B. (1957), Consumption Patterns and Permanent Income, American Economic Review, vol. 47, no. 2, 536–55.

Frietsch, H. (1991), Bestimmungsgründe der Sparquote, Berlin: Duncker & Humblot.

Fuhrer, J.C. (2000), Habit Formation in Consumption and its Implications for Monetary-Policy Models, American Economic Review, vol. 90, no. 3, 367–90.

Fullerton, D., Rogers, D. L. (1993), Who Bears the Lifetime Tax Burden? Washington, DC: Brookings Institution.

Galbraith, J.K., Kum, H. (2005), Estimating the Inequality of Household Incomes: A Statistical Approach to the Creation of a Dense and Consistent Global Data Set, Review of Income and Wealth, vol. 51, no. 1 (March), 115–43.

Gale, W., Sabelhaus, J. (1999), Perspectives on the Household Saving Rate, Brookings Papers on Economic Activity, no. 1, 181–224.

Gale, W., Scholz, J. (1994), Intergenerational Transfers and the Accumulation of Wealth, Journal of Economic Perspectives, vol. 8, no. 4, 145–60.

Garcia, R., Lusardi, A., Ng, S. (1997), Excess Sensitivity and Asymmetries in Consumption: An Empirical Investigation, Journal of Money, Credit, and Banking, vol. 29, no. 2, 154–76.

Gibson, J., Scobie, G. (2001), Household Saving Behaviour in New Zealand: A Cohort Analysis, New Zealand Treasury, Treasury Working Paper Series no. 01/18.

Giovannini, A. (1985), Saving and the Rate of Interest in LDCs, Journal of Development Economics, vol. 18, no. 2–3, 197–217.

Gourinchas, P., Parker, J. (2002), Consumption Over the Life Cycle, Econometrica, vol. 70, issue 1, 47–89.

Graham, J.W. (1987), International Differences in Saving Rates and the Life-Cycle Hypothesis, European Economic Review, vol. 31, no. 8 (December),1509–29.

Granger, C.W.J. (1969), Investigating Causal Relations by Econometric Models and Cross-spectral Methods. Econometrica. vol. 37, no. 3, 424–38.

– (1988), Some Recent Development in a Concept of Causality, Journal of Econometrics, vol. 39, no. 1–2, 199–211.

Gross, D.B., Souleles, N. (2000), Consumer Response to Credit Supply: Evidence from Credit Card Data, Manuscript, University of Pennsylvania.

Guariglia, A., Rossi, M. (2002), Consumption, Habit Formation, and Precautionary Saving: Evidence from the British Household Panel Survey, Oxford Economic Papers, vol. 54, no. 1, 1–19.

Guiso, L., Jappelli, T. (1991), Intergenerational Transfers and Capital Market Imperfections: Evidence from a Cross Section of Italian Households, European Economic Review, vol. 35, no. 1, 103–20.

– (2002), Private Transfers, Borrowing Constraints and the Timing of Home-ownership, Journal of Money, Credit and Banking, vol. 34, no. 2 (May), 315–39.

Guiso, L., Jappelli, T., Terlizzese, D. (1992a), Earnings Uncertainty and Precautionary Saving, Journal of Monetary Economics, vol. 30, no. 2, 307–37.

– (1992b), Saving and Capital Market Imperfections: The Italian Experience, Scandinavian Journal of Economics, vol. 94, no. 2, 197–213.

Hahn, F., Solow, R. (1997), A Critical Essay on modern Macroeconomic Theory, Cambridge/Mass.: MIT Press.

Hall, R.E. (1978), Stochastic Implications of the Life-Cycle/Permanent Income Hypothesis: Theory and Evidence, Journal of Political Economy, vol. 86, no. 6, 971–87.

– (1999), The Stock Market and Capital Accumulation, NBER Working Paper no. 7180 (June).

– (2000), E-Capital: The Link between the Stock Market and the Labor Market in the 1990s, Brookings Papers on Economic Activity, vol. 31, no. 2, 73–102.

Hall, R.E., Mishkin, F. (1982), The Sensitivity of Consumption to Transitory Income: Estimates from Panel Data on Households, Econometrica, vol. 50, no. 2, 461–82.

Hamburg, B., Hoffmann, M., Keller, J. (2008), Consumption, Wealth and Business Cycles in Germany, Empirical Economics, vol. 34, issue 3, 451–76.

Handel, A. (2003), Die Entwicklung des Geldvermögens der privaten Haushalte in Deutschland, Arbeitspapier, Institut für Statistik und Ökonometrie, Johannes-Gutenberg-Universität.

Hauser, R. (2002), Die Entwicklung der Einkommens- und Vermögensverteilung in Deutschland – Ein Überblick, Gesellschaft-Wirtschaft-Politik, Heft 3, S. 373–94.

Hey, J.D. (1983), Whither Uncertainty, Economic Journal, vol. 93, 130–39.

Hill, M.S. (1992), The Panel Study of Income Dynamics: A User's Guide, Newbury Park, Calif./London: Sage Publications.

Holloway, T. (1989), Present NIPA Saving Measures: Their Characteristics and Limitations, in: Lipsey, R.E., Tice, H.S. (eds.), The Measurement of Saving, Investment, and Wealth, Chicago: The University of Chicago Press.

Horioka, C.Y., Watanabe, W. (1997), Why Do People Save? A Micro-Analysis of Motives for Household Saving in Japan, The Economic Journal vol. 107, no. 442 (May), 537–52.

Hubbard, R.G., Skinner, J., Zeldes S.P. (1994), The Importance of Precautionary Motives in Explaining Individual and Aggregate Saving, Carnegie-Rochester Conference Series on Public Policy, vol. 40 (June), 59–125.

– (1995), Precautionary Saving and Social Insurance, Journal of Political Economy, vol. 103 (April), 360–99.

Huggett, M. (1996), Wealth Distribution in Life Cycle Economies, Journal of Monetary Economics, vol. 38, no. 3, 469–94.

Huggett, M., Ventura, G. (2000), Understanding Why High Income Households Save More Than Low Income Households, Journal of Monetary Economics, vol. 45, issue 2, April, 361–97.

James, J.A., Palumbo, M.G., Thomas, M. (2006), Have American Workers Always Been Low Savers? Patterns of Accumulation Among Working Households, 1885–1910, Research in Economic History, vol. 23, 127–75.

Jappelli, T., Pagano, M. (1989), Consumption and Capital Market Imperfections: An International Comparison, American Economic Review, vol. 79, no. 5, 1088–1105.

– (1994a), Saving, Growth, and Liquidity Constraints, Quarterly Journal of Economics, vol. 109, no. 1, 83–109.

– (1994b) Personal Saving in Italy, in: Poterba, J.M. (ed.), International Comparisons of Household Saving, Chicago: The University of Chicago Press.

– (1998), The Determinants of Saving: Lessons from Italy, Inter-American Development Bank, Research Department Publications no. 3012.

Jappelli, T., Pistaferri, L. (2000), The Dynamics of Household Wealth Accumulation in Italy, Fiscal Studies, vol. 21, no. 2, 269–95.

Jung, S. (2001), Privater Verbrauch in Deutschland. Eine empirische Untersuchung der Ausgaben auf Grundlage der Einkommens- und Verbrauchsstichprobe 1993, Deutscher Universitätsverlag.

Juster, F.T., Lupton, J., Smith, J.P., Stafford, F. (2004), Savings and Wealth; Then and Now, EconWPA, Series Labor and Demography no. 0403027.

– (2006), The Decline in Household Saving and the Wealth Effect, The Review of Economics and Statistics, February, vol. 88, no. 1, 20–7.

Kennickell, A.B., Starr-McCluer, M. (1994), Changes in Family Finances from 1989 to 1992: Evidence from the Survey of Consumer Finances, Federal Reserve Bulletin (October), 861–82.

- (1997a), Household Saving and Portfolio Change: Evidence from the 1983–89 SCF Panel, Review of Income and Wealth, vol. 43, issue 4, 381–99.
- (1997), Retrospective Reporting of Household Wealth: Evidence from the 1983–89 Survey of Consumer Finances, Journal of Business and Economic Statistics, vol. 15, no. 4 (October), 452–63.
- (2000), Recent Changes in U.S. Family Finances: Results from the 1998 Survey of Consumer Finances, Federal Reserve Bulletin (January), 1–29.

Keynes, J.M. (1936), The General Theory of Employment, Interest, and Money, San Diego, New York, London.

Kiley, M.T. (2000), Identifying the Effect of Stock Market Wealth on Consumption: Pitfalls and New Evidence, Federal Reserve Board (July), Mimeo.

Kopits, G., Gotur, P. (1980), The Influence of Social Security on Household Savings. A Cross-country Investigation, IMF Staff Papers, vol. 27, no. 1 (March), 161–90.

Koskela, E., Virén, M. (1983), Social Security and Household Saving in an International Cross Section, American Economic Review, vol. 73, no. 1, 212–17.

Kotlikoff, L.J. (1988), Intergenerational Transfers and Savings, Journal of Economic Perspectives, vol. 2, no. 2, 41–58.

Kotlikoff, L.J., Summers, L.H. (1981), The Role of Intergenerational Transfers in Aggregate Capital Accumulation, Journal of Political Economy, vol. 89, no. 4, 706–32.

- (1988), The Contribution of Intergenerational Transfers to Total Wealth: A Reply, NBER Working Paper no. 1827 (also Reprint no. r1093).

Kott, K., Krebs, T. (2005), Einnahmen und Ausgaben privater Haushalte. Ergebnisse der EVS 2003 (erstes Halbjahr), Wirtschaft und Statistik, Wiesbaden, Statistisches Bundesamt, 2, 143–57.

Kraay, A. (2000), Household Saving in China, World Bank Econ Rev 14 (3), 545–570.

Kreinin, M.E. (1961), Windfall Income and Consumption: Additional Evidence, American Economic Review, vol. 51, no. 3, 388–90.

Krusell, P., Smith, A.A. (1998), Income and Wealth Heterogeneity in the Macroeconomy, Journal of Political Economy, vol. 106, no. 5, 867–96.

Kuehlwein, M. (1991), A Test for the Presence of Precautionary Saving, Economic Letters, vol. 37, no. 4, 471–75.

Kuznets, S. (1934), National Income, 1929–1932, National Bureau of Economic Research, NBER Chapters no. 2258.

- (1937), National Income and Capital Formation, 1919–1935, National Bureau of Economic Research, NBER Books no. kuzn37-1.
- (1952), Proportion of Capital Formation to National Product, American Economic Review, Papers and Proceedings, vol. 42, no. 2, 507–26.
- (1953), Shares of Upper Income Groups in Income and Savings, National Bureau of Economic Research, NBER Books no. kuzn53-1.
- (1965), Economic Growth and Structure: Selected Essays, New York: Norton.

- (1966), Modern Economic Growth: Rate, Structure, and Spread, New Haven and London: Yale University Press, xvii + 529.
- (1971), Economic Growth of Nations: Total Output and Production Structure, Cambridge/Mass.: Harvard University Press.

Laibson, D., Repetto, A., Tobacman, J. (2000), A Debt Puzzle, Manuscript, Harvard University, 32, NBER Working Paper no. 7879.

Landsberger, M. (1966), Windfall Income and Consumption: Comment, American Economic Review, vol. 56, no. 3, 534–40.

Lawrance, E.C. (1991), Poverty and the Rate of Time Preference: Evidence from Panel Data, Journal of Political Economy, vol. 99, no. 1 (February), 54–77.

Leff, N.H. (1969), Dependency Rates and Savings Rates, American Economic Review, vol. 59, no. 5, 886–96.

Lehmann, H. (2004), Die Modellierung der Konsumausgaben privater Haushalte, Schriften des Instituts für Wirtschaftsforschung Halle.

Lehnert, A. (2004), Housing, Consumption and Credit Constraints, Board of Governors of the Federal Reserve System (U.S.), Finance and Economics Discussion Series no. 2004-63.

Loayza, N., Lopez, H., Schmidt-Hebbel, K., Servén, L. (1999), Saving in the World, Stylized Facts, in: Schmidt-Hebbel, K., Servén, L. (eds.), The Economics of Saving and Growth. Theory, Evidence, and Implications for Policy, Cambridge University Press, 6–32.

Loayza, N., Schmidt-Hebbel, K., Servén, L. (1999), What Drives Private Saving Around the World? The World Bank, Saving Across the World Project, World Bank Research Working Papers, November, 1–32.

- (2000), What Drives Private Saving Across the World?, The Review of Economics and Statistics, May, vol. 82, no. 2, 165–81.

Lucas, R.E. (1976), Econometric Policy Evaluation: A Critique, Carnegie-Rochester Conference Series on Public Policy, vol. 1, no. 1, 19–46.

Lucas, R.E., Sargent, T.J. (1981) Rational Expectations and Econometric Practice, vol. 1, Minneapolis: University of Minnesota Press.

Ludwig, A., Sløk, T. (2002), The Impact of Changes in Stock Prices and House Prices on Consumption in OECD Countries, IMF Working Paper no. 02/1.

Ludvigson, S. (1999), Consumption and Credit: A Model of Time-Varying Liquidity Constraints, The Review of Economics and Statistics, vol. 81, no. 3, 434–47.

Ludvigson, S., Steindel, Ch. (1999), How Important is the Stock Market Effect on Consumption?, Federal Reserve Bank of New York Economic Policy Review, vol. 5, no. 2 (July), 29–52.

Lusardi, A. (1997), Precautionary Saving and Subjective Earning Variance, Economic Letters, vol. 57, no. 3, 319–26.

– (1998), On the Importance of Precautionary Saving Motive, American Economic Review, , vol. 88, no. 2, Papers and Proceedings of the Hundred and Tenth Annual Meeting of the American Economic Association, 449–53.
– (2001), Explaining Why So Many Households Do Not Save, Center for Retirement Research Working Paper no. 2001-05.

Maddison, A. (1992), A Long-Run Perspective on Saving, Scandinavian Journal of Economics, vol. 94, no. 2, 181–96.
Maier, K.M. (1983), Der Sparprozeß in der Bundesrepublik Deutschland. Eine empirische Analyse des Sparverhaltens der privaten Haushalte seit 1950, Frankfurt/M.: Peter Lang, Europäische Hochschulschriften, Reihe 5.
Maki, D.M. (2000), The Growth of Consumer Credit and the Household Debt Service Burden, Board of Governors of the Federal Reserve System (U.S.), Finance and Economics Discussion Series no. 2000-12.
– (2001), Household Debt and the Tax Reform Act of 1986, American Economic Review, vol. 91, no. 1, 305–19.
Maki, D.M., Palumbo, M.G. (2001), Disentangling the Wealth Effect: A Cohort Analysis of Household Saving in the 1990s, Federal Reserve Board Finance and Discussion Series Working Paper no. 2001–21 (April).
Mankiw, N.G., Zeldes, S.P. (1991), The Consumption of Stockholders and Nonstockholders, Journal of Financial Economics, vol. 29, no. 1, 97–112.
Masson, P., Bayoumi, T., Samiei, H., (1995), Saving Behaviour in Industrial and Developing Countries, IMF Manuscript.
– (1998), International Evidence on the Determinants of Private Saving, World Bank Econ Rev, 12 (3), 483–501.
Mayer, T. (1966), The Propensity To Consume Permanent Income, American Economic Review, vol. 56, no. 5, 1158–77.
– (1972), Permanent Income, Wealth, and Consumption. A Critique of the Permanent Income Theory, The Life-Cycle Hypothesis, and Related Theories, Berkeley, Calif.: University of California Press.
Meghir, C., Weber, G. (1996), Intertemporal Nonseparability or Borrowing Restrictions? A Disaggregate Analysis Using a U.S Consumption Panel, Econometrica, vol. 64, no. 5, 1151–81.
Menchik, P., David, M. (1983), Income Distribution, Lifetime Savings, and Bequests, American Economic Review, vol. 73, no. 4 (September), 672–90.
Merrill Lynch, Cap Gemini Ernst & Young, World Wealth Report 2004, 2003, 2002.
Merton, R.C. (1969), Lifetime Portfolio Selection under Uncertainty: The Continuous Time Case, Review of Economics and Statistics, vol. 51, no. 3, 247–57.
Merz, J. (2003), Was fehlt in der EVS?, Jahrbücher für Nationalökonomie und Statistik, vol. 223, issue 1, 58–90.
Modigliani, F. (1966), The Life Cycle Hypothesis of Saving, the Demand for Wealth, and the Supply of Capital, Social Research, 33, 160–217.

– (1970), The Life Cycle Hypothesis of Savings and the Intercountry Differences in the Savings Ratio, in: Eltis, W.A., Scott, M.F.G., Wolfe, J.N. (eds.), Induction, Growth and Trade: Essays in Honour of Sir Roy Harrod, Oxford: Oxford University Press. 197–225.

– (1988), The Role of Intergenerational Transfers and Life Cycle Saving in the Accumulation of Wealth, Journal of Economic Perspectives, vol. 2, no. 2, 15–40.

Modigliani, F., Ando, A. (1980), The 'Permanent Income' and 'Life Cycle' Hypothesis of Saving Behavior: Comparison and Tests, in: Abel, A. (ed.), The Collected Papers of Franco Modigliani, vol. 2: The Life Cycle-Hypothesis of Saving, Cambridge/Mass.: MIT Press, 229–74.

Modigliani, F., Brumberg, R. (1954), Utility Analysis and the Consumption Function: An Interpretation of Cross-Section Data, in: Kurihara, K.K. (ed.), Post-Keynesian Economics, New Brunswick: Rutgers University Press, 388–436.

– (1980), Utility Analysis and the Aggregate Consumption Function: An Attempt at Integration, in: Abel, A. (ed.), The Collected Papers of Franco Modigliani, vol. 2: The Life Cycle-Hypothesis of Saving, Cambridge/Mass.: MIT Press, 128–97.

Muellbauer, J. (1988), Habits, Rationality and Myopia in the Life Cycle Consumption Function, Annales d'Economie et de Statistique, no. 9, 47–70.

Münnich, M. (2001), Einkommens- und Geldvermögensverteilung privater Haushalte in Deutschland – Teil 2. Ergebnis der Einkommens- und Verbrauchsstichprobe 1998, in: Wirtschaft und Statistik, 2, 121–37.

Mulligan, C.B. (1997), Parental Priorities and Economic Inequality, Chicago: The University of Chicago Press.

Oberheitmann, A., Wenke, M. (1994), Strukturveränderungen des westdeutschen privaten Verbrauchs, RWI Mitteilungen, Jg. 45, 103–26.

Obstfeld, M. (1990), Intertemporal Dependence, Impatience, and Dynamics, Journal of Monetary Economics, vol. 26, no. 1, 45–75.

Ogaki, M., Ostry, J., Reinhart, C. (1996), Saving Behavior in Low and Middle-Income Developing Countries, IMF Staff Papers, vol. 43, no. 1, 38–71.

Otoo, M.W. (1999), Consumer Sentiment and the Stock Market. Federal Reserve Board Finance and Discussion Series Working Paper no. 1999–60.

Otterbach, A. (1996), Gesamtwirtschaftliche Einflüsse auf das Sparverhalten privater Haushalte, Frankfurt/M. u.a.: Lang.

Oulton, N. (1976), Inheritance and the Distribution of Wealth, Oxford Economic Papers, vol. 28, no. 1 (March), 86–101.

Parker, J.A. (1999a), Spendthrift in America? On Two Decades of Decline in the U.S. Saving Rate, in: Bernanke, B., Rotemberg, J. (eds.), NBER Macroeconomics Annual, Chicago: The University of Chicago Press, 317–87.

– (1999b), The Reaction of Household Consumption to Predictable Changes in Social Security Taxes, American Economic Review, vol. 89, no. 4 (September), 959–73.

- (1999c), The Consumption Function Re-Estimated. Mimeo, Princeton University (August), Mimeo.

Paxson, C. (1996), Saving and Growth: Evidence from Micro Data, European Economic Review. vol. 40, no. 2, 255–88.

Pemberton, J. (1993), Attainable Non-Optimality or Unattainable Optimality: A new Approach to Stochastic Life-Cycle Problems, Economic Journal, vol. 103, no. 416, 1–20.

- (1997), The Empirical Failure of the Life Cycle Model with Perfect Capital Markets, Oxford Economic Papers, vol. 49, no. 2, 129–51.

- (1995), Income Catastrophes and Precautionary Saving, Discussion Papers in Quantitative Economics and Computing Series E vol. 3.

- (2003), The Application of Stochastic Dynamic Programming (SDP) Methods to Household Consumption and Saving Decisions: A Critical Survey, in: Altug, S., Chadha J.S., Nolan, Ch. (eds.), Dynamic Macroeconomic Analysis. Theory and Policy in General Equilibrium, Cambridge: Cambridge University Press.

Pichette, L., Tremblay, D. (2003), Are Wealth Effects Important for Canada?, Working Paper 30, Bank of Canada.

Pigou, A.C. (1951), Professor Duesenberry on Income and Savings, Economic Journal, vol. 61, no. 244, 883–85.

Poterba, J.M. (1989), Lifetime Incidence and the Distributional Burden of Excise Taxes, American Economic Review, vol. 79, no. 2 (May), 325–330.

- (2000), Stock Market Wealth and Consumption, Journal of Economic Perspectives, vol. 14, no. 2 (Spring), 99–118.

Poterba, J.M., Samwick, A. Shleifer, A., Shiller, R.J. (1995), Stock Ownership Patterns, Stock Market Fluctuations, and Consumption, Brookings Papers on Economic Activity, no. 2, 295–372.

Poterba, J.M. (ed.) (1994), International Comparisons of Household Saving, Chicago: The University of Chicago Press.

Poterba, J.M., Venti, S., Wise, D. (1993), The Effects of Special Saving Programs on Saving and Wealth, NBER Working Paper no. 5287.

Quadrini, V., Rios-Rull, J. (1997), Models of the Distribution of Wealth, Manuscript, University of Pennsylvania.

Ravn, M.O., Schmitt-Grohe, S., Uribe, M. (2008), The Macroeconomics of Subsistence Points, Macroeconomic Dynamics, vol. 12, 136–47.

Rebelo, S. (1992), Growth in Open Economies, Carnegie-Rochester Conference Series On Public Policy, vol. 36, no. 1, 5–46.

Robinson, J. (1962), Economic Philosophy, Chicago; Aldine Publishing.

Runkle, D. (1991), Liquidity Constraints and the Permanent Income Hypothesis, Journal of Monetary Economics, vol. 27, no. 1, 73–98.

Sabelhaus, J. (1992), Development and Use of the Consumer Expenditure Survey (CEX) Consumption, Income, and Wealth Data Set, Mimeo.

– (1993), What is the Distributional Burden of Taxing Consumption, National Tax Journal, vol. 46, no. 3 (September), 331–44.

– (1997), Public Policy and Saving in the United States and Canada. Canadian Journal of Economics, vol. 30, no.2 (May), 253–75.

Sabelhaus, J., Groen, J.A. (2000), Can Permanent-Income Theory explain Cross-Section Consumption Patterns, Review of Economics and Statistics, August, vol. 82, no. 3, 431–38.

Samuelson, P.A. (1969), Lifetime Portfolio Selection by Dynamic Stochastic Programming, Review of Economics and Statistics, vol. 51, no. 3, 239–46.

Sargent, T.J. (1987), Dynamic Macroeconomic Theory, Cambridge/Mass.: Harvard University Press.

Schmidt-Hebbel, K., Servén, L. (2000), Does Income Inequality Raise Aggregate Saving?, Journal of Development Economics, vol. 61, no. 2, 417–46.

Schnittker-Reiner, U. (1987), Der Erklärungsbeitrag des Konsumklima-Index für das Nachfrage- und Sparverhalten privater Haushalte, Frankfurt/M.: Lang.

Schönig, W. (1996), Ersparnisbildung und Vermögensanlage privater Haushalte. Zur Fundierung einer Verhaltenstheorie des Sparens mittels einer Auswertung des sozio-ökonomischen Panels, Frankfurt/M. u.a.: Lang.

Schrooten, M., Stephan, S. (2002), Back on Track? Saving Puzzles in EU-Accession Countries, DIW-Diskussionspapiere no. 306.

Scobie, G.M., Gibson, J.K. (2003), Household Saving Behaviour in New Zealand: Why do Cohorts Behave Differently?, Dec., New Zealand Treasury, Working Paper no. 03/32.

Serres, A. de, Pelgrin, F. (2003), The Decline in Private Saving Rates in the 1990s in OECD-Countries: How much can be explained by Non-Wealth-Determinants?, OECD Economic Studies, no. 36, 2003/1.

Siegel, J.J., Thaler, R.H. (1997), Anomalies: The Equity Premium Puzzle, Journal of Economic Perspectives, vol. 11, no. 1, 191–200.

Shapiro, M.D., Slemrod, J. (1995), Consumer Response to the Timing of Income: Evidence from a Change in Tax Withholding, American Economic Review, vol. 85, no. 1, 274–83.

Shea, J. (1995), Myopia, Liquidity Constraints, and Aggregate Consumption: A Simple Test, Journal of Money, Credit, and Banking, vol. 27, no. 3, 798–805.

Skinner, J. (1988), Risky Income, Life Cycle Consumption, and Precautionary Savings, Journal of Monetary Economics, vol. 22, no.2, 237–55.

Slesnick, D.T. (1992), Aggregate Consumption and Saving in the Postwar United States, Review of Economics and Statistics, vol. 74, no. 4, 585–97.

– (1993), Gaining Ground: Poverty in the Postwar United States, Journal of Political Economy, vol. 101, no. 1, 1–38.

Smith, J.P. (2004), Inheritances and Bequests, provided by EconWPA, Labor and Demography no. 0408012.

SOEP Group (2001), The German Socio-Economic Panel (GSOEP) after more than 5 Years – Overview, Vierteljahreshefte zur Wirtschaftsforschung, vol. 70, no. 1, 7–14.

Sommer, M. (2001), Habits, Sentiment and Predictable Income in the Dynamics of Aggregate Consumption, Working Paper no. 458; updated 2006, Johns Hopkins University Department of Economics.

Souleles, N.S. (1999), The Response of Household Consumption to Income Tax Refunds, American Economic Review, vol. 89, no. 4 (September), 947–58.

Starr-McCluer, M. (2002), Stock Market Wealth and Consumer Spending, Economic Inquiry, vol. 40, no. 1, 69–79.

Stiglitz, J.E., Weiss, A. (1981), Credit Rationing in Markets with Imperfect Information, American Economic Review, vol. 71, no. 3, 393–410.

Stoker, T.M. (1986), Simple Tests of Distributional Effects on Macroeconomic Equations, Journal of Political Economy, vol. 94, no. 4 (August 1986), 763–95.

Takayama, N., Kitamura, Y. (1994), Household Saving Behavior in Japan, in: Poterba, J.M. (ed.), International Comparisons of Household Saving, Chicago: The University of Chicago Press.

Thurow, L.C. (1969), The Optimum Lifetime Distribution of Consumption Expenditures, American Economic Review, vol. 59, no. 3, 324–30.

UNIDO (United Nations International Development Organization), Industrial Statistics Database (2001).

UNU/WIDER-UNDP World Income Inequality Database, http://www.wider.unu.edu/wiid/wiid.htm (2000).

Uzawa, H. (1989), Time Preference, the Consumption Function, and Optimum Asset Holdings, in: Preference, Production, and Capital, Selected Papers of Hirofumi Uzawa, Cambridge University Press, 65–84.

Viard, A. (1993), The Productivity Slowdown and the Savings Shortfall: A Challenge to the Permanent Income Hypothesis, Economic Inquiry, vol. 31, no. 4, 549–63.

Vissing-Jørgensen, A. (1999), Limited Stock Market Participation and the Equity Premium Puzzle, University of Chicago (December), Mimeo.

Weil, P. (1993), Precautionary Savings and the Permanent Income Hypothesis, Review of Economic Studies, vol. 60, no. 2, 367–83.

Weinert, G. (1991), Der Rückgang der Sparquoten in den großen westlichen Industrieländern im vergangenen Jahrzehnt, Hamburger Jahrbuch für Wirtschaft- und Gesellschaftspolitik, vol. 36, 231–242.

Wolff, E.N. (1999), Wealth Accumulation by Age Cohort in the U.S., 1962–1992: The Role of Savings, Capital Gains and Intergenerational Transfers, Geneva Papers on Risk and Insurance, Issues and Practice, vol. 24, no. 1, 27–49.

Wortmann, W. (1976), Sparverhalten und strukturelle Einkommensverteilung, Göttingen: Vandenhoek und Ruprecht.

Zeldes, S.P. (1989a.), Consumption and Liquidity Constraints: An Empirical Investigation, Journal of Political Economy, vol. 97, no. 2 (April), 305–46.

– (1989b), Optimal Consumption with Stochastic Income: Deviations from Certainty Equivalence, Quarterly Journal of Economics, vol. 104, no. 2 (May), 275–98.

Political Science

campus.de/wissenschaft
Ab September 2013 mit neuem
Konzept und mehr Inhalt!

NEU

campus

Frankfurt. New York